UNORGANIZED CRIME

To: Steve

Synora Cantrell

Sidney James Heart

UNORGANIZED CRIME

As told to:

Synova Cantrell

DEDICATION

To my friends and family who endured the years of
research and anxiety.

To James for his patience and understanding.

Thank you to all the librarians who spent countless hours
searching for old records.

Most importantly, thank you Lord for bringing such a
testimony into my life.

Chapter 1: Jail Break

What makes a successful gangster? Is it the amount of money he launders, the number of women chasing him, or perhaps the body count he's left behind? None of these factors make a successful criminal career. The best gangster is a faceless one, or so I was told when I interviewed said gangster in person. (Yes, he did possess a face.)

Sidney James Heard was raised in a small mob-controlled suburb of Chicago and grew up not wanting to be a fireman or a doctor like most other children. He grew up dreaming of becoming a professional criminal. By the time he was thirteen, he was already on probation and well on his way to a career in the well-connected underworld. In his world, there weren't a lot of options. You were either dirt poor or a criminal. The facade of middle class was almost nonexistent.

"A good con man must be a chameleon," Sidney explained to this wide-eyed preacher's daughter over a meal at Applebee's one afternoon. An accomplished conman should be able to walk into a crowded bar looking like a million bucks, patronize the women, buy a round of drinks for the rowdy group, and walk out again without leaving one clear description of himself behind in the minds of the witnesses. It sounds impossible, but after working with Sidney Heard for five years I believe he could pull it off.

It is nearly impossible for the common law abiding citizen to fully comprehend the mind of a professional criminal. We strive to find a reason for the person's actions and a cause for their mental degradation. What causes a man to commit an evil act of violence? Our world has become so inundated with psychology we seek a cause for such immorality when evil itself is the cause. There is no plausible excuse for the actions Sidney chose, nor is there a reason for them. I set myself on this course to find a justifiable cause for this man's actions only to discover greed and evil were the only cause for the story about to unfold in the upcoming pages.

For the next five years, I would interview Sidney, search through old newspaper files, contact librarians all over the U.S., contact the archivist for the United States Supreme Court, and the curator for the U.S. Treasury Building in Washington D.C. This is the story as it was told to me by the very man himself. I have tried to verify every detail of this fantastic tale, but must admit some stories are not verifiable and must be strictly taken at face value.

****

April 20,1960, wasn't overly monumental for the vast majority of Earth's population. No, the planet continued its age-old rotation. The sun still splattered the western sky with pink and gold over the city of Wheaton, Illinois. People were scurrying around their houses getting ready for their next workday, never considering the sinister plot would soon unfold. Children were whining about their early bedtime, and getting ready to go to school in the morning. All the while three desperate county prisoners were busily conjuring up a supposedly infallible scheme to escape from the DuPage County Jail. The very safety of the entire neighborhood was at stake yet as usual, not one person took notice.

Lights-out was called throughout the newly built county jailhouse at 8 pm. sharp. Eighty-five inmates were rounded up like cattle, herded toward the barred cells, and carefully dispersed between them. The second-floor inmates were marched into a six-man bullpen and the steel barred doors quickly slammed to a close. The dismal clanging sound reverberated through the heavy walls, striking a chord in each criminal reminding him of his dilemma. A uniformed guard slowly stomped down the large hallway precisely following the prison schedule. He carefully checked the "locked" lights on each cell block, rattled each cage door, and muttered a few obscenities as he plodded along his way. The new state-of–the- art, $960,000 jailhouse still suffered from kinks in its electrical system leaving the overworked staff with another headache to manage. Several would-be incidents had been circumvented already.

"This light burned out a few days ago, sir," a young prisoner named Sidney Heard reported to the examining guard. In reality the light was in perfect working order. The teenaged conman knew of several previous jailhouse issues and chose to use them to his advantage. A good criminal must also be a quick-witted schemer. The guard's cold eyes pierced between the steel bars and carefully examined the youngster's expression looking for truth. Sidney's cool gaze never wavered as he stood his ground. The guard shook the gate a couple of times and, after a critical stare at the innocent looking lad, the uniformed man slowly moved on to check the next cell. It was a well-known fact the young gangster had been one of the first inmates to be sent to the 1959 Wheaton jailhouse when he violated his probation from a previous case a year earlier. Unfortunately, the guard's resume didn't include clairvoyance so he had no way of knowing Sidney would soon be the institution's first escapee.

Sidney's insolent blue eyes followed the guard until the large man was well out of sight. A smirk crossed Sidney's face, and then his busy hands quickly freed the intentionally jammed door. The usually rowdy prisoner quietly signaled his cohorts and the daring escape plan was underway. A makeshift rope had been previously prepared from bed sheets. Sidney, along with the other escapees, grabbed the rope and slid open the barred cell door. The three men crossed the six-foot threshold to an open window.

They could smell freedom in the cool night air as they slipped the sheet-rope through the small opening.

Their hearts pounded with excitement as the first man slid through the open window and down the sheet, followed by the other two. As soon as their feet hit the grassy jailhouse lawn below the sheets were hoisted up by a fellow inmate. The remaining collaborator hurriedly untied the sheets and returned them to the bunks. All the sheets had to be replaced quickly. He only had a few minutes to complete his task before the guard would make another round. On the ground, the escapees meandered down the street trying to avoid attention.

To complicate matters, the new brick jailhouse stood adjacent to the county courthouse. Together the buildings formed two sides of the town square. The square itself was not much more than a neatly mowed city park with a few shaded picnic tables and a quaint little gazebo. Even at this hour the park was lightly littered with townspeople. Some were just getting off work and trying to make it home; others were out shopping, but somehow they all were completely oblivious to the criminals' actions.

The escaped convicts knew better than to take off running through the middle of the town square. So, to avoid attention, they tried to walk calmly down the sidewalk and across the street from the park. Unfortunately for Sidney, a flabbergasted housewife had witnessed the daring escape from her front door. In a panic, she quickly locked her doors and phoned the police station, but to no avail. At first the officials didn't believe her account, but they would eventually run a quick head count just in case.[2]

It seemed as if the simple escape plan might work. Fate frowned upon the young escaped cons, however, and a mere nine blocks away from the county jail a patrol car popped over the hill. As soon as the car's lights flashed, Sidney knew they were in big trouble.

"Go!" Sidney hissed to his companions. "I'll take care of it," and he continued walking. The other men quickly disappeared, leaving Sidney alone to take the rap. Moments later the white patrol car pulled up alongside the lone juvenile delinquent. Two officers spotted the lad, and barreling from their car quickly surrounded him with their hands resting precariously on their weapons. Much to Sidney's amazement, the officers hadn't heard of the escape. The uniformed driver was merely surprised at seeing Sidney walking freely down the sidewalk. His face was well known to local law enforcement. This fact did little to bolster the teenager's massive ego, however.

"What are you doing out here, Heard?" one uniformed man bellowed. Everyone in the county knew of the young criminal. His father, Ralph Heard, was a member of the Chicago-based Moose Club, and a local businessman. Ralph also happened to rub shoulders with all the "professionals"—criminals, that is. Sometimes having a shady reputation in a small suburb like North Lake could be troublesome. Sidney couldn't care less about his reputation. He was too busy trying to impress his mobster counterparts and of course the girls.

"Oh, I made bail," Sidney shrugged nonchalantly, trying hard to sound convincing. His scheming mind raced for another escape option, but none came.

"I didn't hear about any bail, Heard. You better get in and we'll check it out," the rugged officer ordered, and nodded toward the back seat of the police car. It was at this point in time Sidney Heard learned an important life lesson: When staring down the wrong end of a few guns, it is always best to follow orders. He reluctantly slipped into the back seat of the white patrol car. His disappointed blue eyes watched freedom pass him by as the police car returned to the same three-story brick building he had worked so hard to escape. Sidney was escorted into the jailhouse office politely enough. Disbelief quickly filled the deputy's face when he looked up to see the tall dark headed teen standing before him.

"What the heck are you doing out here, Heard?" the deputy cursed, using more expletives than will be mentioned here. "I just locked you in the upstairs cell block!"

Upon the guard's outburst, the arresting officer quickly cuffed the fugitive's wrists.

"Well, I'm not there now," Sidney, retorted with a grin. His teenage smart mouth would get him into more trouble than his cunning and schemes throughout his criminal career. Sidney was not Italian by any means, but he was definite proof you don't have to be a Made Member of the *La Cosa Nostra* to be a wise guy. [*La Cosa Nostra*, meaning "this thing of ours" is the official name used by the Italian mafia. You would never catch someone connected to the organized underworld using the generic term "mafia." Instead real mobsters use the words "family," "connections," or even "friends"; but never mafia, or "the mob." The news media and Hollywood coined those terms, and many more to label organized crime.]

After the count was taken of Sidney's former cell block, the deputy soon discovered others were also missing. Sidney was immediately interrogated.

[It should be noted while Sidney distinctively remembers having three cohorts in this escape attempt, the media reported one renegade backed out of the escape plan, and stayed behind in the cell block. He was the one who let the others down through the window and stashed those bed sheets afterward. At this point in the narrative only one man was missing. Sidney of course was too distracted by his escape plan to keep track of the other prisoners. After his feet hit the grassy ground, Sidney was totally focused on obtaining freedom and nothing else. This was no time for babysitting. It was every man for himself.]

"Where is your partner, Heard?" the officer growled slamming his fist on the wooden table in front of him. The teenager sat back in his seat facing the officer and silently stared at the irate man. Sidney had been subjected to harsh interrogations before, so the man's angry tone didn't intimidate the teen in the slightest bit. He was used to the hostile interrogation techniques of many local authorities. Sidney knew his rights well, along with his underworld connections, so he didn't let the man's bad attitude disconcert him.

"You guys are cops. You go find him. That's *your* job," Sidney spat vehemently. The cops wouldn't get any information out of him. Their mind games and dialogue had no effect on the hardened criminal. The term hardened criminal sounds odd when you realize it refers to a boy of seventeen. Sidney had no information to give if he had been cooperative. The other prisoner ran off when the cops showed up and Sidney had no idea where the man had gone. Sidney wouldn't tell the police even if he had known the man's whereabouts. He wasn't a rat.

The officials knew there was no sense in interrogating the smart-mouthed hooligan any further. Sidney was finally led away in handcuffs. He expected them to return him to his cronies in the cell block, but this time the officer leads him to a holding cell in the woman's section of the jailhouse. It was separated from all the other prisoners and offered the inmate a quieter setting where he couldn't get into any further trouble—supposedly. The testosterone-driven teen was disappointed, however, when he realized he wouldn't be allowed to see any of the women.

In this new cell Sidney, would receive his "three-square-a-day" along with a new attempted-escape charge. This charge was neatly placed on top of his ten previous B&E (breaking and entering) charges. But Sidney honestly couldn't care less about the legal matters. He just wanted out. While most teenagers take on odd jobs in hopes of building an impressive resume, Sidney just piled more arrests and convictions onto his criminal record. The more trouble he got himself into, the better his gangster resume would look to his underworld connections. It sounds insane, but unfortunately that's the world Sidney grew up in.

The woman's tiny holding cell where Sidney was assigned granted the teenaged gangster a sense of privacy the six-man cell block he'd been in had lacked. Here Sidney could think without the dull roar of the other prisoners' conversations and arguments. The bland gray room was furnished with a cot bolted to the wall and a flat, lumpy mattress. But the best part was the small toilet in the corner of the cell he had all to himself. In jail one quickly learns to cherish the small things, or so I'm told.

Chapter 2: Sidney's Unfortunate Childhood

Sidney James Heard was born on October 9, 1942, to Ralph and Betty Heard. His family lived in North Lake, a suburb of Chicago in DuPage County, Illinois. As a boy, Sidney was what is now called a Latch Key Kid. He spent his afternoons unsupervised and bored at home after school. Of course, this was before the public-school system offered after-school programs for kids. This lack of supervision led the boy into all sorts of illicit chicanery with the neighborhood girls, including paying them to take off their shirts in his clubhouse.

In an effort to guide his son onto brighter paths, Ralph strongly encouraged his son to spend the afternoons with him at work where at least he would have some similitude of adult supervision. Ralph Heard owned the Mobil Gas station in North Lake. The plan was for the young boy to learn the basics of running a business. Regrettably, in a desperate attempt to lead his son in a better way of life, Ralph unknowingly introduced Sidney to the life of organized crime. You see Ralph's gas station just so happened to be the local hangout for all the big-time Italian "family members" in the Wheaton/Chicago area. Criminal men of all ages flowed through the station regularly.

Sidney couldn't help noticing how the criminal constituents drove the fastest cars, had the prettiest women, and seemed to live life to the utmost. The connected men always wore the finest of clothes and their hair was always perfectly groomed. They seemed like sordid movie stars to the young boy. In this era families were dirt poor, or filthy rich criminals. Economically there weren't many options and society itself was shifting as the sixties began. Strict moral values were being pushed to the breaking point as the young began to fight the establishment of the elder.

As an impressionable child, Sidney was blind to the dark side of his new friends. To make matters worse, the older guys took the rowdy boy under their wings. Soon the preteen began to emulate his so-called heroes in every way. At the tender age of sixteen Sidney found himself classified as a professional criminal with a massive resume of his illegal activities. At an age when most young boys are just learning to drive, Sidney found himself being arrested in Laramie, Wyoming, for armed robbery and trying to cash a phony check.

[Sidney's childhood is filled with stories of typical boyish orneriness and petty crime. To make the first sixteen years of his life compact enough to fit in this narrative I have chosen to highlight the more memorable exploits. I have also arranged them in sub-chapter headings for easier reading.]

Sidney's bully:

Nowadays, everyone complains about being bullied on the playground. Bullying is practically a crime today, but Sidney had a different approach for bullies. When he was eight or nine years old, Sidney remembered being beat up by a certain older boy every day at school. Instead of whining about it, or talking to an adult about it, he chose another option. Of course, it wasn't a good option.

After having his guts full of the physical and verbal abuse, Sidney slipped a baseball bat into his backpack and waited for his intended victim. When the older boy approached Sidney at recess, Sidney clobbered him with the bat as hard as he could. earned Sidney a trip to the principal's office for the incident, but the bully never bothered him again. In his mind the only way to deal with a bully is to hit first and hit harder. The members of Sidney's new found criminal brotherhood found this story quite amusing and gave the boy a big pat on the back for his schoolyard chicanery. Now the bully no longer bothered Sidney, but with his brutish ways the youngster had become the new bully of the school.

Sidney's Church Attendance:

At ten years of age, Sidney thought of a cunning way to hustle the local Catholic congregation as they were leaving Sunday morning mass. Sidney would pay a quarter to get a newspaper from a vending machine, but when the machine opened, instead of just taking one copy of the paper, he would take them all. He would repeat this process at four or five newspaper vending machines before heading over to the local Catholic Church.

The young conman would then wait on the sidewalk outside the church and sell the papers for a dollar apiece. In just half an hour the youngster would be at least ten dollars richer. Even as a child he enjoyed the thrill of a good hustle. His parents always told him how proud they were of him for going to Sunday school alone every week. Unfortunately, they would never learn the truth behind their son's "faithful church attendance." I'm not an overly judgmental person, but I sincerely doubt this type of attendance would earn him a trip through the pearly gates.

Sidney's Wool Coat:

Somewhere along the way Sidney had acquired an ugly wool coat. The baggy jacket was adorned with several visible pockets. It was hot, itchy and uncomfortable. It was a far cry from the flashy mobsters he so worshiped and he hated it, but he wore it all the time anyways. Sidney had carefully added several hidden pockets by cutting large slits in the lining of the coat.

When his mother sent him to the store for groceries he would steal half of them from the store's shelves and stash them inside the coat's open lining. Then he would return home with all the groceries, and pocket the money he hadn't spent for them. Of course, this was in the days before security cameras. So, if he was quick-handed he wouldn't get caught, and his mother could never figure out why her absent minded eleven-year-old never brought home a receipt.

Sidney's first Arrest:

I asked Sidney about his first crime. He told me it had all officially started with a small petty crime at the age of thirteen. Sidney had volunteered to stay late after school one day to clean the blackboard and the erasers. After completing his task, he was instructed to close and lock all the windows. Instead he left one window unlocked. The next night he was to have a boy scout meeting at the local Lutheran church a few blocks away.

After the meeting was well underway, Sidney slipped out of the crowd and ran down to the schoolhouse. Being careful not to run into the janitor, he crawled through the unlocked window. Going from one room to another the young hoodlum stole all the student's money set aside for their milk and lunch. It wasn't a big "haul," but it wasn't the money itself that grabbed Sidney; it was the thrill of the theft. He quickly exited the schoolhouse filled with adrenaline from his first big crime. The excitement of getting away with it was intoxicating.

Unfortunately, Sidney didn't get away with it. Another classmate named Frank Bauman had been a co-conspirator but backed out at the last minute. The boy easily broke under police questioning and snitched on Sidney. Although school officials couldn't prove it, Sidney was blamed and punished for the crime. It was okay with Sidney though; he never held a grudge. He just got even.

The next day Sidney, the smooth talking young bully, caught Frank on the playground and pulled him aside away from the other students. Once out of sight Sidney's fist landed squarely along Frank's jaw. Sidney could feel the crunch of the boy's jaw beneath his knuckles. Frank face planted in the dirt. When the brawl was over, Sidney could hear the snitch crying and vomiting on the ground. The sounds made Sidney's feet fly even faster over the hedge and down the street.

Sidney was arrested and sent to what locals referred to as the "Audi Home." This Chicago-based facility was for juvenile prisoners, and at the time there was no bond set on the juvenile offenders. Sidney had an ace in the hole, however with his family connections. His father had a lot of influential friends both legal and otherwise. Also, Sidney's grandmother had previously married a local Italian bookie and we shouldn't have to explain his connections.

While Ralph Heard would have let his son rot behind bars to teach him a lesson, he came home to find his lovely wife had other plans. Betty had moved his belongings to the front room and wouldn't allow her husband in his own bed.

"You will not sleep in my bed until my boy is out of horrible jail," she informed her somewhat surprised husband. Ralph immediately went to work. Somehow between his father's friends and his step-grandfather, Sidney only spent three days in jail.

In North Lake, Illinois, having a criminal record was commonplace and now Sidney had an official record of his own. After his extremely brief jail time he was given six months of probation and fined a whopping $20. One day a few months later the young hooligan went in to the county office to report to his probation officer. He waited but was eventually told his probation officer was no longer working there, because he was in jail for murdering a man. Yes, you read it right. The "happily married" officer had gotten drunk at a local bar and had decided to fight over a barmaid. When the man jumped him, the officer drew his gun and shot the man dead in front of an entire crowd of witnesses. There was no other officer available to be assigned to Sidney so the teenager never bothered to check in again.

At one point Sidney told me the FBI had investigated the small suburb for signs of corruption. They quickly discovered every officer in town had a criminal record of some sort. To the young man it seemed the only way to get ahead in the world was to be crooked.

Boy scout Camping Trip:

The next summer Sidney was invited to go on a camping trip with his local Boy Scout troop. By now the rowdy youngster had been a part of the troop for nearly a year. He proudly donned the uniform, packed his bags, and told his father goodbye. While everyone was sidetracked with setting up camp, Sidney slipped into the troop leader's tent. He rummaged around until he found the troop's treasury and ran off into the woods with it. Obviously, Sidney didn't earn very many Boy Scout merit badges. He did, however, earn a reputation as a punk. If the mob gave out merit badges, for being a punk, Sidney would have been wearing a shirt full of those badges before he even reached adolescence.

Instead of focusing on getting an education, Sidney's rowdy childhood was filled with petty crime and girls. He even sunk so low as to steal money from his own mother. When I asked him, what motivated him to commit these crimes he would shrug and say he liked buying the affection of the local females. I guess that's a nice way of putting it.

These pilfering stories and more, Sidney would share with his mobster heroes. They would merely laugh at the youngster's shenanigans, thus encouraging him in his criminal endeavors. One might resort to psychological reasoning here and point out if his father had given him the attention he needed, perhaps Sidney wouldn't have turned to the mobsters for his emotional support. Howbeit, Sidney does not blame his father to this day. He still holds some resentment for the man, but admits something deep within himself craved the thrill of a good hustle; thus, blowing "psychology" out of the water.

At the age of fifteen Sidney was attending Fenton High school and played as a linebacker on the football team. At six-foot-one and 185lbs, the teenager was one of their best defensive players. He loved plowing through the opposing team and tackling them to the ground. Perhaps one might suspect Sidney's life was looking up. He was off probation, he was a star football player, and he had girls flocking to him. Unfortunately, Sidney's rowdy ways would bring this to an abrupt end one day when he decided to light a cherry bomb and throw it into study hall. The school board waited until the end of football season, but promptly and permanently expelled the wannabe gangster. Of course, they couldn't disrupt their football season. Heaven forbid.

To complicate Sidney's life even further, his mother passed away on October 3, 1958 just six days before his sixteenth birthday. He mourned the loss of his mother like any child would, but instead of letting his grief and anger out; he chose to harden himself to the pain. He took a job at the gas station to help pay the medical bills and officially quit school. Without his mother's guiding light, Sidney's mere boyhood games would slowly turn into the dastardly crime of armed robbery. It seemed the only thing he wouldn't do to make a few bucks was kill someone. His hesitance to pull the trigger on another human being, and the fact he was not Italian were the only two reasons why Sidney would never become part of the mafia. [One must have an Italian father to become a made member of the *La Cosa Nostra*. The mother's lineage was not as important, but the father's was considered a "deal-breaker."]

The petty crimes of Sidney's childhood paled in comparison to all the breaking and entering charges the seventeen-year-old now faced. Since right after his mother had passed away Sidney had been breaking into stores and homes. He would steal money, guns, and jewelry then he would drive from the small rural suburb into the city and sell all his stolen goods on the black market. The cops charged him with ten "B&E" charges, but Sidney told me he had hit quite a few more places. The police had only charged him with a few.

On one such run, Sidney had a bout of road rage. He had a carload full of stolen guns and was waiting at a red light around 1:30 am. It was a rural light and no one was around, but the malfunctioning light wouldn't change. Sidney sat and stewed with his illegal merchandize for several minutes, and then in a fit of rage he grabbed a stolen Colt .45 handgun. He took aim and shot out the irritating light, climbed back into the car and drove off.

"That thing kicked like a mule," Sidney told me later in an interview. I laughed and wondered how many times other commuters (myself included) would have liked to shoot out an irritating stop light. It was these robberies that landed the teenager in Wheaton jail for the second time. His first incarceration in the new jailhouse had come less than a year earlier.

Ralph Heard finally remarried a woman named Ann. While they were gone on their honeymoon Sidney stole some Old Crow whiskey left over from the wedding. After picking up a few friends and finding girls they ended up in a nature preserve doing what drunken teens do when the police showed up. The officer immediately arrested Sidney for having an open liquor container and told him to follow them to the police station. Well the teen did as he was told—eventually.

The kids piled into Sidney's car in a panic. Come to find out every one of them were on probation for one violation or another. Sidney took off and started cutting through back roads and ditches trying to lose the cops. He eventually lost his tail, but broke the car's a-frame when he hit a large hole and could only turn to the left from then on. It took quite a while, but Sidney took all his friends home before he headed to the county jail. He ditched his crippled car, walked to the town square, and climbed up onto a picnic table in the park right in between the city hall and the jail. Eventually the officers found him and of course they didn't believe he had slept on table for over an hour.

Sidney Heard was the first inmate to be assigned to the newly opened jailhouse. His first sentence was thirty days. During this time, he helped the staff carry over all the furniture and helped set up all the supplies in the new facility. The next time he would be incarcerated there he wouldn't be quiet so helpful.

As Sidney lay stiffly on his standard issue prison cot in the new Wheaton jailhouse, he pondered his childhood: the mistakes of his father, the loss of his mother, and the never-ending hope of escape from one incarceration after another.

Sidney didn't mind being alone in the women's holding cell. The seclusion afforded his young mind the peace and quiet he needed to daydream about his beautiful wife of a mere two weeks. While most newlyweds are blessed with the opportunity to spend some special, private time together, unfortunately, Sidney just found himself *doing* time — so goes the life of a gangster.

In one of our many lunch interviews, Sidney described his first wife, Elizabeth Louise Baumgardner, as a gorgeous Elizabeth Taylor look-alike. He seemed to be drawn to

Hollywood doppelgangers and would end up marrying several of them during his lifetime. Elizabeth Louise worked in the office at *Vogue Magazine.* Her biggest dream was to become a full-fledged cover model someday. The tall, slender model-in-training made a perfect trophy wife for the wannabe gangster. And, of course everyone knows a gangster should have a trophy wife; it's just part of the deal. All Sidney's mobster friends had trophy wives and even a few trophy girlfriends on the side. He emulated the gangsters in every other way, so why not have some arm candy of his own, right?

The couple had recently, in December of 1959, traveled to Kansas City to visit her folks. While in K.C. the couple discovered the marriage laws in Oklahoma were very lenient. Instead of having to wait three days for a marriage license in Missouri, they could legally get married right away in Oklahoma.

On January 1, 1960, Sidney and Elizabeth took off with plans to elope to Miami, Oklahoma. They rode in Sidney's 1951 Pontiac Catalina. He recalled when he filled the car's gas tank the gas prices were a mere 15 cents a gallon. [At the time of this writing gas prices are $3.70/gallon as a national average.]

Unfortunately, his life in the fast lane would come to a screeching halt a few weeks after their marriage when he was caught and arrested for an armed robbery he had committed weeks before. Sidney's fleeting memories of the good life were no match for his dismal surroundings, so he tried to brush the thoughts of his beautiful bride from his mind.

"Would she wait for him?" he wondered. *"Probably not,"* he surmised grimly. *"Who cares anyways?"*

The one part of a gangster's life Sidney hated was the jail time. The actual imprisonment was not the problem. In fact, it was to be expected at some point in his chosen vocation. In the criminal underworld imprisonment, could almost be compared to a boy scout's merit badge. Every gangster eventually ends up in jail. The boredom of doing time, however, was another story. To combat this archenemy, Sidney tried to distract himself with the sparse, happy childhood memories he shared with his father, Ralph Heard. And, they were indeed sparse, to say the least.

After brooding for two weeks in the county's holding cell, Sidney was moved to the west side of the building up on the third floor. The new cell held three other prisoners.

Normally, Sidney would have rotted away in idleness in a woman's cell until his court date, but a young Italian man used his pull with the guards to arrange the move. *(We will call him "Freddie C" to protect his true identity-and ours.)* Everyone in town knew Freddie had underworld connections. It was obvious since the Italian garbage truck driver lived in a million-dollar home, wore only the finest designer clothes, and of course drove a brand-new Cadillac. More importantly, Freddie C. owed Sidney a favor.

A few weeks before Sidney's escape attempt, a fellow inmate had jumped Freddie with a knife. Sidney happened to be near the attack and wrestled the knife away from the assailant. From time on Freddie C. knew he owed Sidney big time, but Sidney was wise enough to never cash in on the debt. Life lesson number two: It is always best to have a guy with connections owe you a favor rather than the other way around. Owing the mob, a favor can be deadly.

Sidney appreciated the better-furnished surroundings in the new location, as well as the kindred fellowship. Freddie was kept in a cell block across from Sidney only the small walkway ran between the rows of cells. Of course, none of this mattered because the only thing on Sidney's mind was planning his next attempt to escape. Sidney, however, did enjoy running with Freddie, when they were briefly let out of their cells for exercise.

"Let out for exercise"—it sounded like he was a caged animal. And in a sense, he was. His mind wandered back and forth from one side of his "cage" to the other like a caged tiger at the city zoo. Sidney steeled his countenance as tough guys are known to do, but in his mind, his imprisonment was driving him loco. He would try to calm his nerves by persistently dreaming up a new escape plan. It was the only thing could keep him sane. Most of the other men in the cell were much older than him and had no trouble slowing down, but to the hormonal adrenaline laced teen the monotony was torturous. All he could do was think about the past and hatch an escape plan.

Sidney's Second Escape:

Sidney's second attempt would have to be well planned if he hoped to succeed. He studied the door's locking mechanism for hours on end. In all his examining, he soon realized the screws would require an Allen wrench. With this problem in mind, his clever but devious mind immediately went to work looking for a solution to the problem. Other, more well behaved inmates might have access to a screw driver or an allen wrench in the workshop. But after his escape attempt there was no way the jailor was going to let Sidney have access to tools. He quickly overcame this obstacle. It was a simple trick—he would just have to snatch an ordinary spoon from his lunch tray. Filing the spoon down to a sharp tool by grinding the edges of it on the concrete floor, however, was time-consuming and required persistent patience. But really, he figured, what else did he have to do?

When the time was right, Sidney was ready to launch his cunning plan. This time, his cohort would be a 16-year-old criminal named Jimmy Woods. Woods was awaiting trial on charges of rape, armed robbery, and assault. Although Sidney's charges seemed mild compared to Jimmy's, the pair had one thing in common—deep within their souls raged a burning desire for freedom. Incarceration was not in either of their plans. When asked about his choice of "running buddies," this is what Sidney had to say:

"I needed someone crazier than me to take care of the cops if need be." Sidney would explain his remark in an interview nearly fifty years later. "It's not right, I know, but that's the way my mind worked back then." Of course, by choosing Woods as his partner, Sidney unwittingly placed himself in a different rank of criminals—a vicious one, one would give the police license to kill.

Sidney quickly jammed the lock of the door to his cell and called the guard over.

"I think this door is messed up again," Sidney said, giving the door a convincing tug. The guard nodded and called the maintenance department all the while keeping a wary eye on the escape artist. A maintenance worker promptly arrived and managed to work open the cell door. The rigged door was easily fixed and slammed shut by the guard a few moments later. Sidney watched with a gleam in his young eyes. This seemingly inconsequential event took place on a regular basis. After several days, Sidney was sure the door's bolts were worn down enough so he could use his makeshift spoon-tool to open them.

On June 23rd, as the huge clock on the courthouse tower began to chime the eight pm. hour, jailer Hugo Themer made his rounds. He carefully checked each cell block as he moved on by. He counted every man in every cell, and made sure they were all locked away tightly. [3] After the jailer passed by his cell block, Sidney bent his spoon-tool to shape it as a pry to work loose the panel on the gated door; then he quickly removed the already loosened screws. A moment later six small screws tumbled into his hands. While no guards were around and the other inmates slept, Sidney lifted the latch on the cell door—and he was nearly free once again.

Two dark figures crept across the third-floor hallway and pried open a screen-covered window. The thin screen wire was easily torn from the opening. Then the desperate fugitives climbed through and dropped themselves through the portal. He let gravity stretch his body to its full length until his fingers winced then let himself drop. The twenty-foot leap from the window sent pain shooting up Sidney's leg, but he refused to think about it as he hobbled through the woods behind the jailhouse. His mind was focused on finding new clothes, money, and guns. Because of Sidney's clever planning, the two teenagers had officially escaped from the county jail—and he was a so-called free man once again.

The *Daily Journal* reported on Friday, June 24, 1960, the electrical locking system had worked fine for years until it was subjected to the ingenuity of a teenage boy.[4] Sidney would get a kick out of line nearly a half-century later when I read the article to him over the telephone. It's not like he needed anything else to bolster his ego back then. Sidney knew he was smart and literally thought he could out strategize the local law enforcement. He thoroughly enjoyed making fools out of the cops.

At 9:30 pm. the local police department set up roadblocks around Wheaton and various other locations in DuPage County in hopes of capturing the fugitive teenagers. A short time later Heard and Woods stumbled onto a house on Orchard Road, which was owned by a Robert F. Nelson. No one was home, so the despots quickly kicked in the back door of the Nelson residence[5]. They stole some clothes and armed themselves with a couple of Nelson's rifles and a pistol. They rummaged around until they found the ammunition and snatched $500 cash.

Now armed, the two convicts followed the railroad tracks ran along the back of the property. A few yards down the line they came across a pump trolley and hopped aboard its platform. They then proceeded to manually pump their way south toward Warrenville, Illinois, like a couple of sordid cartoon characters. The two young jailbirds hid from authorities in a nearby wooded area for a while until they were sure the coast was clear. Bugs and boredom tormented the anxious teenagers until well after sunset. Sidney was restless. He wanted to keep moving, but he knew better than to leave their makeshift hideout, so he calmed his nerves and waited.

Around 11 pm on June 24th, Sidney suggested they steal some wheels. During their flight, they stumbled across the yard of the Horne Lumber Mill. They scurried from wood truck to wood truck until they finally found a red 1948 Dodge with the keys still in the ignition. [This just goes to prove you should never leave your keys in the vehicle.] Sidney planned to use the loaded truck to his advantage if they found themselves pursued by the authorities. The lumber could easily be dumped onto the road to deter any officers in their pursuit. Fortunately, this plan was never put into play and no officers had to face an avalanche of cord wood.

When the news was first reported in the local papers, the police were still not certain if the theft at the lumber mill was connected to the fugitives. For the next few hours any crime was committed within DuPage County and the surrounding Illinois areas was blamed on the missing young men. At this point the *Chicago Daily Journal* reported "Shoot to Kill" orders had been issued on the heads of Sidney Heard, age 17, and Walter Woods, age 16.6

When copies of this news article were shown to Sidney during an interview years later, he was shocked by the headline. Of course, his record didn't warrant such violence, but Jimmy's did. Someone must have been watching out for this rebel lad, or Sidney's life could have ended before it even began.

Now they had wheels, but they ran into another problem. Jimmy couldn't drive a vehicle with a standard transmission, so Sidney took the wheel of the wood truck and the two desperadoes headed southwest toward St. Louis, Missouri. When their gas tank ran dry, they simply ditched the lumber truck and hitchhiked their way westward across the states toward California. The *Chicago Daily Journal* reported finding the abandoned truck along Route 31 on Saturday, June 25, 1960. When Sidney and

Jimmy reached Oklahoma City the pair stayed in a nice hotel and ordered a huge steak dinner at the most expensive restaurant they could find. They enjoyed the luxury accommodations, but knew their money wouldn't last long if they continued spending it so recklessly. Normally they would just steal more, but they needed to lie low for a while.

While the news media blamed every illegal incident in the vicinity on the pair over the next few days, in reality the rogue villains had escaped the great state of Illinois within twenty-four hours after jumping from the jailhouse window. Life on the run was a pure adrenaline rush for Sidney. If they needed anything, they just stole it, or conned it from an innocent bystander. If they wanted girls, they played the gangster card. Sidney knew rowdy women love gangsters, and of course his marriage vows meant nothing unless Elizabeth was around. He knew the authorities probably had her under close surveillance so he dared not contact her.

Being spotted by the authorities was the only real worry Sidney had at this point. One day while they were waiting in a bus stop, Sidney looked up at the bus station's television set and saw pictures of himself and Jimmy flash across the screen on the news. They quickly decided to forgo their bus ride and continued to hitchhike. It was a much safer option for the pair of despots, and it was cheaper.

Their stolen bankroll was running low by the time they finally reached Los Angeles, California, so Jimmy decided to rob a tavern on Santa Monica Boulevard. Sidney held on to Jimmy's change of clothes and waited in the city park for his accomplice to return. Before long Jimmy ran up to their set meeting place with $1,200 cash in his pocket. The two split the haul and hurried to the next town. On the way Sidney learned another essential life lesson: one cannot plant any roots while living life on the run.

Not wanting to stay in one place for too long, the two criminals decided to hitch a ride to Reno, Nevada. They "thumbed" for what seemed like an eternity, but no one would stop and pick them up. It was getting extremely cold and the two decided they were going to hijack the next car. There was no need for it, however, because the next car stopped and offered the frozen scoundrels a ride. They were dropped off at a 24-hour gas station several miles down the road.

Sidney soon discovered the perverted cashier in the station liked to watch women using the bathroom through a tiny hole in the wall. It seemed to Sidney twisted minds were everywhere. Of course, in his mind this man was a worse criminal than he ever was. He never stopped to think about how badly he hurt people with his criminal escapades. After spending a few hours at the mangy truck stop, Jimmy and Sidney finally found a traveler who was willing to take them to Reno. Sidney was glad to get away from the dump and the disgusting cashier.

Sidney later applied for a draft card under the name of Sidney James Cudto in hopes of obtaining some sort of "legal" identification. Much to his chagrin, the cashier told Sidney the card would have to be mailed to him later. Impatient, as usual, Jimmy decided to forgo the ID filing process by stealing some blank draft cards and making his own. So, the plan was set. They found a nearby park where Jimmy donned his "robbing clothes." This time Sidney didn't have long to wait on him. A mere fifteen minutes had passed when he spotted Jimmy racing across the little footbridge into the once peaceful park. He was being chased by a mob of angry people. Jimmy turned back, holding a gun, as if to shoot into the crowd and they all quickly dispersed. Sidney handed his co-fugitive some new clothes and stashed the weapon.

"Meet me in Sacramento," Jimmy whispered before racing out of Sidney's life forever. With Sidney was left alone, without an accomplice, no place to sleep, and without any identification. As hopeless as it sounds, Sidney was not discouraged. He had money so he could always find a cheap hotel, or a local prostitute to spend the night with.

Chapter 3: Life on the Run

Alone in the world Sidney wandered through the streets of Los Angeles for a couple of hours before finally thumbing his way to Sacramento. Many people might feel lonely and lost, but not Sidney he enjoyed the solitude. He scooped out the California sights for a few days, but Jimmy was nowhere to be found. Growing impatient, Sidney finally headed north toward Maryville, California. He wasn't sure if he wanted to meet up with his deranged cohort anyways. Like most people in young Sidney's life, Jimmy Woods had served his purpose and now Sidney was ready to move on. Jimmy was nothing more than a tool had outlived his usefulness.

While hitchhiking his way north, the weary con man ran into a couple of brothers named Charlie and John Smith. They were on their way to work in the apricot fields and invited the young escaped convict to tag along. The Chicago native was curious. He had never even seen an apricot tree before, and he could use a little money. Besides, wandering alone in the world without an identity can be difficult, to say the least.

Sydney took the alias of "Bob Smith" and joined the apricot field crew as the third Smith brother. For the first few days he climbed ladders and picked apricots off the trees for a measly $1.25 an hour. The money was not great, but, hey, at least he was not behind bars. Out in the apricot fields Sidney got more than his fair share of sunshine and fresh air. The three new recruits shared a small bunkhouse with several rowdy Mexican men. After three days, Bob Smith was given a 25-cent raise and was promoted to loading boxes onto the trucks. Bob could take the trucks to the dry loading area where the women were. He longed for a few moments alone with one of them, but his daydream was never realized. Of course, the fact he was already married never entered his mind.

One Friday night, the "Smith" boys returned home late from a night on the town to find the Mexican men drunk in the kitchen. The three so-called brothers headed off to bed in hopes of catching a few hours of sleep before going to work the next morning. The rowdy crowd in the kitchen, however, grew louder by the hour. "Bob" politely asked them to quiet down several times. Finally, one of the wasted men brandished a knife and threatened to castrate Bob if he dared to return to the kitchen. Of course, the poor man had no idea who he was messing with.

With his anger flaring to a boiling point, Sidney stormed back to his bunk and grabbed the stashed gun from under his pillow. A moment later the kitchen door flew open under the force of Sidney's boot.

"I said shut up!" Sidney yelled, pistol in hand. The drunkards took one look at the gun in the angry gringo's hand and quickly vacated the premises. One man even dove out the kitchen window to escape the blue-eyed tyrant. The "Smiths" got a couple hours of sleep, then left early the next morning in fear of what the boss might say when the details reached his ear.

The now unemployed brothers traveled south for nearly four hundred miles to Chino, California, to stay at their parents' place. Sidney was raised in the suburbs of Chicago and thought he had seen everything, but he was in for the surprise of his life. The Smith family lived without electricity or even a real roof over their heads, but they did have one amenity to offer their fancy house guest. Their makeshift shack stood next to a drive-in movie theater, and the Smiths had stretched a wire from the theater to the place they were staying so they could watch the movies for free. They may not have had a roof or running water, but they could keep up with Hollywood's latest releases. Who needs a roof and a bathroom anyways, right?

The Smith family was strawberry farmers, and the three guys spent the next day working in the field. Sidney was used to the cooler weather of Chicago, and lasted only four hours in the California heat. Sweat poured from his furrowed brow as he picked yet another bucket of strawberries. The young gangster quickly decided the strawberry-picking hobo life was not for him. He would much rather have worn the classy three-piece suits, and con his way through life like his mobster counterparts. This gig was too much work and too little pay.

A couple of days later the Smith boys left their ramshackle home and traveled to the picturesque town of West Yellowstone, Montana. The snow-covered mountains were the perfect backdrops for the quaint little town. The main streets were lined with old storefront buildings. Sidney thought photo of the town would have been perfect on a Christmas post card. Sidney and the Smith brothers parted ways for good in West Yellowstone. He found a job washing dishes in the town at the Shamrock Cafe making $6.50 a day plus meals. It was nowhere near the luxury accommodations he and his gangster friends were used to, but at least it was indoors and out of the heat. Sidney focused on his work and was promoted to cook soon afterward.

He rented a room and soon found a girlfriend named Maryland. After hours Sidney, would take his earnings and gamble over a game of cards in the back of the café. He would usually win and take his opponents money, but he didn't stop his betting fun with card games. One opponent bet Sidney couldn't name all 50 states in the union within two minutes. Sidney was off on a roll, but he couldn't remember the last state. His girlfriend kept coming in, passing out fresh beer and making strange gestures, but Sidney paid no attention. When it was all over, he lost his wager and his girlfriend reminded him of her name; Maryland. It was the last state.

Life was good for a while, but soon Sidney's restlessness set in and he made a trip back to California in hopes of finding a better job. After an unsuccessful job search, he quickly realized his mistake and decided to return to the charming little town of West Yellowstone. On his way back, he walked along the sunny California beach looking for a car to steal. Instead, he found a man's jeans and a wallet. Sidney snatched the man's identification and easily slipped into the personage of "Miles Kenneth Leathergood." He did however leave the poor man his pants. I suppose stealing a man's identity is okay if you don't make him walk naked on a public beach.

Now he had identification, he decided to head for Las Vegas. With his quick eye and sharp memory, he knew he could gamble his way into a small fortune. He never did find a car to steal so he was back to hitchhiking. Along the way a blond woman driving a convertible Cadillac passed the weary vagabond as he plodded along the highway. Cadillac. It was his favorite mode of transportation. She quickly swerved onto the road's shoulder and waited for Sidney to jog up to the car. Not only did she offer him a ride, she offered him a place to crash for the night. The exhausted gangster was thankful for both favors.

Over time Sidney began to learn the rules of the road. He would knock on the back door of a truck stop and ask if he could wash dishes in exchange for a meal. worked and usually someone would feel sorry for him and give him a little money to boot. Sidney hitchhiked all over America before deciding to look up an old friend in Florida. He had a little money in his pocket, and a new alias. At one point when he was stopped for hitchhiking, Sidney quickly discovered from the officer who stopped him, Mr. Leathergood was a fine upstanding citizen and didn't have a warrant out for his arrest. Thank you, Miles Leathergood. Life finally seemed to be turning up for the outcast criminal.

Just outside Jacksonville, Florida, Johnny Lane and his girlfriend Jacquelyn Ann stopped along the road to pick up the hike-weary teen. The couple was from Ohio and seemed nice, so Sidney squeezed into the back seat alongside their friend, Eugene Blanton. As they all became acquainted, Sidney learned they had more in common than he first realized. For example, when they wanted money they would just stop and steal it and life for them was one big party. The four desperadoes proceeded to go on a sightseeing tour through Florida's everglades with their ill-gotten gains. Life was fun for all them for a short period, but soon Sidney would be smacked in the face with another one of life's difficult lessons. Karma has a peculiar way of catching up with you – even when you're flying down the fast lane.

When the money ran out a few days later, the band of misfits decided to rob a convenience store in Inverness, Florida. They had broken into several homes to steal money, but they had never robbed a business. This robbery would change Sidney's life forever. The bold cashier would have none of their attempt at robbery and began to struggle to reach his hidden gun. Sidney quickly hit him over the head with the butt of his own gun, grabbed the money, and ran. Unfortunately, "petty" things like consequences never crossed the young criminal's mind. Survival, fun, and money were the most important aspects of his life at time.

After the robbery, the foursome drove off into the night. Something was said in conversation and Sidney started to get a sinking feeling the car they were driving may have been stolen. He asked his new-found friends about this, but the question was repeatedly shrugged off. A few hours later the crew of misfits were flying down HWY 10 just south of Bonifay, Florida, when an officer pulled them over for speeding. Sidney's feelings were confirmed when the officer ran the car's plates for a background check and the report came back it was stolen. Dread settled around the escaped con the moment he heard a siren.

Sydney tried to convince the officer he was just a hitchhiker, but Jacquelyn's big mouth quickly spilled the entire story of the past few days. She related every robbery in specific detail and they all included their new friend "Miles."

After Jacquelyn's damning confession, they were all immediately arrested and taken to the city jailhouse in a nearby Florida town. Sidney was booked as Miles Leathergood. He was fingerprinted and the paperwork was sent off to Washington D.C. for verification. Unfortunately, Sidney knew the routine well and, after undergoing the booking process, he was thrown into a tiny room behind another barred door. He had been on the run for nearly four months. Life would soon take a drastic turn for the now eighteen-year-old convict.

Two weeks after his arrest Sidney's fingerprints returned from Washington D.C. and successfully exposed his identity. He was no longer a first-time offender. He was a big-time criminal from Chicago. Along with his prints came a massive laundry list of charges stemmed back over the previous two years of his professional criminal career. Once they discovered whom they had behind bars, Sidney was immediately put under heavy guard. The South had bagged a big game prize from the North and they weren't going to run any chance of him escaping.

Several hours later Sidney was called to join a lineup. He stood against the wall alongside a few other criminals he had never seen before. A bright spotlight blinded the handcuffed men in the line. It was hot and bothersome, and Sidney couldn't see anything but the shadows of the men standing before them. The convenience store manager was brought in from the Inverness robbery and easily identified Sidney as his assailant.

"Yeah, that's the guy. I would have killed that Yankee if I could have got to my gun," the man spat vehemently. "That punk knocked me over the head." The man ranted and raved all the way as an officer led him out the door. Sidney knew he was doomed.

With the damming testimony, Sidney was quickly charged with armed robbery and aggravated assault. The new charges were piled on top of his previous armed robbery and escape charges. A feeling of dread settled deep in the pit of his stomach. Another life lesson smacked the teenaged gangster across the face. Whether anyone wanted to admit it or not, "Northerners" were still hated in the South in the 1960s.

Three monotonous weeks later a gruff guard ordered the young man to the front of the jailhouse. "You have a phone call, Heard."

The whole situation seemed strange to the nervous teen. Who would be calling him? His own parents hadn't returned any of his messages or letters. The uniformed officer unlocked Sidney's handcuffs, handed him the phone, and then took a seat across the desk from him. His large body sat rigid and motionless, his cold eyes casing the inmate's every expression. Sidney's quick gaze noticed a pistol sitting on a shelf well within his reach and the open door behind his chair. Everything within him screamed, "run," but a still, small voice echoed for him to beware. The guard's eerie stare, the obviously placed hand gun, and the open door all added up in Sidney's mind as a setup.

He tried to steady his heartbeat as he listened to his wife's voice on the phone. Oh, how he missed her, but being married to a man doing hard time was not in Elizabeth Bumgardner's plans. Honestly, hard time was not in Sidney's plans either. If he could find a way out he would be running wild and free. Of course, this also meant he could never return home to her. He wondered if he would even get to see Chicago again. Oh, how his soul longed for Chicago.

"Do you hear me, Sidney? I want a divorce." Elizabeth ranted on the other end of the line. "I am not going to be married to a criminal."

While most men would be upset by the threat of divorce, Sidney simply refused to care. There were plenty of other women out there, and gangsters could pick up another trophy wife any day of the week.

"I understand," he mumbled. His mind was too preoccupied with escape plans to care what the woman was saying. In his lifestyle, women were a dime a dozen. When asked if he ever loved his wives, Sidney would coolly reply, "I did at the time." In reality, each woman Sidney would acquire along his criminal path would serve a specific purpose for an allotted time. Then Sidney would move on to the next female object waiting in line, bedazzling her with expensive trinkets; sometimes he would marry her and sometimes he would just drag her along on his criminal escapades.

Sidney could feel his hands tremble as he handed the phone back to the jailer a few moments later. *Don't do it,* his mind screamed. *Run,* yelled every nerve in his body. His cold blue eyes carefully cased the pistol as his body slowly rose from the chair. The jailer, as a uniformed hunter, patiently waited for his prey to take the bait. He would soon be disappointed, however, when Sidney held out his hands to be re-cuffed. Sidney's suspicions were confirmed moments later when two armed guards walked through the door directly behind him. It had been a deliberate setup, but Sidney hadn't taken the bait. The young Chicago gangster would live to see another warm Florida morning even if it was behind bars.

In his cold, dark cell, Sidney stared at the ceiling and refused to sleep. Every creek of the cot made him jump. He knew the jailors wanted him dead, and they wouldn't stop their treachery until they had succeeded. For now, he would have to wait and stay alert. He steeled his nerves once again and prepared himself to face whatever the South could throw at him.

[Sidney was quick to tell me although he was a nervous wreck at this point he would never have shown it.

He has told me repeatedly he has not related most of this tale to anyone; not even his wives. To reveal this much emotion to him, even now, is a sign of weakness.

"I would say you know me about 99% and that's a whole lot more than any of my wives," Sidney explained to this unassuming writer.]

The next day Sidney was called to appear before the local judge. He was quickly cuffed and stuffed into the back of yet another patrol car and taken to Inverness, Florida. The nonchalant officer shoved the teen into the Citrus County Courthouse to wait his turn. After waiting a torturous few hours, they were finally ushered inside the courtroom.

Sidney thought the black robed man seemed amiable, but the naive teenager was sorely mistaken. Sidney was quickly ushered into his assigned seat behind the defendant's table. Unfortunately, one valuable piece of information had been hidden from the convict. The convenience store owner Sidney had pistol-whipped a few weeks earlier was the county judge's nephew. Of course, a good attorney would have pointed out this obvious conflict of interest to Sidney, but he didn't have the luxury of an attorney. No, the teenaged boy would stand alone to face his crimes without the benefit of a public defender. The formidable black-robed judge motioned for Sidney to approach the bench.

"Listen, son, if you plead guilty to this armed robbery, I will send you back to Chicago where you came from," the judge assured the young man standing before him. "You don't belong in the South, son."

Sidney couldn't agree more. Besides, he knew he could get his case dropped in Chicago with all his mob connections. Those connections, however, were useless in the South. He was not Italian (therefore he was not a "Made Man"), and he didn't know any of the criminal families in Florida. Sidney pondered his chances and quickly agreed with the judge. He decided to plead guilty to the crime without the assistance of an attorney.

[At this point I must point out in 1962 people accused of a crime didn't have the right to a public defender unless they were accused of murder. This right would come later with the *Gideon vs. Wainwright* case; in which Sidney played a big part. In fact, at the time of this writing, Sidney Heard is the only surviving petitioner in this landmark case we know of.]

As the judge's gavel slammed into its base the ominous echo sent chills up Sidney's spine. He immediately realized his grave error even before the man spoke a single word.

"Sidney James Heard, I hereby sentence you to twenty-five years of hard labor in the Florida State Penitentiary," the judge declared with a laugh. He then ordered court officers, "Take Yankee Son of a ... away." [We will not repeat the exact words of the "honorable" judge here. I think you get the idea.]

Sidney stood stunned by the sentence. Twenty-five years sounded like an eternity to the youngster. A uniformed officer slid the cold steel cuffs around the dejected teenager's wrists and sent him back to his tiny jailhouse cell.

The next day Sidney, along with his three male cohorts, were escorted back to Bonifay, Florida, to face more burglary charges before he was to be transferred to the Florida State Penitentiary for the next quarter of a century. As anger grew within him, Sidney determined to escape from the south—or die trying. The Florida State Pen, or Raiford, was rumored to be one of the worst prisons in the country. To make matters even worse, Sidney was a *white* northerner. He knew he would have a better chance of escape from the Holmes County jailhouse in Bonifay than he would if he made it to the state penitentiary in Raiford.

Sidney's well-trained eyes scoped out the county jailhouse as the patrol car driver parked in front of the building. The officer slowly lumbered around the car and opened its back door for the handcuffed criminal. The two-story white building would be an easy escape, or so Sidney thought. Instead of steel barred windows, the openings were covered with a thin mesh material. Sidney's mind took in every detail of the building's layout as he was escorted into his assigned cell. He knew this would be a temporary placement, and he only had a few days to make a break for it. He spent the next couple of hours trying to plot his way out of the state. Sidney knew the Alabama state line was just a few miles to the north. If he could get across it, he might have a chance for freedom. His chance would come the very next night.

Jacquelyn heard about Sidney's unfair sentence and felt awful about it. She knew her damming testimony had gotten him into this mess. Whether it was her supposed guilt over Sidney's arrest, or her fatal attraction to bad boys, Jacquelyn was determined to help the young Chicago man escape. There was only one jailer on duty night. So, when he came into her cell to "hook up" with her cellmate, Jacquelyn slipped the keys from his discarded pants and quickly ducked out of her cell. With the guard busy getting busy she left completely unnoticed. She made her way down the hall to the men's ward and slipped down the hallway to Sidney's cell. She opened the barred door and motioned for Sidney to follow her. Afterward she released Johnny and Eugene as well. Together the four escapees made their way to the front door of the jailhouse. They quietly opened the front door and hit the ground running as fast as they could. The fierce winter wind tore at the four jailbirds as they raced toward the Alabama border.

The rag-tag band of misfits ran along the road, ducking behind signs, trees, and even dumpsters every time a car passed them by. After a short time, the bitter cold became too much for Jacquelyn's meager apparel, so when her boyfriend Johnny decided to go back to the jailhouse, she gladly went with him. Of course, Eugene decided to tag along behind the pair as usual. Sidney had no choice, however. His rap sheet was as long as his arm, and he was not going back without a fight. He simply couldn't return to tiny cell. After trudging through the nearby woods for a couple of hours, Sidney came across a bridge ran along the state line. He waited inside the timber's edge as a few cars passed, then made a dash toward freedom.

Just across the Alabama line, two men from the local militia armed with guns and dogs closed in on the escaped convict. Without warning, a third man hit him from behind with the butt of his rifle. Searing pain shot through Sidney's skull, and before he knew what hit him another large fist found its mark along his jaw. The world began to spin around him. Blood filled his vision, his ears exploding with the constant barking of the vicious dogs. Moonlight shone on the blood red snow. Fear, pain, and confusion overwhelmed his body. Slumping to the ground helpless he tried to cover his head, but the brutal beating continued. Boots crammed into his ribcage causing him to cough up blood. The pummeling continued for several harrowing minutes until the blood lust of his attackers finally subsided.

Blood poured from Sidney's face as the men literally threw his limp body into the back of a pickup truck. Their scent-sensitive dogs jumped in the truck alongside him and began to lick his wounds. The driver pulled his dogs away and proceeded to kick Sidney in the back of the head once more.

"That dog's too good to be licking your Yankee blood, boy," snarled the truck driver. He let out a low guttural laugh and hopped into the cab of the truck. Sidney trembled in fear as the vehicle bounced its way back to Bonifay. The cold wind stung his wounds as he huddled against the truck's cab trying to stay warm. The world around him still spun and the bouncing truck turned his stomach. The pain in his skull throbbed to the beat of his heart as his life's essence poured from his wounds and stained the freezing cold truck bed beneath him.

At the jailhouse, mobs of angry farmers surrounded the truck as Sidney was pulled from the pickup's bed. His limp body fell to the ground among angry shouts from the onlookers. The officers slammed cuffs on the subjugated teen's wrists, and then proceeded to drag the beaten young man up the jailhouse steps. Sidney was too weak to protest or even walk.

"You're lucky, boy!" shouted one of the farmers. "I wish I'd a caught ya. I'd a got fifty bucks for you alive and a hunerd' for ya dead."

Sidney was not sure if the farmer was telling the truth, but it still struck fear deep within him. Unfortunately, being heckled by an angry lynch mob would soon turn out to be the least of the young man's concerns.

Sidney stumbled into the jailhouse with his hands cuffed behind his back. The cuffs were so tight he thought his wrists might bleed. The blood and snow soaked prisoner was thrown into a metal cage-like cell with a wire mesh ceiling. Pain shot through Sidney's head as he slumped onto the cold concrete floor. He tried to huddle into a ball to stay warm, but his bruised ribs made it nearly impossible. Nights in Northern Florida could get very chilly, and Sidney would find this out the hard way. At least when he was running he was working up some heat, but lying motionless on the cement floor sent chills straight through him.

The next day, Sidney made the terrible mistake of asking for a drink of water. The jailer smiled an evil grin and promised the bruised man a drink. A moment later the man turned the fire hose on the inmate. The powerful burst of water stung Sidney's wounded flesh and offered little in the way of a refreshing drink. Time for another life lesson: Don't ask for *anything* when you have been beaten half to death and held in a cage like an animal. Sidney spent the second night in the cell huddled on the cold floor; soaking wet.

The third day, Sidney was finally pulled from his cage and escorted to Sheriff Cletus Andrew's office. His wrists were raw from being handcuffed behind his back, but he kept his swollen lips closed. Sidney watched silently as the sheriff gnawed on juicy steak and slurped a cold beer. Sidney's stomach knotted with hunger, and his soul seethed with hatred.

The uniformed man ordered everyone else to leave the room. Sidney watched the officers leave and panic began to set in his mind. Once he was left alone with Andrews, Sidney was informed in a not so subtle manner he would be killed if he tried to escape again. The sheriff owned several profitable businesses around town and practically ran the county. He had a good business reputation to maintain—he was not going to let a little Yankee punk ruin it for him. Scared stiff, Sidney couldn't wait to return to his cell.

In all reality, Sidney was not concerned with the twenty-five years so much; he just wondered if he could survive the night. This grim truth settled deep around him like a dark dense fog. Death peered at him from the shadows. Mental images of the warden waving a steak knife at his throat tormented Sidney's sleep. The sheriff's mind games had worked on the terrified teenager.

[To me this seemed like a sick Hollywood script when Sidney first relayed it to me. I was immediately angry at the jailors and the sheriff, but Sidney wasn't. that's what I found so refreshing about him. Nowadays people want to blame everyone else for their consequences, but Sidney is a completely different breed. He told me the sheriff was a good guy, and he was just doing his job. Then he told me another story about the sheriff's kindness helped me understand his way of thinking.]

While Sidney was waiting for his transfer to Raiford a drunk man started a fight and ended up throwing a jar of sorghum at Sidney. He was behind bars and when the glass jar hit the steel it shattered into a million pieces. The trustees were called in to help clean up the mess and the drunken man was hauled off. Sidney kept telling them something was wrong with his eye. The medic examined him, but couldn't find anything. A tiny shard of glass had embedded in his eye.

The next morning Sheriff Andrews personally walked Sidney down the street to the eye doctor. He didn't handcuff him or anything. He did inform the young man he would have to shoot him if he tried to run, and Sidney didn't dare try. During their trip the sheriff told Sidney he was going to try to help him with his sentence. Sidney was set to receive five years for a robbery Jacquelyn had ratted about, and another three to ten years for his escape attempt.

The sheriff talked with the judge and got the five years to run concurrently and instead of the maximum of ten years for the escape he got Sidney only three. He tried to get it to run concurrently, but the judge ended up stacking sentence. Instead of having to serve up to forty years the sheriff had knocked it down to twenty-eight. In Sidney's mind, whatever the man's tactics, Sheriff Andrews was a good man and he never forgot it.

Chapter 4: Florida State Penitentiary: July, 1961

Sidney watched out the patrol car window as the car slipped through the barbed-wire gates of the Florida State Penitentiary. The yard was precisely trimmed and the landscaping was somewhat appealing to visitors. In the warm summer sun, the place might have looked inviting to someone on a tour. However, to know you couldn't step a foot beyond the neatly painted sign or on the meticulously mowed lawns for a quarter of a century was enough to drive Sidney to the brink of insanity. Many inmates cannot withstand the anxiety and eventually snap. It would take all the teenager's mental fortitude to withstand the meltdown. Once inside the complex the troubled teen was stripped of his identity, his clothes, and whatever dignity he may have had left. By this point in time, there wasn't much left for the state of Florida to take from him.

[Being naive in nature I was shocked to find penitentiaries strip their inmates during the processing procedure. It may be done differently now, but this wasn't done in a private room. They were all marched along in a line naked as jaybirds. I guess this would make an inmate think twice about running off.]

At this point Sidney James Heard, for all intents and purposes, ceased to exist. The inmate number "001818" became his name. His few earthly belongings were placed in a storage box and he was issued a set of blue prison clothes. His greatest "fashion accessory" was a set of leg irons. Diamond pinkie rings and three-piece suits were a thing of the past. His inmate number was printed in large block letters down the legs of his blue prison pants so the guards could identify their target from a distance if he tried to run away. All his hopes and dreams were left at the door as the surly jailer barked orders to the group of new arrivals. Time quickly became nothing—and yet everything. Only one who is or has been in prison can truly understand this anomaly.

Sidney quickly became accustomed to the standard grits for breakfast and green vegetables for lunch and dinner. Meat was a rare commodity came in the form of Mullet on Fridays. A new inmate usually spent an average of thirty days in the Diagnostic's Dormitory.

Diagnostics was set up like a large dorm room with rows of bunk beds; it housed sixty men on average. During this time, each inmate's IQ would be tested; they would be given a full medical examination, and be assigned a job within the prison. The warden would spend this time piecing together each inmate's criminal record. This process could take quite a while in the years before the convenience of the Internet. Everything had to go through the U.S. Postal service, and might as well have been the pony express. To make matters worse, Sidney had a criminal record a mile long. Not only did his legal infractions span several states they had also piled up over several years. It sounds strange since he was only a teenager at the time, but it was true none-the-less. [Remember, Sidney was on probation by the age of thirteen.]

While the men were being shuffled through the receiving department like a herd of cattle, Sidney ran into a well-connected man named Henry T. from the Tampa Bay area. [His last name cannot be mentioned because it happens to be a household name everyone in America might recognize, and I'd like to keep my head thank you.]

Henry was serving a short sentence for something less serious, like tax evasion. The Feds had tagged him with a minor charge just to get him off the streets. It was not like it bothered the big-time gangster in the least. As with most mobsters, Henry T's illegal business ventures still ran smoothly while he was tucked away behind bars. His "soldiers" still ran all his deals on the street. That's the way underworld crime works. It is not built on the shoulders of one man. Each boss has an under boss, a vast array of captains, or "Capos" and an army of soldiers. Not only did this keep business running smoothly in the boss' absence it also insulated the big man making it hard to get a conviction. Sometimes their attorneys were a major part of the criminal network. This allowed the boss to send and receive messages the prison officials wouldn't have access to.

Henry T. was in charge of the prison laundry room when Sidney came through the line. Henry had heard of the young gangster with Chicago connections, and respected the teenager's gall. Not many men had the guts to try and escape from the sheriff in Bonifay, Florida. Whether it was guts, desperation, or outright stupidity is still up for debate.

Henry discreetly questioned Sidney about his connections as he was moved through the laundry line.

Sidney dropped a few big underworld names, and low and behold he was given the best clothing available. is the way it worked behind bars both then and even now. If you had connections and friends in high places you were treated like some sort of odious royalty. Sidney was smart enough to use this to his advantage. [As his biographer I've noticed his actual connections were never quite as illustrious as his assumed ones. Of course, Sidney kept this tidbit of information to himself.]

Not everyone respected the teenager however, and one evening during shower time a large brute of a man made the mistake of complimenting his view of Sidney's rear end. The egotistical teen boiled back to his bunk bed and waited there fuming until lights-out was called a short time later. He listened and waited for the walking guard to pass by before quietly slipping down from his bunk. Tiptoeing through the dark, Sidney made his way across the room to his "admirer's" bed.

"Hello, I am glad you came," the man whispered. Sidney knelt as if to crawl into the bunk next to the man. While kneeling he quickly grabbed the man's footlocker from under the bed and bashed it over the man's skull a few times. Sidney whispered a few expletives about liking women before quietly making his way back to his own bunk. The men in the surrounding beds did nothing to stop the viscous attack. They simply rolled over in their beds and ignored the situation.

Nothing was said the next morning as the MTA cleaned up the inmate's face. Not one witness could be found to give an explanation. The injured man was immediately hauled away and put into protective custody, but no one ever dared question Sidney's sexual preference again. No one ever "rolled over" on him either. For those of you who don't already know, the term "rolled over" simply means to snitch on someone.

One particularly bland morning, Sidney was asked if he wanted to try out for the prison boxing team. Every inmate was usually given a job to do inside the prison system, but Sidney's past escape attempts kept him firmly grounded for a while. Longing for something to do, he volunteered for the boxing team and was ushered to the building across the yard, nicknamed the White Rock. The name was not derived from the building's color, but rather from the skin color of its occupants. In 1961, prisons were still segregated. The prison yards wouldn't be integrated until later year. Even then, integration rules only applied to the weekends. This reprehensible regulation would still be in force long after Sidney's release.

The White Rock building was crammed with rowdy inmates looking for some action, entertainment, and a chance to gamble. The tall, lanky teenager was pushed toward the boxing ring among shouts of profanity and excitement. Waiting in the makeshift ring was the prison's current boxing champion, Doc Gaines.

A bell sounded signaling the start of the fight. A moment later Sidney found himself crumpled in a heap on the mat. Sidney's black and blue eyes opened to the sound of the referee yelling, "Seven!"

The disoriented teen tried to get up, but found his limbs were immobile. The match was over before the mighty wannabe gangster could even throw a punch. The crowd jeered at the bloody inmate lay on the floor. Obviously, no one lost any bets on Sidney day.

The dazed teen tried to remember what happened between the numbers one and seven, but his muddled mind couldn't conjure up the memory. Yet, somehow, despite the humiliating loss, Sidney could join the prison boxing team. He had nothing else to do, and this would give him access to the prison's gym. His "flight risk" status had left the bored teen little options, and Sidney decided he would rather be pummeled in the ring than decay alone in his cell. Mental boredom had always been one of Sidney's worst enemies. This change in routine gave him time away from his cell and more importantly it gave him an outlet for his anger.

Later evening, after his disgraceful defeat in the ring, the ego-bruised prisoner climbed into his bunk. His muscles still ached from the beating. He lay on his bunk bed and watched the crowd of men pour into the dorm. The scene never changed. Sixty men would cram into one drably painted room lined with bunk beds. Every day the routine was unwavering and exasperatingly monotonous.

The morning bell rang just a few hours later. It didn't bother Sidney; he never slept much anyway. He longed for the day when he didn't have to be bossed around by a buzzer. At the sound, everyone crawled out of bed grumbling and spitting profanity. Sidney sighed, pulled on his blue uniform shirt, and slipped into his ugly blue pants. For a moment, his mind receded and he longed for the good old days of three-piece suits, fast cars, diamond pinkie rings, and beautiful women. It was the women he longed for most of all. Oh, the women. They were fast, loose, and perfectly beautiful. If women were classed from one to ten, his women were required to be elevens. Long, tall, plastic Barbie dolls were his type and he'd die for one right about now.

He hastily brushed those depressing thoughts out of his mind, swallowed his raging hormones, and quickly filed into a line leading down the hall along with the rest of the convicts. Once in the hallway, he watched the guard torment a smaller inmate. It was a familiar scene. Anger again welled up deep within him and he determined he wouldn't be the man's next victim, whatever it took.

Inside the blandly painted walls of Raiford the rowdy, fun-loving teenager would slowly develop into a hardened conman. His very existence in prison depended on his survival instinct, his wit, and his physical strength. One wrong move and he was history...or worse. [It could be asked at this point if America's prison system is rehabilitating criminals—or creating them. I believe the question would make even Albert Einstein ponder.]

Setting politics aside, this day would be a turning point in the young criminal's life. He was sent to the Rock to learn how to box. He spent the day learning the basics of the sport, and soon discovered the boxing teams were the "celebrities" of the yard. Suddenly Sidney was eating the best of food, wearing one of the best-looking prison uniforms, and was even given more yard privileges than most other inmates. Yeah, Sidney was finally living the good life—if such a thing existed behind bars. Slowly he began to pack on a few pounds of muscle and after a little training he became quite the contender in the boxing ring. After a while the inmates began betting *on* him instead of *against* him and he was making them a lot of money. He was also transforming from a tall, lanky kid into a massive brute of a man.

After spending a month in Diagnostics, Sidney was relocated to the White Rock Building where he was crammed into a ten-man cell. His little box of "home" was shoved under another worn out bed and the rigid routine began again: a bell told him when to get up, when to shower, when to eat ...even when to go to bed. The only thing the warden couldn't control was Sidney's scheming mind. The only highlight to his new surroundings was his new running buddy, Big John from Chicago. It was nice to find someone from his hometown and the two inmates quickly hit it off.

On one particularly monotonous day, Sidney decided to act as a backup man for Big John while the Chicago thug collected a debt. When the indebted inmate balked, and refused to pay voluntarily, Sidney watched his friend proceed to "shake down" the fellow inmate with a knife. [The term "shake down" simply means to take something from someone by force.] Sidney would later learn his buddy Big John was robbing the guy. It seemed his buddy from Chicago had set him up. Either way, Sidney refused to snitch on Big John, and so as punishment Sidney was thrown into the *Hole.*

He knew to keep his mouth shut. Every gangster knew about "Omerta," the mafia's vow of silence. This rule was to be honored whether you were Italian or not. By keeping his mouth shut, Sidney earned a greater respect from his peers. And, respect is more valuable than gold when you are behind bars, or even on the street for matter.

Sidney's diminutive cell consisted of four gray walls, a concrete floor for a bed, a cemented-in toilet, and a blanket if you were lucky. He was not lucky. The inmates were not even allowed to flush their own toilet. The toilets would have to be flushed from the outside by a prison guard. The Hole's greatest punishment, however, was its total, petrifying darkness. The hole was so dark an inmate could only catch an occasional glimpse of light seeping in from under the door. Some of these cells were even built underground to add to the darkness and silence of the chamber.

It was in the Hole Sidney discovered the greatest diet plan of all time. Women of the world, listen up: Breakfast was always an eight-ounce bowl of oatmeal. The remaining two meals were soup made from mashed peas and carrots. was it. Sidney walked into the Hole weighing 175 pounds and exited at a mere 140 pounds…a weight loss average of 1.2 pounds per day for those of you who were counting. [Okay so it's not exactly the Hollywood Miracle diet, but I am sure if it could be packaged and sold, millions of women would buy it.]

When Sidney's chastisement was over he was reckoned as a troublemaker and was quickly transferred across the river to the Star building. This decrepit, maximum-security prison also housed at least one hundred bugs per man in each cell. Without exaggeration, cockroaches and ants outnumbered the inmates a thousand to one. Sidney quickly learned to collect Lanolin every time the medic cart came by. The only way to sleep bug-free was to line the bunk with the yellow ointment. The bugs wouldn't cross the application of Lanolin, thus allowing a somewhat comfortable night's sleep. For those of you who are unfamiliar with Lanolin, it is a cream often used by breast-feeding mothers to help heal chapped skin. [You would think the prison officials would wonder why all those men needed Lanolin. I know I would.]

Inmates were not allowed to talk in the Star building, so they resorted to their own version of sign language. The cells were arranged in long rows resembling Alcatraz with a wide walkway between the rows. Inmates would have to sign to the inmate across the hall from them if they desired communication. Small items could be passed from cell to cell if the guards were not looking. Of course, nobody had much to share, but everyone was good about sharing their books and magazines with their fellow inmates.

Sidney lay in his bunk and watched the bugs zigzag across the cold, cement floor. Soon his mind grew bored with the tiny creatures and memories of his mother floated through his head. He missed their loving relationship badly. Betty Ann Heard had passed away at a critical point in the young adolescent's life. The emotional scar would never completely heal. Of course, this would never be vocalized. How would it look for a hardened conman like Sidney Heard to admit he missed his mama? No, just like in every other difficult situation the man faced, he merely hardened himself to the pain and refused to show emotion.

The desperate teen had written a letter to his father and stepmother nearly every day since his arrest in Bonifay, but he hadn't received a single reply from them. The despondent teen watched the other inmates open CARE packages at Christmas time, but he never received a thing. This exclusion caused pain to shoot through his heart for an instant, but it was soon replaced with anger. He knew his dad could help him out of his current mess if he really wanted to. Ralph Heard had enough connections to keep his son out of hot water even in the south. was the problem. Ralph didn't want to get involved, and his son knew it.

Betty Heard came back to Sidney's tormented mind as he closed his tired blue eyes. He thought of his mother's smile and slowly the anger melted. He remembered the time she kicked his father out of their bedroom and made him sleep on the couch.

"You are not sleeping in my bed until my son is out of horrible jail," she had declared. Those better memories made the lonely teenager smile as he drifted off to sleep. Sidney hadn't stayed in jail very long time. Unfortunately, however, Betty Heard wouldn't be able to save her son this time around. The now nineteen-year-old youngster would be a forty-six-year-old man before he would taste another moment of freedom.

East Unit: P-wing:

In 1961, Florida State Prison, or Raiford, opened their new East Unit. Construction wouldn't be completed however until 1968.[2] The new facility would be able to house up to 1,400 inmates at a time; it is still considered to be one of Florida's largest prisons. The prison also provided lodging for convicts in one of Florida's three death rows, as well as the state's execution chamber.

Sidney was one of the first groups of inmates to be transferred to the new facility. Here the inmates could go to the Mess Hall to eat. This was quite an agreeable change for the young convict. Every day at mealtime all the inmates were marched down the long hallway to the large mess hall. The mess hall was not much more than a giant cafeteria lined with tables. Each table was bolted to the floor and surrounded on two sides by narrow benches, which were unmovable as well. Four inmates would be seated at each table. This new privilege provided Sidney with the opportunity to socialize—and the best part of the new building was its lack of bugs. Life was looking up for the dejected criminal.

Shortly after moving into the East Unit, Sidney ran into a large German man with a crew cut and an unusually creepy demeanor. Carl Gargiulo spoke very slowly with a slight European accent, and had a strange gaze fixed in his fierce eyes. Everyone avoided the hulking brute thinking he was insane. One day as Gargiulo passed Sidney's cell block he stopped and slowly turned to the man seated in his cell.

"You got any cookies, Heard?" Gargiulo asked very slowly. Sidney nodded and handed his little box of cookies to Gargiulo through the bars. The German smiled saying, "You are my friend," and slowly sauntered away.

A few days later Sidney was playing cards with other inmates in the day room when Gargiulo slipped into the room. Sidney was wining of course. No one could beat his photographic memory. One man quickly grew tired of losing and began to cuss Sidney out. Instantly Gargiulo grabbed the cussing man and lifted him nearly a foot off the floor.

"That's my friend. Don't talk to him like that!" Gargiulo growled in a maniacal tone. The man quickly stopped his ranting and nodded in understanding. The German dropped the man before turning heal and walking away. The disgruntled man slowly rose from the floor, his gaze darting from Sidney's grin to the doorway. He never complained about losing a game of cards again.

Gargiulo eventually let Sidney in on his own little scam. He wasn't insane, but he knew if he acted way he would eventually be sent to the Florida State Hospital in Chattahoochee, Florida. He knew he couldn't escape from prison, but he thought he could escape from the white washed mental institution. So Gargiulo started throwing fits; it would take half a dozen guards to hold him down. Finally, he pulled a scam guaranteed his transfer.

Gargiulo purchased a Baby Ruth candy bar from the prison commissary. He went back to his cell and cleaned his toilet out really well and dropped the candy inside. When a guard came by Gargiulo picked up the candy from the toilet and took a big bite. Then he asked the man if he wanted a taste. Gargiulo was immediately classed as insane and transferred to the mental hospital. A few days later Sidney read in the prison copy of the newspaper his German friend had escaped from the train on the way to the hospital —and the cops had lost his trail in the Okefenokee Swamp. You can bet Sidney got a good laugh out of that.

[As hard as I tried I couldn't find any newspaper articles on Carl. With Sidney's gangster mumble it is hard to understand various names and places. I must research every name he has given me because it is never spelled or pronounced quite like he says it. I have also noticed every surname on the planet comes out sounding a bit Italian with Sidney's mumble.]

It wasn't long before three disgruntled inmates looking for a chance to escape approached Sidney for help. They had the manpower, but they needed a sharp mastermind to plan the ordeal. Everyone already knew of Sidney's past escapes. Of course, Sidney was obliged to help his new-found compadres. The four men sat at the lunch table, and tried to not draw any attention from the guards as they quietly planned an escape.

Sidney returned to his cell day with a spring in his step—and a spoon in his shoe. Frank Beck, Jack McDermott, and Lee Wilson also swiped spoons from their lunch trays before they parted ways in the hallway. Why the prison officials don't stop and count the silverware I will never understand. I'm sure they have remedied this situation by now. I hope.

Now Sidney remembered Frank Fredrick Beck as quite a character. He was a mathematical genius and a master at card counting in the game of blackjack. No one could beat him, and he didn't cheat either. Frank was also a health nut, according to Sidney and he was constantly working out. He was the type would do a hundred push-ups as soon as his feet dropped from his bunk in the mornings. And before the days of Arnold Schwarzenegger, the tall, blond haired, blue-eyed body builder could have given Charles Atlas a good run for his money. The handsome, well-built man looked rather out of place wearing prison garb. So, Sidney was surprised when the pretty boy joined his rowdy group of renegades.

To understand the plan, first you must understand the layout of the prison. All the cells were built with two solid concrete walls on either side of the room. The front wall was made of heavy bars, and the back wall was an electric door could only be opened from the outside. Sidney was fortunate enough to have a cell where the front barred wall faced the outer windows. He could look through the window bars and catch a glimpse of the outside world as it spun on without him. His restless soul longed for freedom—and now he had a plan to get freedom back.

It didn't take long for the new lunchtime routine to become boring for Sidney once again. He was granted a three-minute cold shower on Mondays, Wednesdays, and Fridays. Getting out of his cell for anything was great, but this also grew into insane boredom. As usual, lunch, shower, and bedtime were all announced by the sound of a bell, and to make matters worse it was an irritating buzzer with a high-pitched squeal. If Sidney had a gun he would have loved to use it for target practice. Of course, if he had a gun he would be too busy escaping to shoot the irritating noise maker. To this day Sidney does not have a loud buzzer for an alarm clock. After years of getting up before dawn, he doesn't have to use an alarm clock at all.

Prison regulation mandated every worn out or empty container in all the cells must be returned to the jailers for disposal. To receive another roll of toilet paper, an inmate was required to turn in the empty cardboard roll. So, if you wanted paper to wipe your butt you would comply. This rule was also applied to the used toothpaste tubes. This process eliminated the chance of an inmate using these meager supplies as some clever means of escape. One might wonder what someone could possibly do with a cardboard toilet paper roll, but you would be surprised by the ingenuity of a desperate prisoner. It's been reported prisoners have used raincoats to make rafts, sheets to make ropes, and even soap to make guns. Desperation breeds innovation, or so the proverb goes.

One of Sidney's accomplices happened to work at the prison hospital and he informed the mastermind he had access to hacksaw blades. Why would prisoners have access to such things? Who knows? Lee would snatch one blade periodically and "carry it bodily" back to his cell thus avoiding attention during the routine pat downs. [Yes, it is a very bad mental image. I apologize, but as a writer I must be truthful here.]

The plan was to sharpen the stolen spoons into knives and then the prisoners would take the guards hostage. Construction on the prison's outdoor fence was incomplete; the barbed wire band hadn't yet been added to the top of the fence, and the watchdogs hadn't been brought into the prison yards so far. Sidney knew the prisoners could use these facts to their advantage. And, as always, Sidney could keenly observe and memorize his surroundings, adapt to them, and in the right timing use them to his advantage. The fence would be completed within a few weeks, so they didn't have much time to plan. Why they were worried about a little string of barbed wire after "carrying" hacksaw blades is beyond me.

The inmates planned to take the guards hostage and cut through the barred windows with the stolen hacksaws. Then it would be a short jump out the second-story window before climbing the fence to freedom. Lee's sister lived nearby and would be parked outside the prison fence waiting to drive them to safety. He had sent her a coded message with his last letter to her. Anyway, was the plan. It was hardly foolproof, but it was a good one, nonetheless.

Sidney, of course, was all for it. He had watched his life slowly ebb away behind bars for too long.

Chapter 5: Escape Attempt

Sidney and Lee studied the prison's layout every day during their short escapades outside of their cells. The first floor held cell block One. Cell block two was on the second floor; a small landing halfway down the steps separated the two stories. The landing housed a small lock-box geared to open and close all the cell doors, a phone to signal the control room, and an electric door locked from the outside. Most importantly, the landing had a bar-covered window.

Proven prison routines are essential in order to keep the inmates in check. However, routines can also be studied and manipulated. Sidney's quick eye took note of the steady routines and found a fatal flaw. While one guard would march the inmates up the stairs, another guard would wait at the stairway landing for the uniformed man's return. After all the prisoners were in their cells, the guard would open the box and press the button to close all the cell doors. The first-floor inmates would be locked up first, then the second, and so on.

One cool evening early in December, Sidney decided it was time to put his daring escape plan into action. The meal-buzzer signaled it was time for everyone to go to mess hall. Sidney stood at his cell door and waited patiently for it to open, then he stepped into his place in line behind the long string of inmates at the mess hall door. After being handed his platter, he quickly found a seat near his cronies. Frank quietly assured his friends all was in place. Sidney nodded slightly and continued chomping on the tasteless meal before him. His pulse quickened with anticipation of carrying out the escape plan filled his mind. Life started to spark deep within his dormant soul once more.

Soon chow was over and the buzzer sounded the close of dinnertime. Sidney calmly dumped the remains of his less-than-tasty meal in the trash bin and placed his tray in the stack to be washed. He watched as Frank and Jack did the same thing and slipped into the back of the outgoing line. Everyone marched back down the hall toward cell block One. Everything went like the usual clockwork. Sidney watched as one of the two guards marched up the steps to the landing while the other guard waited with the rest of the inmates at the end of the hallway.

Once in his cell, Sidney stood and waited patiently as the door slid closed. He quickly slipped his spoon-knife from under the "mattress" pad of his cot and waited for his friends to reopen the door. Meanwhile, Frank and Jack eased out of the slowly moving line of inmates and scrambled into the nearby shower room while the two guards were preoccupied with distributing prisoners.

After the guard who was leading the line marched the second-floor inmates up the stairs from the landing, Frank and Jack jumped the guard stayed behind on the landing. Then they took the other guard captive as he came back down the stairs. The two prisoners opened the doors to their cohorts' cells and the plan was on a roll.

Sidney and Lee waltzed out of their cells, down the hall, and to the landing to help their friends stifle the guards. Frank and Jack started sawing on the four-by-six-inch bars with their improvised tools. Those little strips of metal were all separated the desperate inmates from freedom. The next hour went by smoothly. Every thirty minutes Lee would grab the hallway phone and call the main control room and say, "P-wing checking," as if he was a guard. He would wait for an affirmative response and then continue guarding their hostages. It was beginning to look as if they would pull it off.

"Don't worry. We don't want to hurt you," Sidney told their captive prison guards. "We just want to get out of here."

He lit a couple of cigarettes and gave one to each of the two men. Sidney knew from experience he had best be nice to the hostages, because if his plan failed they would most likely extort revenge.

There was one problem the cons hadn't considered when working out their plans. In 1962, all the prisons in the south were still segregated. The third-floor housed cell block Number Three, which held all the African-American prisoners. To complicate things, every couple of hours the third-floor orderly would bring coffee and donuts down for the second-floor guards. Sidney could have no way of knowing this. He hadn't even seen an African-American man since he had arrived at Raiford, except on a few occasions in the prison yard.

Without warning, the second-floor door opened and there stood a black orderly holding coffee and donuts for the guards. He was, of course escorted by a prison guard. The two men glanced around the landing and saw Sidney and Lee standing there holding the guards as hostages. The nervous trustee quickly dropped the tray. The guard slammed the door closed and the black trustee ran screaming down the hall.

"Them white boys are holding the guards hostage up there on the second floor!" he shouted to an outside guard.

Immediately, sirens started wailing, doors slammed closed, and dozens of guards converged on the second floor from all corners of the prison. Armed guards even gathered below the second-floor window on the outside waiting for the men to jump from the small opening. Frank and Jack threw their saw blades out between the bars of the window and Sidney opened all the cells to make it look like they were rioting instead of escaping. Of course, this didn't work out as planned either. Obviously, the hostages could attest to what the men were up to.

"Let them go, boys, or I will come up there and shoot everyone!" yelled Warden Sinclair when he arrived on the scene a moment later. "You have fifteen minutes."

"Wait, what about us?" screamed one of the captured guards.

"Suck it up, boys. You knew the risks when you took the job. You have fifteen minutes to make a decision," the warden growled at the prisoners through the locked door.

Everyone knew of the Warden's hardcore ways and the rest of the inmates began to shout at the cons begging them to surrender. All the prisoners started scrambling back to their cells in a panic. No one wanted to be out of their cell when the warden decided to bust through door. A few minutes later Jack knocked on the second-floor door.

He called, "Hey, Warden! Are you still there?"

The warden and his men cocked their shotguns in reply, the sound reverberating through the empty hallways and up Sidney's spine. Whether he wanted to admit it or not, he knew the jig was up and despite his efforts towards freedom he had prolonged his torment.

"We want to talk to Major Godwin," Jack negotiated with the warden through the closed door. This was a strategic move on the criminal's part, because Godwin's father had been a warden at Raiford many years earlier. Godwin's father had been killed in a similar insurrection, and Jack wanted to use this fact to his advantage. He also knew Godwin's word was as good as gold. Besides, no inmate in the entire prison system trusted Warden Sinclair.

"Will you promise not to hurt anybody if we surrender?" Jack tried to negotiate with the Major through the locked door.

"You have my word. Just surrender and no one will get hurt," came the gruff reply from Godwin. With that, the siege was over and the escapees raced back to their cells. Sidney tried to lie down on his cot and pretend like he was asleep, but the ploy didn't work. A few minutes later he was jerked from his cell by a few guards and arrested. Shackles were placed around his legs, wrists, and waist.

Outside his tiny cell, Sidney was stripped of his prison garb, searched, and taken to the warden's office. Then nine guards shoved the naked criminal down the hallway toward the Hole in the infamous Q-wing. The Q-wing was where the death-row inmates were kept, along with the electric chairs. Death loomed in the air and jarred the nerves of the steel blue eyed punk from Chicago.

"What'cha think you're doin', boy?" the degenerate old warden growled.

"I hate your @*%# prison!" Sidney smarted off, using a few more expletives than required. "Your food is disgusting—and I don't like *you*!" Obviously, his outburst only worsened his plight, but at this point the Warden couldn't take much else from him, or so Sidney thought. He was wrong; dead wrong.

"Take him away," the warden yelled, shaking his cane at the naked man. Sidney was marched to the Hole, while trying to cover what was left of his dignity with his cuffed hands. Every other prisoner cursed and jeered at the humiliated criminal as he was paraded to the Hole. So much for Sidney's great escape plan.

The cell in the Hole had no bed, so Sidney was forced to sleep on the cold concrete floor in the dark. Naked and freezing, Sidney began to wonder if he would ever get out. The only light he could see was the tiny glow tat slid in under the cell door. Studies have shown complete isolation from everyone including prison staff can cause anxiety, hallucinations, paranoia, and even mental instability. After a while the utter darkness begins to play tricks on the mind and becomes almost like a form of blindness.

The Hole would be Sidney's abode for the next thirty-three days. There in darkness and isolation Sidney would spend the Christmas holiday. The regular Hole menu consisted of a soup made from squashed peas and carrots and a glass of water to drink. The Hole didn't have a sink. The toilet was basically a bordered hole in the floor and it would be flushed from the outside.

After a couple days in complete isolation, Sidney's sensitive ears heard footsteps coming down the hallway towards him. Hope of human interaction sprang up within him, but it was short lived. When the door opened two black orderlies stepped inside and glared down upon the prisoner. These two were a member of the prison's dog boys." Dog boys were the inmates in charge of handling the vicious canines would chase down escapees. Most of the time the handlers were just as savage as their beasts.

The pair were a gift from Sidney's prior hostages and they immediately began the pummeling as soon as the door closed behind them. During the years of segregation, the prison officials were fond of using black trustees to beat white men, and white trustees to beat black insurrectionists. Of course, this only furthered the racial hatred between the inmates. It had been nearly a century since the official Civil War ended, but the battle still raged behind the prison walls and the generals were none other than the prison staff themselves.

The all-out brawl lasted for several minutes, but it felt more like an eternity to the bloody prisoner on the floor. The two brutal men finally left Sidney lying on the cement floor with a broken nose, broken ribs, and blood dripping from his face. Sidney lay on the floor in excruciating pain. Blood trickled from his wounds. He could feel the warm liquid run down his face and neck. His head pounded with every heartbeat and every muscle in his body ached. It was a sickening feeling to feel a river of warm blood flow down your own face. One accustomed to bar room brawls, or a boxer might not take notice of such a stomach-turning sensation, but in the darkness, everything other than sight was overly magnified.

If a medic had been sent to help the young man, the guards would have to confess to their treachery, so no one ever came by his cell to bandage him up. Painfully rolling onto his back, his swollen eyes turning up toward the hidden ceiling, Sidney seethed with hatred. He reasoned the cold concrete was the floor beneath him, so the ceiling would have to be above him—or maybe not. He might be crunched against a wall with his "ceiling" being the opposite wall. Who knew?

The suffocating darkness closed around him like death. Unfortunately, thousands of prisoners are subjected to this kind of mental torment every year, whether they have done something wrong or not. Very few of the prisoners are strong enough to endure it. Many more of them succumb to the perceptual distortions.

"God, am I going to survive this place?" Sidney whispered through his bloody, swollen lips. It wasn't necessarily a call for help to an omnipotent creator, as much as a statement of an utter loss of hope.

Outside the fortified walls of Raiford, the majestic sun rose and fell from the horizons on its burning trip around the sky. The light never touched the eyes of the lone human in the hole, but somehow time still healed his wounded body. His heart and mind, however, would never be the same. Pain and anger slowly seeped deep into his soul. Darkness encompassed his inner being like the plague. Eventually word came the two guards had sent the dog-boys after Sidney were fired right after Christmas. Major Godwin was a hard man, but he was true to his word and he had promised nobody would get hurt over the ordeal.

The news did little to remedy the pain Sidney had endured. His anger continued to grow until it reached a boiling point. Sidney survived his time in the Hole. Maybe it was his youthful vitality; maybe it was his wit; but more than likely it was his rage got him through the mental torment of isolation.

To this day every year around Christmas time, Sidney suffers a bone-chilling cold sensation throughout his body. He knows it is merely psychological, but sometimes nightmares are hard to forget; especially when you've lived through them.

After thirty-three long days Sidney was finally released from the Hole and could take a shower for the first time. The ice-cold water ran down his back and washed the dirt, blood, and grime from his body. The short three minutes felt like heaven after his time in the Hole. He was once again given an inmate uniform and taken to solitary confinement back in the P-wing. His new cell number would be P1S4. And cell would be his home for the next two-and-a-half years. His fellow inmates felt sorry for him and shared their food with the emaciated inmate. The nasty prison food tasted like gourmet steak to his deprived taste buds.

The new cell was still small, but at least it had a bed, a sink, and a toilet. In Solitary confinement, he could listen to the radio through earphones plugged into the wall, or read books and magazines. During his stay in P1S4 Sidney would look forward to Saturday nights when he could listen to the *Grand Ole Opry*. The simple country and gospel melodies somehow spoke to the hardened criminal's soul. Sidney still loves type of music to this day. He will still travel all over to hear some old-fashioned country/gospel and even some bluegrass style music.

Boredom was the inmate's archenemy in the solitary confinement wing. To combat this problem inmates could read books and if they had money they could order up to five magazine subscriptions. Sidney didn't have any money. He couldn't work in the prison industry and his family wouldn't send him money, but the other inmates were kind enough to share their books and magazines. One inmate would get a new book and pass it to the next cell when they were finished reading it. Most inmates could average reading a book a day, at least those inmates who were not illiterate. Sidney read everything he could get his hands on.

The first year Sidney was in P1S4, the prison gave out paperback westerns for all the inmates to read. Sidney once told his biographer, "there were so many westerns floating around the prison you could almost smell the horse manure and gun smoke."

The prison would only allow inmates to order *Reader's Digest*, *Cosmopolitan*, *Redbook*, *Field & Stream*, and

Outdoor Life. was all. If you wanted to read *Time Magazine* you were just out of luck, or you would have to get someone to smuggle it in as if it were drugs.

In his new location, three times a week Sidney would be released from his cell to allow him to take a three-minute shower. However, the best part of Solitary confinement for the lonely inmate was the dim light bulb in the room. He might be locked up and alone, but at least he could see around him in room. Even the dull gray paint on the walls was like a rainbow to his color-deprived eyes. Sidney cherished the simple pleasure the little light bulb provided. He would also have the luxury of human interaction once again. He wouldn't be allowed to socialize with his fellow inmates, but he could speak to a guard on occasion. With these sparse amenities, Sidney discovered life was better in solitary confinement. [Here one must point out the outside world tends to merge Solitary confinement and the Hole. But in reality, especially in Sidney's case, Solitary confinement was a definite step up from the Hole.]

Three months passed slowly by. Normal inmates of the general prison population were given a job of some sort. Every inmate was assigned a regular task to keep the prison system running smoothly and to supposedly keep them out of trouble. This goes back to the old "idle hands" adage. Unfortunately, this didn't apply to those inmates in solitary confinement. Prolonged isolation threatened to destroy the young inmate, but then something happened would change Sidney's destiny, and his entire outlook on life.

Judge Joseph ("Joe") Peel was convicted of hiring someone to murder Judge Chillingsworth and his family. By time Joseph Peel hadn't been a judge for quite a while, but everyone still called him "judge." Peel was assigned to cell number P1S5, next to Sidney's cell. While interaction between inmates in solitary was forbidden, the two men still conversed through the cell wall when there were no guards around. Days would pass and Peel would tell Sidney of all the cases he had won, and Sidney would eventually relate his case to the disgraced judge.

The young Sidney Heard was impressed by Joe's charisma, and his legal mind. Sidney would refer to him later as a legal genius. Intelligence doesn't matter when you must depend on someone else to do the dirty work. This human fallacy was Peel's only error in his criminal planning.

When Joe was still a fledgling attorney he had won a case for a hunter charged with murder. The man and his dog had been out hunting one day and the dog drank from a nearby pond. Later the dog died a painful death, and the hunter realized the pond had been poisoned. He quickly tracked down the farmer and informed the man of his poisoned pond, expecting to find concern.

Instead, the farmer just grinned from ear to ear and said, "Yep, I know it. I poisoned it myself to keep you pesky hunters away." I guess the guy had never heard of a No Trespassing sign.

The hunter in a fit of rage pulled out his hunting rifle and shot the farmer dead right on his own front porch. The case seemed to be destined for an obvious "guilty" verdict.

Joe was assigned to this man's case and nobody expected him win it. Undeterred, Peel argued the hunter suffered from temporary insanity because he loved his dog so much. Through Joe's slick wit, smooth talk and knowledge of the law, the hunter got off Scott-free. This was just one case the silver-tongued attorney had won on his way to becoming judge.

Joe liked to play both sides of the law, however, and this would eventually lead to his downfall. Joe would still be free if he hadn't depended on Floyd A. "Lucky" Holzapfel and George "Bobby" Lincoln. These two would eventually turn "State's Evidence," and would be the end of Judge Joseph Peel.

Joe's reputation as a "legal mastermind" soon flooded the prison and, of course, everyone in the prison argued they were nothing more than an innocent victim. Any time someone was incarcerated knew a little about the law, the inmates would gravitate to person for help in their own cases. Judge Joseph Peel was no exception, even if he was in solitary confinement. Once Joe heard Sidney's story, he knew he could help. Peel had already decided he wasn't going to appeal his own case until Holzapfel was put in the electric chair. Florida law stated there had to be two witnesses to the crime to receive a death sentence and, with Holzapfel dead, Joe thought he'd have a chance at appealing his case and avoiding execution. Meanwhile he had nothing to do but help his fellow inmates.

Legally, Joe thought Sidney had a solid case, but just in case it happened to fail, they came up with an escape plan. Sidney knew he had been railroaded and the ex-judge agreed. They were determined to have their case heard and they would file a writ of *habeas corpus* and appeal all the way to the Supreme Court if need be.

By this time the famous Clarence Gideon had appealed to the Supreme Court claiming he had been tried without an attorney's assistance. Clarence claimed all suspected criminals should have the right to an attorney no matter what type of crime they had been charged with. [8] This case was causing quite a legal uproar, and its ripple effect was affecting all the prisons in the United States.

In Florida State Prison during the 1960s, inmates were welcome to use the broom-closet-sized prison library to write letters to their attorneys and such. Inmates, however, were not allowed to take anything with them when they went to the library. A guard would frisk each man when he exited his cell and again when he left the library. The tiny "legal library" was furnished with a desk, prison stationary, and a pencil.

Sidney wouldn't have access to even the simplest of law books for his legal appeals. To solve this problem, Joe Peel would write legal writs on long strips of toilet paper, slip it through the bars, and around the end of the wall to

Sidney when the guards were not looking. Sidney would quickly wrap the makeshift legal documents around his arms and legs underneath his clothes before the guards made their rounds. When he was patted down, no one could tell he had legal writs all over his limbs.

One might notice if too much toilet paper went missing so the two cohorts had to carefully plan each square was used. Herein lies a great math question for those algebra lovers out there. How many sheets of two-ply does it take to write out twelve pages of legal jargon? Also, have you tried to write on toilet paper with a pencil? Trust me it takes a lot of patience, determination, and if you know a few swear words it might take a few of those too. Of course, as the pastor's daughter I'm not allowed to swear so I was just down to patience and determination. I know for a fact it was twelve pages. I contacted the archivist for the United States Supreme Court and he so graciously supplied me with a copy of the hand-written writ.

Sidney's plan was to get his case appealed; then he would subpoena Joe to be his attorney. The two inmates were required to be moved to a local city jail during their trial. There the pair planned to escape the low-security jailhouse and head straight for South America.

Joe had an underworld acquaintance in the country named Salvarini ran a scheme of his own. Anyone interested in adopting a child would take on a temporary name and wait outside the border until Salvarini's representative brought out an orphaned child. Then those seeking to adopt would enter the country under their real name and go through the legal process of adopting the child. At the time, South America had a law no one could be extradited out of the country if they had gone through the adoption process. [Caring for the children obviously was not a necessary requirement for adoption in South America at the time.] This was all part of Sidney and Joe's plan anyway.

Chapter 6: The Laws of Justice

Eventually, Sidney was called to stand before the local judge to be sentenced for his escape attempt and for holding the guards hostage. His inmate cronies Frank, Jack, and Lee stood in the line beside him. He hadn't seen them for quite some time, but the sordid family reunion was unhappy and short lived. He wondered if they had also been beaten, or if Sydney had received special treatment since he was the ringleader. Sidney noticed for some unknown reason, four African-American men were thrown into the line along with Sidney's crew. Although they were not involved in Sidney's attempt to escape, they were to be sentenced right along with the rest of those unfortunate souls in the lineup. To this day, Sidney doesn't know what they did, or if they did anything.

Since not one of the accused men had the benefit of an attorney, the judged asked each defendant to submit his own plea. Each inmate pled "not guilty" to his accused crime. After each plea, there was a small pause, and then a smug look crossed the judge's face. The gavel slammed to the desk with a dull thud, and every man was pronounced guilty of attempted escape and assault on a guard.

Afterward, the judge started handing out five and ten-year sentences like he was dealing cards at a poker table. Unfortunately, Sidney ended up with a sentence of five years for the escape attempt and eight years for the assault on the guards. meant within a matter of an hour, Sidney had another thirteen years added to his twenty-eight-year sentences. His total time to serve was now forty-one years. Sidney stood in the courtroom completely numb with shock.

After sentencing, the forlorn teenager was hauled back to solitary confinement in chains. It appeared the nineteen-year-old boy would be a sixty-year-old man before he could taste freedom again. As the despair of solitary confinement closed in around him, Sidney began to wonder if suicide would be a better option. Yet even in this man-made hell, God touched the young man's heart and kept him from ending his own life. To this day Sidney credits a higher power for his long life. There were too many instances when he should have died.

Determination now welled up inside Sidney, and he dropped to the cold cell floor and did as many pushups as his forearms would allow. *I'll show them. I'll bounce out of here in the best shape of my life.* After about twenty pushups, Sidney slumped against the wall, and tried to brush off his caged-animal feeling. He tried to pace to ease his anxiety, but it was hard to pace with his long legs in such a tiny space. Pacing consisted of two steps, turn, and then repeat. He stared at the floor while he paced. He knew every hairline scratch in the concrete, every dimple in the painted ceilings, and every smudge on the walls. If a new dust bunny showed up, Sidney would notice. What else did he have to do? He felt as if his brain might explode.

Life quickly became monotonous for the hyperactive young man. The only relief Sidney had was when he could talk to Joe through the wall separated them. Late evening, after the guards had made their rounds, he related his sentencing fiasco to his neighboring ex-judge. Joseph Peel was his only ray of hope in this desolate place. He was the type of judge who would represent both parties in the same divorce case. While anyone else who tried such a thing would be disbarred, Peel would get a slap on the hand or a shake of the head and continue. Joe knew Sidney hadn't received a fair trial ever since he had been arrested in Florida, and the ex-judge was going to prove it—or at least escape while trying to prove it. The two men never could imagine the success was just around the corner for one Sidney James Heard.

From point on the charismatic Judge Joe Peel took on Sidney's case with a renewed vigor. In fact, any inmate who could get to the pair would ask them for legal advice. The two quickly became sort of celebrities inside the prison walls. Every inmate wanted a piece of advice and, of course, the pair would happily dish out the advice for a price.

Joe knew if he could get Sidney's appeal denied in the Florida Court System they could head for the U. S. Supreme Court. Sidney didn't expect to win the case. Joe would provide the legal mind to start the process; Sidney was the escape artist would mastermind a plan to get them both out of the low-security jail in the progress of the trial. Escape was all was on their minds.

With that, the long process of commuting Sidney's sentences began. Sidney habitually spent time in the prison library, or "writ room" as the inmates called it. Sidney would carefully copy the legal jargon Joe had provided for him onto prison stationery with a blunt pencil. With time, Sidney slowly moved up the ladder of the justice system and soon his case was filed alongside the famous Clarence Gideon in the U.S. Supreme Court.[9] [To the best of our knowledge Sidney Heard is the only surviving petitioner as of this writing.]

Gideon vs. Wainwright Case:

Although this case is standard reading for any entry level law student many Americans take their right to an attorney for granted and assumed they have always had this right. This was not the case until the Gideon decision was handed down from the U.S. Supreme Court on March 18, 1963. The story would culminate in one of the most land mark Supreme Court decisions of all time.

Clarence Earl Gideon was reported to be a poor drifter born on August 30, 1910. After quitting school and running away from home in eighth grade, he wandered his way through the states of Missouri, Kansas, and Texas leaving a string of petty criminal escapades in his wake. June 1961 found Gideon in Florida where his hobo life would come to a drastic end. On June 3rd, a local pool hall was robbed. The bounty included $5 in change, a few beers, a few bottles of soda, and $50 worth of quarters stolen from the jukebox.

A local resident stated he *might* have seen Gideon leave the establishment with his pockets loaded with coins and drive away in a cab. On this vague testimony, the local homeless man was arrested on burglary and theft charges.

Here I must make a logical interjection. Have you ever tried to carry $55 worth of change in your pants pocket? Also, the testimony does not describe him carrying a bag. So, where did he carry a few bottles of beer and a few bottles of soda? Being of a curious nature I decided to conduct my own experiment. I gathered up $55 in random change and piled it high upon my bathroom scales. The change weighed approximately 3 pounds. Now I don't know about you but I cannot fit $55 worth of change in the pockets of my skinny jeans. Of course, I realize a hobo in the sixties most likely was not wearing knock-off designer denim. He was probably wearing tacky looking slacks. Whatever the case unless he was wearing M.C. Hammer pants brimming with quarters I doubt this theory is plausible.

To complete my investigation, I went online and found a glass bottle of beer weighs approximately one pound each and a glass bottle of soda weighs the same. In 1961 bottles were made of glass and not plastic like they are today. So, depending on your definition of "a few" Gideon was supposedly carrying three pounds of change in his pockets and an armload of bottles. If "a few" meant six of each drink, then this little man was hauling approximately twelve pounds of bottles. I find this also highly unlikely. After viewing many photos of the emaciated Clarence Gideon, I don't think a man resembling a walking skeleton could carry such a load. Even with my feeble attempt I could cast a reasonable doubt as to this man's guiltiness. Of course, if Gideon had the benefit of an attorney he or she could have conducted a more scientific experiment.

When Gideon was brought before the judge, he requested an attorney be granted to defend his case. The judge denied it saying the State was not required to assign a public defender to anyone unless it was a capital offense.

With no other option, Gideon struggled to defend himself and proclaimed his innocence long after being sentenced to five years in prison. Instead of giving up, he decided to petition the Supreme Court claiming his right to a fair trial had been declined. Of course, Gideon had no money to file by regular means so he simply hand wrote his appeal on prison stationary with a pencil and sent it in the mail.

The Supreme Court has a category called *In Forma Pauperis*. The phrase is derived from *Latin* meaning "in the state of a pauper." This is a way for the poorest people of the nation to have their voices heard even though they lack the financial means to file a proper lawsuit.

Hugo Black was a Supreme Court Judge at the time and he thought poor people shouldn't be placed at a disadvantage in court because of their financial state. He had been fighting for this concept in the Supreme Court for nearly twenty years. "Equal Justice Under Law," is chiseled across the front of America's most powerful courthouse, and Black believed in this concept wholeheartedly.

In October 1962, the law was passed with a unanimous vote and now everyone would have the right to an attorney no matter the crime, or the defendant's financial state. Clarence Gideon was classed as a Constitutional Hero, but he was not alone. Several other petitioners sent their cases alongside Gideon. While history has forgotten these names, one man's name is printed alongside the land mark case. name is Sidney J. Heard.

Sidney hadn't expected to get his sentence commuted; he was fighting to get a chance for retrial. He never dreamed of his case's positive outcome as he opened the official letter. Sidney stared at the printed words for quite some time before uttering a sound.

Instead of the twenty-eight-year sentence he had received, Sidney's sentence had been commuted by the judicial system to a mere thirteen-year sentence. He could barely believe his luck. Sidney would usually file another writ of *Habeas Corpus* to the Florida court system requesting a retrial. However, after the passing of the *Gideon vs. Wainwright* case, Florida officials realized they would be inundated with similar cases. To avoid the tsunami of retrials and a possible breakdown of the entire legal system, Florida officials came up with the Criminal Proceeding Rule One: Criminals would file their case under this ruling and the courts system would be given the option to class the case as "time served," or it could be sent back as a retrial. In Sidney's case, he was granted a "time served" status, thus dropping his sentence down drastically.

Rampant Illiteracy:

In prison your "identity" is everything, and Sidney had acquired the persona of an "educated gangster" from Chicago. Unfortunately, most inmates, as well as some guards in the Florida institution were totally illiterate. Sidney was somewhat surprised, however, when one of the guards banged on the bars of his cell late one night. Sidney quickly approached the man with a, "yes sir" on his lips. He was a little startled to see a box of the highly coveted "free world" cigarettes resting between the steel bars. Sidney wasn't sure what the bribe was for, but he was determined to find out.

A large guard by the name of Mr. Baker quietly slipped a piece of paper into the inmate's hand, and motioned for him to read it aloud, but quietly. Sidney's pale blue eyes perused the paper for a moment then glanced back up at the guard. The letter was to inform Mr. Baker a storage building was scheduled for demolition and the building's owners needed him to move his truck. Sidney relayed this message to the man and slipped the man's letter back through the bars.

Baker grumbled a few profanities and informed no one in particular that he would have already moved the truck if he wanted the truck moved. After a short tirade, the guard pointed his club at the inmate's head and threatened a beating if anyone found out about his illiteracy. Sidney quickly assured the man his secret was safe and thanked him for the cigarettes. It was not like Sidney had anyone to tell, anyway. Little did either man know they would be reunited fifteen years later at a New Mexico racetrack.

After getting his sentence radically reduced, Sidney hoped to be moved back into the prison's general population, but this was not the case. Years of solitary confinement would be enough to drive anyone crazy, so Sidney jumped on the bandwagon and started collecting spiders in matchboxes. After a while, he had quite the collection of every hideous looking spider he could find. Friends even sent spiders to him from the cafeteria. He was determined to get out of solitary confinement even if it meant donning temporary insanity. The conniving criminal had a plan; an insane one.

On one particularly boring Wednesday, Sidney set his plan in motion. He packed his few belongings into his pillowcase and waited at the cell door. The entire P-wing was scheduled for a new paint job and everyone was going to be hustled over to the R-wing while the job was completed. The somewhat deranged inmate shoved his pockets full of the spider filled matchboxes and eagerly waited at the gate for his escort. Soon the armed man stomped down the dismal hallway towards P1S4. Sidney ruffled up his hair and opened his eyes as wide as they would stretch.

"You ready, Heard?" Lt. Alvarez grumbled, not caring if the scrubby looking inmate was ready or not.

"Yes, Sir." Sidney quickly responded in the required manner. The barred gate slowly opened. Sidney assumed the usual position with his hands on the concrete wall and his legs spread wide. The guard's large hands made their way down Sidney's body and stopped abruptly at the inmate's pockets. Sidney pressed his face against the wall to hide his grin.

"What is in there, Heard?"

"Match boxes, sir."

"Why do you have match boxes?"

Sidney turned and looked at the guard with a strange looking gleam in his eye.

"To keep my spiders, sir"

"What?" Alvarez stepped back a few paces. "You have spiders in there? Why do you have spiders, Heard?"

"To keep the crabs away sir," Sidney chuckled psychotically.

"Crabs? You have crabs, Heard?" The guard asked somewhat perplexed.

"No sir. is why I have spiders."

Well, as he had expected, Sidney was transferred to a regular cell first thing the next morning. Finally, after two-and-a-half years, he was given the regular blue colored uniform and could become part of the general inmate population. His bluff had worked, and he wore his new clothes proudly. They might not be the flashy gangster wardrobe like he had back in Chicago, but to him blue was wonderful.

Chapter 7: Florida Chain Gang

After getting his case overturned and being released from solitary confinement, officials knew Sidney wouldn't dare to risk his chance of being granted parole by trying to escape again. Years of isolation had finally given the young punk a bit of wisdom. So, for the first time since he was originally arrested, he could work in the sugar cane fields as part of a chain gang. Every morning at the crack of dawn, Sidney became one of fifty fellow-inmates who were marched out to the fields. Four armed guards and a harsh looking walking boss escorted them down the long hallway and outside.

The first day Sidney stepped outside of confinement, he sighed deeply with relief. He might have just been outside the prison walls, but to him it felt like he was in heaven. He could feel the gentle breeze wafting on his cheek. He could hear the birds singing sweet melodies in the treetops. Yeah, after solitary confinement this was heaven. In this crazy fast paced world, we live in people tend to ignore Mother Nature's bounty, but to this nature deprived criminal it was amazing. His wandering eyes took in every tree, every bird, and every detail along the path.

Although the sunshine was a welcomed sight, Sidney's crystal blue eyes took quite a while to adjust to the light of the outdoors. After nearly three years in solitary confinement, the blinding sunlight was more than Sidney's now light-sensitive eyes could endure. Pain shot through his eye sockets, and threatened to water them profusely. The "tough guy" somehow worked through the pain and managed to keep his rough exterior in place. After several days, the pain finally eased down to a more bearable level. Later in life, he would need surgery to repair the damage to his eyesight. There's no way of knowing how the nearly three years in P1S4 truly affected his vision.

One morning the walking boss marched briskly toward the Chicago native. The boss's face wore a serious expression. Sidney stood tall and toughened his jumpy nerves. He was fully expecting a verbal berating from the short, wide man. Inside, however, Sidney wondered what he had done wrong. He couldn't remember breaking any of the rules. He had been on his best behavior ever since being released to work in the sugar fields. Of course, Sidney knew he didn't have to "do" anything to receive a verbal thrashing in this place. Yelling and nagging were commonplace.

"Heard. Come with me!" the boss demanded.

Sidney obeyed and was ushered by the guards to the front of the line. All the rest of the inmates watched and glared at him with envy for receiving special treatment.

"Read this aloud," the guard ordered. The man shoved the daily role call sheet into Sidney's hand.

Sidney's nervous eyes gave a quick glance at the guard and immediately realized the man wasn't giving him special treatment, he simply couldn't read the list himself. Sidney pitied the man, but only a little. Never mind the educational differences, the guard was still a free man, and for reason alone Sidney despised the stump of a man.

From that day on, Sidney was put in charge of the roll call in place of the illiterate walking boss. Sidney was used to working with illiterate inmates, but it still surprised him how many of the free men were illiterate as well. To him there was no reason why anyone free shouldn't be able to read. It seemed like such a waste of opportunity.

Each prison squad was made up of fifty inmates. Sidney's squad had four shotgun-toting guards and a walking boss who was quite literally as wide as he was tall. One cold morning Sidney's squad was ushered out into the sugar fields to clean up the debris left over from the harvest. Sidney called fifty inmate names and received fifty verbal responses. The crowd then moved out and began working in the fields. The guards paced back and forth keeping a sharp eye on the group. They knew if a riot broke out it would be hard to handle fifty rioting prisoners all at one time. The guards had four shotguns, but even would barely even up the odds against the crowd of desperate, angry men.

Around noon, the disheveled crew moved under an awning to eat lunch away from the sun's rays. Sidney called role again as the inmates sat to eat and again received fifty responses. But when the walking boss began to count the seated men, he only came up with forty-nine inmates. After recounting heads several times, he ordered Sidney to call role again. This time the men were ordered to step forward in response to the call their name.

This time when Sidney read the name "Art Retoli," no one responded on behalf of their friend Art. He was missing, which was not an easy feat since the ground around them was so flat anyone could easily see a mile in every direction.

As the guards' keen eyes slowly scoped the horizon, they caught sight of a stream of small puffs of smoke rising in the cool air in a spot across the field. The armed guards hurried to the spot. There they found the desperate inmate Retoli had dug himself a ditch, covered himself up with dirt and some discarded sugar cane stalks; he was breathing through a hollow sugar cane reed. The forlorn fugitive was promptly yanked from the ditch and thrown into solitary confinement. Everyone referred to him from then on as "Earthworm."

After leaving the confinement of P1S4, Sidney met a six-foot-six-inch man named Elwood Duncan Taylor. His nickname was Yankee Taylor. He was a giant of a man with a deep gravelly voice. Most inmates considered him arrogant and creepy. Yankee was right up Sidney's alley. The tall, skinny man challenged the younger Sidney to a game of gin rummy. For once Sidney lost the game, but he refused to give up. Yankee took a liking to the Chicago gangster and took it on himself to teach the youngster how to become a master at the ten-card game. Sidney was a quick study with a sharp memory and soon even Yankee himself couldn't beat him.

Back to school whether you need it or not:

Just before Sidney was to be paroled and released from Raiford, the Florida governor finally decided the state should offer some sort of reform for the inmates before they were released back into society. Although Sidney had already graduated from the eighth grade, he was sent to the prison's makeshift school. There he was required to study history, math, science, and government. Sidney already knew all this, but he was happy to be let out of his cell for a few hours every day.

Well-educated inmates were sometimes set up as instructors. Two of Sidney's former friends served as teachers at the so-called school. Sidney's friend Ex-Judge Joe Peel was assigned to teach the inmates about government and history. Frank Beck, another friend of Sidney's, taught math and science.

When the first group of inmates graduated from the program, every dignitary in the state of Florida arrived, along with a massive load of media reps. On one hand, it was a good step in the right direction, but on the other hand Sidney felt it was more of a publicity stunt, than an actual educational experience. (Sidney had already graduated from eighth grade; another eighth-grade diploma meant little to the gangster. If they had offered higher learning classes, then it would have been of more benefit still it was a start. Up until this point Sidney's time in Florida's correctional institutions was all about punishment and nothing about reform.)

Paroled at Last:

On March 29, 1965, Sidney James Heard was finally able to drop his inmate numbers and reclaim his identity. [Sidney told me once in a phone conversation he could never forget the date of March 29th. He had once been married on March 29th, and divorced exactly four years later the same date. He also had been arrested previously on this lovely day in March. To Sidney March 29th would always live in infamy.]

On this date, however, he was released from prison and paroled to Thomasville, Georgia, to face one of his many burglary charges. The twenty-two-year-old convict could finally taste the freedom he had been longing for. Honestly at this point I find all Sidney's charges confusing. He had so many B&E charges from Chicago and acquired even more on his Florida road trip with Eugene Blanton and his girlfriend Jaclyn. These charges didn't include all the times he broke the law when he was running with Jimmy Woods.

Much to Sidney's surprise, his father wired $1,000 to Sidney's attorney to help cover the legal expenses. The next day the judge unexpectedly decided to grant Sidney three-years' probation to run concurrently with his parole from Florida. Sidney was grateful for his father's assistance. It was too bad his assistance took five years to show up.

"The laws of justice work in mysterious ways," the judge told Sidney after pronouncing his sentence.

The young ex-con knew the truth. In reality, the "good" judge had accepted Ralph Heard's payoff. Freedom was finally within Sidney's grasp. The young man could almost taste it. Anticipation and excitement filled his heart for the first time in years.

cool Georgia evening, Sidney sat on the jailhouse steps next to a trustee. He looked down at his hands and sighed. There were no cuffs on his wrists, no chains around his waist, and the street clothes he was wearing were not blue.

Sidney slumped against the concrete stairway post and watched the movement of life around him. This time instead of observing the world at a distance, he felt a part of the universe for the first time in five long years. People hustled down the sidewalk; birds chirped in the treetops; and cars slowly passed by on the street. He watched and wondered what all he had missed during his years at the Florida State Prison. Life may have stopped for him, but the world kept spinning on while he had been rotting away behind bars.

As he sat pondering the years he had lost, he noticed cars would stop in front of the abandoned building across the street periodically. The drivers would honk their horn and wait. Immediately a small African American boy carrying a brown paper bag would scamper out of the building to the car. He would hand it to the car's driver, pocket some money from the driver, and then the boy would quickly turn and race back into the building. The strange scenario happened repeatedly during a couple of hours while Sidney watched. Some cars would honk once and others twice. Sidney turned to the jailhouse trustee beside him and asked about the curious incident.

"Well," the man laughed nervously, "this is a dry [alcohol-free] county, and the sheriff confiscates all the moonshine he can find. The "good" Sheriff pays boy to help run his own moonshine racket out of building. One honk means the sale of one pint, and two honks means the customer wants two pints." The man shrugged and smiled. "I suppose it's a good way to make a little extra money."

Sidney shook his head in disgust and tried to figure out the logic of the situation. It was not legal for all the locals to make and sell whiskey, but it was somehow okay for confiscated brew to be sold by the sheriff. Here the Chicago native discovered the moonshine racket was still big business in the south.

Sidney sat out there on the porch until well after dark. He hated to go inside, but finally he reluctantly went in and crawled back onto a hard cot and slept soundly.

The next morning an officer from Kindle County, Illinois, arrived to transport Sidney to court to face more burglary charges. When the stern-looking officer saw Sidney was loose and sitting on the porch steps, he immediately gave the trustee sitting next to him a severe verbal thrashing.

"What is prisoner doing unshackled?" the officer cursed and quickly pulled out a pair of steel cuffs for the rather amused inmate.

"Aww, he's okay, man. He has sat out here watching the world pass by for two days now, and has not made one escape attempt," the trustee replied calmly. Sidney had more than his fill of the iron bracelets, but he reluctantly held out his hands for the cuffs. The officer slipped the cool metal rings around the gangster's wrists. It was a feeling the young man would never get used to.

During his five-year stint in the Florida prison, Sidney had the opportunity to study a great deal about the procedures of law. Some of this information came in the form of law books in the prison library, but most of it came from his friend ex-judge Joseph Peel. Armed with this knowledge, Sidney quickly reminded the Kindle County judge in the statute of limitations had run out on his previous case. The judge agreed, and Sidney was quickly awarded another three-year probation to run concurrently with the rest of his probation. It was a good deal for Sidney. If all his years of probation had run consecutively, Sidney would still be on probation until the day he died.

Homecoming: DuPage County, IL

Finally, Sidney was escorted back to DuPage County where this criminal narrative began. By now he knew most of the guards at the county seat's Wheaton Jail, and they all visited him regularly at his cell. He found he had become somewhat of a celebrity after surviving five years in the terrible Florida State Prison. Sidney enjoyed every moment of his sordid "homecoming" and used it to his advantage to gain the best accommodations possible behind bars. To his amazement his father even came down and went with him to court. The young gangster wannabe had earned his so-called stripes.

The next morning, Sidney stood before the judge for the burglary charges had landed him in jail originally. Sidney knew his local connections had to be working wonders because he had never seen a judge come in on a Saturday morning before. The judge quickly read through the charges against Sidney. For some unknown reason the judge decided to dismiss all the ten, armed robbery charges against the young man. He claimed Sidney had already done enough time in Florida. He surprised Sidney further by dismissing the two escape charges from the DuPage County jailhouse as well.

The young con man asked no questions; he assumed he owed a debt of gratitude for his connections with the local Italians. Now, after nearly six years, Sidney Heard was a free man. He had been granted a fresh start, and he was determined to make the most of it. He reluctantly made the trip back to his parents' home in Glen Ellyn, Illinois. Emotional pain shot through his heart as he thought about the five lonely years without so much as one response to all the letters he had sent to his father and stepmother. He quickly stifled his feelings, swallowed his pride, and followed his father through their front door.

Chapter 8: Life after prison

Sidney was now nearing the age of twenty-five. He had no home of his own, no money, and no one wanted to hire such a well-known ex-convict. Life for Sidney was becoming difficult to say the least. His father offered him a job painting houses for a family friend whose name was Joe. The deal was to paint two large houses for $2,000. was better than nothing, so Sidney took on the job; he gladly got up before sunrise and headed off to work. For the first time in the previous six years, Sidney would work for a paycheck. In prison, everyone works to keep the prison system working. Some inmates would work to repair the buildings, others served as janitors or cooks, but everyone had a job, unless they were confined to the hole. [Of course, no one in prison ever receives an actual paycheck for his or her efforts.]

Working for his father, Sidney happily spent a week painting the first two-story house on the list. However, when Sidney came home for a paycheck, his father quickly made an excuse as to why he couldn't pay him; instead he paid Sidney twenty dollars to hold him over. When the second week of painting for his dad's business ended the same way, Sidney decided he'd had enough of his father's chicanery.

In reality, Ralph Heard owed Joe a debt and the 'loving father' had conned his son into fulfilling the overdue debt. Sidney took the measly twenty dollars and bought a train ticket to Chicago. The young con decided to give up his straight living and make real money instead. At the time, it seemed easier to play in the "fast lane" than to struggle through life like everyone else had to do.

By the time the desperate young man made it to Chicago he had to use his last dime in the payphone. Sidney made a call to a former "business connection" and was told to report to a specific hotel in Hyde Park, on the south side of Chicago. The next day, Sidney arrived at the hotel at the scheduled time. The well-dressed doorman paid Sidney's cab fare and immediately ushered him toward the elevator.

Waiting for Sidney in an extravagantly furnished room was a well-connected Cuban gentleman named Dr. John Landon Anderson. Anderson was a dentist whose office was on the south side of Chicago; his legitimate dental work was primarily for welfare patients. This made him appear to be charitable, but he was well compensated for his work by the federal government. Anderson had been given this well-paying job by a mutual underworld connection he happened to share with Sidney. As the saying goes, "one good turn deserves another," well so it works with the underworld. One favor leads to another, just make sure you don't end up owing the wrong guy a favor.

Sidney was quickly hired to be the man's clerk without so much as an interview. The connection had been given sparse details about the situation, and Anderson was directed to contact Sidney's parole officer to offer proof of employment. The parole officer was happy to hear Sidney had landed a job and gladly granted his parole transfer request.

's the way the underworld works. No questions are asked if you have the big names behind you. Anderson also owned a beautiful apartment complex in Chicago called the Twin Fountains. Sidney was furnished with an apartment in the lavish building as part of his salary. The luxurious accommodations included a rooftop swimming pool, and a parking place in an underground parking area. With his first paycheck, Sidney donned his standard gangster attire, which consisted of an expensive three-piece suit, plenty of jewelry and, of course, a perfectly placed felt fedora.

With his one desperate phone call, Sidney was now living among the upper echelons of society. Judge Julius Hoffman, nicknamed "Julius the Just," lived in the same building alongside the gangster's apartment. Hoffman achieved his fame from judging the infamous "Chicago Seven" trial. One of his favorite quotes was, "the man with the gun must go, and the man with a crow bar should follow." Julius the Just had a thing about armed robbery. It didn't matter what the circumstances were, he wouldn't bargain with the defendant. He would always issue a life sentence. [10]

Some of Chicago's most popular city aldermen— even the controversial comedian and activist Dick Gregory— routinely rubbed shoulders with the newly released convict. Sidney also met some of the famous Chicago White Sox players when they stayed in the building, or in the Del Prado Hotel[11] a mere five blocks away.

Chicago's White Sox player Pete Ward also lived in the Twin Fountains building at one point. Sidney and Pete were running-buddies for a while and enjoyed betting on baseball games together until Sidney left town. Of course, Sidney never let any of his associates know the truth behind his luxurious lifestyle and if anyone was foolish enough to ask he would simply refer to his legitimate clerk job. Across the street from his new Chicago home was one of the city's most popular nightclubs, the Idle Hour, and just three blocks to the east flowed beautiful lake Michigan, the size of a small ocean. Sidney enjoyed taking his dates to the rooftop of his apartment building to enjoy the majestic view of the lake water while swimming in the rooftop pool.

Flatfoot hustling:

During this chapter of the gangster's life, Sidney began what he would call "Flatfoot Hustling." In other words, Sidney hustled anything and everything, anywhere and everywhere he could. This usually meant Sidney would be walking the sidewalks hence the name "flatfoot." Sidney soon found a couple of guys who were looking for work and lined them up as part of a painting crew for the University Club of Chicago. Sidney would work with them from early morning until early afternoon. Then he would hop aboard a commuter train and head for the racetracks on the northwest side of the city where he would double and sometimes triple his money by gambling on the horses.

During his one of his frequent visits to the racetrack, he ran into some old acquaintances had "obtained" a check-perforating machine a short time earlier. They had been dabbling in check fraud, but hadn't scored a huge profit. Sidney assured them all they needed was good leadership, and he quickly come up with another moneymaking scheme. Before the days of computers, electronic checks, and debit cards the bank issued documents were fairly easy to forge.

As with any business it is always best to have connections, and Sidney spent his time gathering underworld acquaintances like a lady collects jewelry and stilettos. To make his check fraud scheme really work he needed to have false identities made for each of his crew.

The criminal mastermind put in a call to another talented acquaintance and ordered multiple ID cards for himself and his cronies. This would allow the conman to cash the phony checks anywhere using various names. At the time, banks wouldn't investigate an insufficient funds check if it were under their $300 limit. With this fact and the use of several names they were almost guaranteed success. To complicate the trail further, Sidney would cash the checks in various police districts. Sidney negotiated a 20% commission for himself on every check he successfully cashed.

After several months, this scheme grew tiresome and someone in their group came up with a better idea for passing the phony checks: the counterfeiting ring would start targeting the larger investment companies instead of the small banks. Defrauding the investment firms would enable them to receive larger payouts, and greed demanded a pay raise. Sidney never thought of this as hurting the common people. In his mind, he was taking on the greed of corporate America and the banking system. He was fighting the establishment like many others in the late sixties.

This is how the new scheme worked: under his chosen alias, Sidney would call one of the company representatives and make an appointment for just before closing time preferably on a Friday. He would explain how he had received an insurance settlement and how he would like to do business with their company. The eager investment rep always obliged. Sidney would enter the building all spiffed up in his sharp business clothes and quickly start his smooth-talking charade. This is where Sidney's Type A personality, and his quick talking gangster mumble came in real handy.

With his mind running faster than his mouth, he would make a mental note of the things sitting on the representative's desk to see if he could find common ground with the man. If he couldn't find it, he would manufacture it. Sometimes he would make a favorable comment on a photograph, or perhaps a golf trophy, or even a sports cap, and quickly he would win the man's trust. After the paperwork was completed, Sidney would offer the rep a phony insurance "check" for $8,500. Then Sidney would invest $2,500 in the unsuspecting company and ask the rep to cut him a check for the difference. He would walk out of the building a few moments later with a $6,000 "clean" check he could cash anywhere without leaving behind a single clue to his true identity. After a quick stop at the investment company's bank, he would return with $6,000 cold cash. His commission for this endeavor was 30% so he would be $1,800 richer by dinnertime.

"Greed begets more greed," as the saying goes, and soon Sidney became bored with the check-cashing game altogether. The restless conman started looking for other ways to hustle his next paycheck. Soon he discovered another moneymaking game in book sales. He found a place would sell him little square books, each neatly wrapped in plastic. The wholesale price was twenty-five cents per book for a box of one hundred books or $25.00 per box. The books were simply titled, "What Can You Do with Sex After Sixty." Of course, Sidney would find the perfect audience. He would wait outside on a busy street corner during the noon rush hour and sell each book for a dollar apiece to anyone looked over fifty. Within an hour all the books were gone, and he was $75 richer.

On the surface, this may not sound much like hustling, except when customers opened the book's plastic wrapper they would find the entire book was filled with blank pages. Sidney made sure to never work the same street twice. [In my exhaustive research I found these gag gift books are still published today by a publishing house in Chicago and are available for purchase through Amazon's online bookstore. Of course, they are clearly marketed as "gag gifts" so the consumer knows what they are getting right up front. The pages are still blank. Although if I were the book's author I would start and finish the book with one word—Viagra.]

Another hustle Sidney liked to pull was what he called the "knock-off watch game." And in Sidney's sordid mind it was a game—a game with no consequences. At time, there were 980,000 bars in Chicago. Sidney would make a trip to Maxwell Street on the southwest side of the city to a little shop sold off brand watches for one or two bucks apiece. Sidney would purchase an armload of the rip-off watches, and then dress up in his flamboyant suit and head to a bar on the wealthier northeast side of town. He would remove his $4,000 Omega Seamaster watch with a diamond bezel set in 18k gold and replace it with a cheap imitation. Once inside the smoky, dark room of the bar he would enter looking like a million bucks and no one would suspect his watch was worth two bucks. Sidney never pulled a con job without dressing the part. His jewelry alone was worth over fifty thousand dollars. Anyone who paid attention could have told when he was working a job because he never wore it normally unless he was pulling a con.

After a few drinks, he would ask the bartender if he knew of a guy would loan him $25. He would follow up with some sort of sob story about falling on hard times, wife left him, lost millions in stocks, etc. He would reluctantly offer one of his knock-off watches, which he purported to be the only one of its kind as collateral. In the darkness of the bar room, the watch could easily be mistaken for the real deal. Sidney would assure the man it would effortlessly bring in $1,000. So, the bartender would quickly dip into the bar's till and hand Sidney whatever amount he had asked for in exchange for the watch. Sidney would hit an entire block of bars with his pocketed "rare" watches and be a few hundred dollars richer within an hour or so. Of course, with any paycheck he received, he always made a quick trip to the racetrack. There he would compound his winnings by betting on rigged races and go home with an extra load of cash.

This lifestyle bought him all the attention and affection from women he had been craving during his five captive years in Florida. Everywhere he went, Sidney had at least one trophy girl on his arm, sometimes more. Still, deep inside, Sidney wanted more. It would just take a short while for him to admit it to himself. Meanwhile, he tried to drown out the nagging loneliness with more girls, more money, and even more booze. At one point, he consciously made the decision to try and have sex with a woman from every nationality on the planet and joked about it with his buddies. I guess the thought of STDs never crossed his mind.

Sidney wasn't overly selective with his choices of sexual partners. He had a map and would put a pin in every major country. When it came to Asia he just lumped them all together because in his words, they were all about the same. Way to offend an entire continent of women buddy! Thankfully his views towards women have changed drastically over the years. If they hadn't this conservative biographer would probably have been arrested for assaulting an old man with a stiletto. OK. Calm down. That's a joke people.

Among his "travels," Sidney ran into another con man taught him the Mermaid Game. "game" would become his next business venture. He would, of course, dress the part—suit, tie, and all—and walk into a classy bar or club. Once inside, he would scope out the place and find a middle-aged man looking lonely and purposely take a seat close by him. After some drinks and small talk with the man, Sidney would start talking about a sensational prostitute he claimed he knew and visited often. He would show the poor man a photo of some beautiful woman Sidney himself didn't even know, and talk her up a storm. After a while, he would ask the guy if he would like a session with her. Of course, the answer was generally a great big yes. At this point Sidney, would step away and make a fake phone call to see if she was available. This was back before the invention of the cell phone so the client would watch eagerly as his new best friend waltzed over to a payphone.

After the "phone call," Sidney would hand the man the picture of the girl. Then the instructions were simple: Sidney would direct the man to a specific hotel and tell him to watch for a tall sharp dressed black man in the hotel lobby. The instructions were to hand man the picture and two hundred dollars cash in a white envelope. Then the victim would be directed to a specific room number. It always so happened to be on the top floor of the twenty-story building. After the man searched for, and failed to find, the specified room, the disgruntled customer would catch on; by then, Sidney and his cohort would be long gone. Friday and Saturday nights, they would usually cash in on six or seven lonely targets with this pitiful scheme.

During this time, Sidney started tending bar on Friday and Saturday nights at the Idle Time Club across from the famous Del Prado apartment building. Sidney was given half the bar's takes, so he quickly got involved in the games played at the bar—chess, liar's poker, gin rummy, and cribbage—and soon became the house player.

His boss wanted the house to win no matter what, so he gave Sidney a pill to take called the "Black Molly." This pill allowed Sidney to drink like a sieve without getting drunk, but he was instructed to act as though he were completely inebriated. This trick made all the bar's clientele think they could beat the house player, since he was "drunk." Unfortunately, Sidney's mind was still sharp as a tack and he could the cards held in his opponent's hands. Using this tactic Sidney rarely lost. He would make a huge bundle of cash for his bosses over the two-night period; his own cut was not too shabby either. He was definitely the Big Boss's golden boy.

In his mid-twenties, Sidney was truly living the gangster lifestyle. He was a far cry from the forlorn teenager was locked behind bars in Florida. When money ran thin, he would just hustle up some more. And, if he had plenty of cash, he had everything else he thought he wanted. If he got a speeding ticket, he would just take the police commissioner's secretary out for dinner. Sidney always kept her happy so she would let him out of his tickets. Most other petty troubles he found himself in, his connections would get him off the hook. If he could keep juggling all his deals it looked like he could live the high life forever.

At the time, Sidney told me he was working for three different underworld bosses. One boss was an Italian man (we will not mention any names here) who had all the legal connections would ever be needed. The second boss was Jewish and had the large bankroll to finance the whole gambling operation; the third boss was Irish and handled all the music and entertainment of various sorts. Between these three bosses, Sidney could get out of almost any type of trouble if he stayed inside the Chicago area. Alas even with all his criminal brilliance, his greed would overtake his common sense and he would leave this "safe haven."

One day a rumor started circulating about a bank in Vineland, New Jersey, was sitting on a huge pile of cash. It wasn't scheduled to be moved any time soon and seemed ripe for the picking. Naturally, the story caught Sidney's attention and without a plan he decided to add bank robbery to his list of crimes. Before he left town to head east, he stopped by his boss Doc. Anderson's office and stole all his credit cards and his ID. The "good doctor" was currently traveling in Cuba so Sidney knew his missing identification and credit cards wouldn't raise a red flag until the man returned to the United States some time later. would buy Sidney enough time to don another alias and hit the bank in Jersey. He could be back in Chicago within days and his boss wouldn't even know his identity had been stolen.

Sidney hoped to rob the bank, grab a boat load of cash, and replace the stolen identification before his boss returned.

Sidney packed up Julie, his trophy girlfriend at the time, and rented a Ford Mustang under his new alias, Dr. John Landon Anderson. Doctor Anderson was Cuban and held little resemblance to the blue-eyed Chicago native, but Sidney figured he would dump the ID after the job was completed anyway. In the meantime, a hat and sunglasses would do the trick. Why no one ever requested these items be removed is completely beyond me.

Sidney and Julie made a twelve-hour trip east to New Jersey to knock over the rumored $40,000 bankroll. Any professional bank robber would case the place for days or even weeks in advance, learn all the employee's routines, and then lay out an elaborate plan. Patience was never one of Sidney Heard's strong suits, so he decided to hit the place without any semblance of a plan. This fool hearty mistake would cost him dearly. Sidney entered the bank all dressed up in the typical three-piece business suit, coordinating fedora cocked "ace/deuce," brilliantly shined shoes, and of course a briefcase. He calmly strolled up to the first unsuspecting teller available. Laying the case on the counter he popped the hatch open. Inside the case lay a loaded handgun.

Sidney quietly informed the teller she was to give him all the money in her till. She nodded anxiously and quickly emptied out her cash drawer. Sidney approached each teller repeating the process. After working his way through the teller line, Sidney pulled the gun out for everyone to see. He ordered the entire banking staff and a few customers into the bank's vault. At this point, Sidney realized the process was taking too long and he began to panic.

Every bank has more than one vault. One vault holds the sensitive documents for everyone's account, and another vault holds the institution's cash reserves. Sidney would have known this if he had taken the time to case the bank's layout. Instead of having the manager open the inner money vault, Sidney left everyone standing in the documents vault, closed the door, and took off. An experienced bank robber would have avoided the teller line, and coaxed an unsuspecting loan representative to open the large money vault. This would have cut down on the entire staff's awareness of the crime. One person in the vault without a silent alarm would have been a lot easier to handle than the entire panicked staff. And, the payout would have been exponentially larger.

Sidney found he only had gained $1,300. He knew he could have done better than at the gaming tables in Chicago. Dejected, he stashed the briefcase under the car seat and changed into regular clothes as Julie drove him toward the New York state line as fast as the rented Mustang would fly.

Along the way, the couple was stopped by the highway patrol at two different turnpikes. Sidney, now in different clothes—wearing regular work clothes with a cap and sunglasses—didn't fit the description of the well-dressed bank robber they were looking for. Each time he was stopped, Sidney would flash the stolen drivers' license and each time the police officer would send him on his way. Let down by the low bank take and the turnpike stops, Sidney and Julie finally made it to Syracuse, New York. After checking into a hotel as Dr. Anderson Sidney quickly contacted another Italian "business" acquaintance in hopes of finding another job and a bit of protection.

His anonymous acquaintance set him up within his construction company and life seemed to continue for a few days. However, Sidney had unknowingly stepped out from under his protective umbrella. Not only had he moved out from under the safety shield of his local mob families, but he had also robbed a bank without checking it out beforehand. He had gotten sloppy, and no one was willing to vouch for him.

Without warning, one of Sidney's underworld acquaintances was arrested in a local bar, and then suddenly Julie disappeared. Panic hit the paranoid bank robber head on. As soon as he learned Julie had been arrested he grabbed a pistol and hit the road in the rental car.

In his race for freedom, he carelessly left everything behind in his hotel room. The police raided Sidney's hotel room within hours of the criminal's quick escape. The officers seized a small armory of guns, a pile of cash, and even Doc. Anderson's missing credit cards.

By this time, Sidney was flying down the highway in the rental car, hoping to escape from the great state of New York. Without warning, the FBI surrounded the fleeing outlaw like he was some sort of Jesse James. They arrested Sidney and charged him with violating New York's Sullivan Law. [The Sullivan law was a controversial law in New York at time prohibited the carrying of guns.] Sidney, tried to deny everything, but Julie had already confessed to the bank robbery and everything else she knew about the gangster Sidney James Heard, including his identity. is the problem with trophy girls; once the money runs out they will snitch every time. Darn the luck.

Chapter 9: Escape Attempt & Federal Prison

Sidney was quickly whisked away to Trenton, New Jersey where he would await his trial and sentencing. The officers assigned a 24-hour guard to keep an eye on the escape artist while they waited for his criminal record to come flooding in from all across the United States. The guard escorted Sidney everywhere he needed to go. Their orders demanded he should not leave the guard's sight. The only privacy Sidney was afforded was the standard three-minute cold shower once a week. When the three minutes were up, a guard would open the door and hand him a towel and a fresh set of clothes. Privacy didn't really matter to Sidney. He was used to the lack of it. He had been through this whole scene before.

I asked him once if he ever thought about not breaking the law so he wouldn't end up in jail, but he just shrugged and said, "no." He was always too busy making money (illegally), buying women (mostly illegally), and partying. The thought of jail time as a consequence for his actions never crossed his mind. When he was out he was only interested in having a high heel time, and when he was locked away his only thought was, "how can I escape." Stupidity is the only word comes to mind here. Oh wait, in our politically correct society I'm not allowed to say "stupid." Oh well, I just did.

One day, Sidney's keen eye noticed the control room door led outside was just beyond the shower room door. His scheming mind immediately went to work on another escape plan. Only one guard stood at the shower door. Sidney figured if he could take guard hostage then he could get him to open the outside door. Beyond door sat a couple more guards, but Sidney knew he could breeze past them if he had a hostage. Then he would be free. It seemed like a simple plan.

Meanwhile, Sidney made friends with a black fellow-inmate nicknamed "Broadway." Broadway was serving a life sentence without parole. Sidney assumed Broadway would have nothing to lose, so he would most likely go along with his scheme. When Sidney approached him about his escape plan, the fellow-inmate appeared to quickly side with him. Over the course of a few days he foolishly laid out his entire plan to the man.

Sidney had read all about "Public Enemy Number One" gang leader John Dillinger as a youngster. He had even studied his criminal tactics throughout the years. In 1934, the media reported the infamous bank robber had fashioned a gun out of wood and had successfully bluffed his way out of the Crown Point Prison. The scheming conman figured if the trick worked for Dillinger it would work for him. So, over the next few days, Sidney collected bread, soap, black shoe polish, and the aluminum foil wrappers from inside his Bugler tobacco can.

He painstakingly pressed the bread and soap into the shape of a colt .45 pistol. After the bread pistol was shaped properly, he wrapped the makeshift gun barrel with the aluminum foil wrappers to give it the sheen of steel. Then he found some black shoe polish and dyed his master creation. Soon the crude firearm was complete. I doubt he could have done much damage with his soap gun, but who knows? His plan was to hold up the prison guard with the so-called weapon and escape through the control room door. One guard and two doors were all stood between Sidney Heard and freedom.

At the last minute, however, Boardwalk decided to snitch on the Chicago native and Sidney's plan was never completed. He was shackled and immediately shipped off to a high-security holding prison on West Street in New York City. This facility was where the Federal Government held all its notorious criminals while they awaited their transfer orders to the various Federal Penitentiaries all over the country. Naturally, Sidney felt right at home. Now every time he had to appear in court the officers would have to escort him from West Street, New York City, all the way back to Trenton, New Jersey. Sidney knew it was a pain in the neck for the officers, but he simply didn't care. In fact, he thoroughly enjoyed every minute of the hour-long car ride to Trenton and this gave him an extra two hours out of his cell every time.

Sidney was assigned a job in the bakery of the West Street facility. Here Sidney met prisoners Anthony "Sonny" Sutera and Frankie Dioguardi, two key players in the was then dubbed the French Connection. Sutera and Dioguardi were convicted of importing heroin into the United States from France. The media reported it was said to be the largest seizure of heroin in American history. The "street" value of the load of heroin equaled nearly one hundred million dollars, and the seized shipment weighed almost 209 pounds.[12]

[Hollywood has created their own rendition of the French connection, but the movie and the book by Robin Moore were both based on a different heroin seizure. Or maybe the facts were changed to protect the writers and directors. Who knows? Feel free to draw your own conclusions at this point. As you may have noticed I have been a little foggy on a few details to save my own neck. No judgement here.]

While in this prison's holding facility, Sidney met a captain of the Colombo crime family named Johnny "Irish" Matera. For those of you who don't know the New York underworld was and still is ruled by five major crime families; the Colombo, the Bonanno, the Gambino, the Genovese, and the Lucchese. The F.B.I. has waged a steady war against organized crime since the eighties and won a big victory when they put John Gotti behind bars for life. Gotti was the boss of the Gambino crime family and some reporters claim he was the last big don. Don't be fooled. The mob still exists and they are still capable of violence.

Johnny "Irish" Matera was serving time after murdering an undercover cop was trying to infiltrate the *La Cosa Nostra.* Matera would later be released from prison only to be "whacked" by one of his own "family" members. His body was chopped up in pieces and left to rot because his associate was upset with his cut of some illegal gambling money. Even though he was really tight with John "Sonny" Franzese, the onetime underboss of the Colombo crime family, Matera was marked for a hit. His only mistake was in allowing the FBI to trail him to a meeting. Obviously it doesn't take much to get "knocked off" when you're a made member of the mob[13].

Every year around Christmas time the prison staff would host huge gin rummy tournaments to keep the inmates occupied during the holidays. To add to the competitive spirit, the prison officials always ended up pitting the Jewish inmates against the Italian prisoners. Sidney was chosen to represent the Italians because of his skill rather than his bloodline, and for a long time the Jews couldn't find anyone to beat him.

When asked if he cheated, Sidney would scoff, "you don't have to cheat when you can remember what cards everyone had in their hands." As usual, Sidney's arrogance and sharp tongue would stave off the naysayers. His six-foot two-inch frame carried an air about him helped dispel any further complaints. Card counting mixed with a bit of skill and a sharp memory were all he needed to beat most opponents.

There was one man always caught Sidney's eye during these prison tournaments. He was a blond haired, blue-eyed man named Donald Duncan. Duncan was part Jewish and always took the Jews' side of the game, so this often pitted him against the Chicago native. With his shiny hair and flashing eyes, Duncan always looked like a million bucks, even in a drab prisoner's uniform. He held himself with an air of confidence and poise Sidney couldn't help but notice. One day Sidney just had to ask him the forbidden question.

"Man, you don't seem to fit in around here," Sidney remembered asking. "What did you do to get stuck in here?"

"Oh, not much really. I just sold some property," Donald shrugged nonchalantly.

"Since when is it illegal to sell some property?" questioned the curious gangster. "What did you do sell property belonged to someone else?"

"Oh, it isn't illegal to sell your own property—except I sold the same property a dozen times over the course of a few years," Donald grinned. Donald owned twenty river front lots in Puerto Rico. He sold them for $50,000 each, but he never figured anyone would want to build on the land, so he kept selling the same parcels of land until someone decided to fly down and see their property. Donald had sold stretch of land until he had earned himself well over two-and-a-half million dollars through the scam.

Sidney shook his head and laughed. He never forgot the blue-eyed conman.

The overworked justice system works at a snail's pace, but Sidney eventually plea-bargained and received a sentence reduced to fifteen years for the bank robbery. He somehow got out of the gun-carrying charge by convincing the judge the gun was already in the rental car when he drove it off the lot back in Chicago. [Why anyone would believe such a thing is beyond comprehension, but it is true nonetheless. Even now Sidney has a very charismatic personality tends to make people like him— even those who are trying to put him away.]

After sentencing, Sidney was shipped to the Lewisburg Federal Prison on January 6, 1966. This maximum-security prison is located only two hundred miles north of Washington D.C. in the Kelly Township of Pennsylvania. Sidney's new inmate number would be 33196. The infamous teamster Jimmy Hoffa was convicted of jury tampering and would be assigned to the same facility a short time later. [14] Of course Sidney, the wannabe gangster, was naturally drawn to the charismatic Hoffa mobster. He was eager to learn anything he could from the man.

Now with a federal rap, Sidney found himself with an entirely different class of criminals. In his experience state prisons were filled with petty criminals, racially biased prison guards, and below par facilities. Sidney entered Lewisburg, a federal prison, and was surprised to find himself in a small metropolis of highbrow gangsters and white-collar criminals. It was a whole different world for the Chicago native. If he had to be in prison, he figured, this was the place to be.

Sidney was assigned a job in the laundry department; he was happy to have something to do. Each prisoner received a small wage could be spent in the prison commissary. The store offered personal hygiene products, stamps, reading material and, of course, the highly coveted free-world cigarettes. As fate would have it, Jimmy Hoffa was assigned to the same department. His job was to repair the torn mattress pads lined the bunks in each cell. Sidney's workstation where he dried all the prisoner's sheets was nearby. Of course, Sidney recognized the highly publicized New York teamster and studied him.

Some newspapers had labeled Hoffa as a mobster with a massive criminal resume while others heralded him as a hero. Although his dealings may not always be aboveboard, the charismatic activist impressed Sidney greatly. Jimmy Hoffa was one of the most powerful men in the United States. His teamsters owned the entire big rig shipping industry. Some rumored his unchecked power to be beyond of the President of the United States. Here he was going to be locked up and he could have put all the trucks in America on strike with just one phone call. He refused to abuse his power this way because he knew would hurt the little guy so he didn't send the order. It seemed like Hoffa was more concerned for the teamsters and the union man on the street than his own well-being. This trait alone gave Sidney a great respect for the man.

While at Lewisburg, Sidney noticed a little old man looked more like a Sunday school teacher than a criminal. He seemed completely out of place in prison. His name was Anthony "Tino" De Angelis.[15] This innocent looking man had embezzled over five hundred and seventy million dollars with his salad oil scheme. Yes, you read right. I said $570,000,000. The conman owned several large tanker-trucks full of soybean oil used to make salad dressing. He would use the trucks as collateral to obtain massive loans from various banks across the U.S. Unfortunately for the banks; most of the tankers were filled with water instead of oil. When the inspectors would stop by they would get a pure oil sample from the unloading pipe, not realizing the pipe was the only thing containing oil. The rest of the tank was filled with water. One would wonder why it took the banks so long to catch on to such an obvious trick. Angelis never sold his tanks of water and never repaid the loans. In the pen, De Angelis earned the nickname, "Salad Oil King."

Life in the penitentiary quickly became stagnant, and the daily routine was mind numbing after a while. Occasionally, something noteworthy would happen to bring a spark of life back to the inmate drones. Sidney was busy working in the laundry department when he witnessed several gang members from D.C. jump a fellow inmate. They began brutally beating and molesting the man. Feeling sorry for the victim, Sidney attacked the men with nothing but a bucket of soapy water and a mop. After a brief scuffle, Sidney helped the inmate up off the floor, dusted him off, and sent him on his way. But this time Sidney's hero complex would get him into terrible trouble. Hoffa was still toiling away at his workstation and witnessed the entire ordeal. But instead of congratulating Sidney's heroics, Hoffa shook his head and quickly urged the young man to request a transfer to Atlanta.

Hoffa warned Sidney, "Those were big D.C. thugs, and now they're out to kill you. You should have stayed out of it."

"I couldn't just stand by and let them do to guy," Sidney shrugged pretending to be unscathed by the warning. Still, he went ahead and requested the transfer. If Hoffa was right, the transfer wouldn't do him any good anyways. It always took forever to get approved and if someone wanted him dead the authorities would find his body stashed somewhere long before he received his approval.

Surprisingly a mere three days later, Sidney was mysteriously transported to Atlanta on the U.S. Attorney's private plane along with a few other inmates. Sidney remembered it was so cold the pilot had a hard time getting the engine to start, but after several attempts they were up in the air. No one mentioned Jimmy Hoffa's name, but there was no doubt in Sidney's mind his life had been saved by the nefarious mobster.

Inmates couldn't get a transfer approved quickly back then, even if their lives were in danger. A mobster might kill you in a heartbeat, but it is nothing personal; it is merely business. On the other hand, many mobsters were known to be kind and gracious. Of course, Sidney had no idea if Hoffa was really connected or not, but he would always be grateful.

Upon arrival at the Atlanta prison, Sidney Heard's inmate number was changed to 90441. Strangely enough, Atlanta felt more like home to Sidney. He had served time with many of the same inmates while he was in the Florida prison system years earlier. Inmates gossip worse than a bunch of pious old women so by the time he arrived everyone had heard what happened to Sidney in Lewisburg. Now everyone assumed the Chicago native had connections with the legendary Jimmy Hoffa. Sidney never corrected them; he simply let them arrive at whatever conclusion they chose. was Sidney's way. This "connection by proxy" concept would take him far in the criminal underworld, but it would also cause him a great deal of trouble with the Feds.

One evening when Sidney was playing gin rummy with a group of other inmates, he ran into his old friend Yankee Taylor. The pair played a few games of Gin Rummy and reminisced on the old times at Raiford, Florida. This reunion would reoccur at both Atlanta and again a few years later when Sidney was shipped to the maximum-security prison in Marion, Illinois.

As usual, every inmate was always assigned a job within the prison to keep things running smoothly, and to keep them busy. This time Sidney's assignment was to work in the prison's records office. Here his curious mind again kicked into high gear, and he began researching the convictions of each of his fellow inmates. He wanted to know what each man was in prison for, and by narrowing down the records of each conviction, he could find out which was the hardest crime for an attorney to convict a criminal of. The answer was arson. Unless somebody rolled over on you, or you got sloppy and left witnesses it was nearly impossible to be convicted of arson in the 1960s.

Nowadays with forensic science it isn't quite so easy to get away with arson. Back tracking through a burned structure the technicians follow the evidence and can determine not only where the fire started, but also how it traveled throughout the building. Many accelerants leave a trail along the floor and these can be analyzed in the lab using gas chromatography (GC) to determine exactly what was used. Also, scientists have discovered by using different types of light they can see fingerprints on various surfaces. While most people would expect fingerprints to vanish in the flames the exact opposite is true. The intensity of the heat will seal the evidence onto the object thus preserving it for the officials. Of course, none of these techniques were available in the sixties.

Sidney soon discovered the prison's outdated filing system still held the original records of inmates dating all the way back to 1906. There were hundreds of useless files needed to be trashed, and yet other inmates had files missing or incomplete. Sidney spent the next two months cleaning, organizing, and re-filing all the dusty folders. FBI agents would frequently visit the expansive record room in search of information on fugitives. Of course, this gave the curious conman an excuse to read all about his fellow inmates. If he found anything really "juicy," he would use it to his advantage. Soon the word got out about the good work Sidney had done in the records department and it would eventually lead to better job opportunities.

Sidney's run-in with death:

Everyone will face death at one point or another in their life and in Sidney's chosen profession he faced danger regularly. There was one incident in Atlanta however could have cut this narrative short and buried the leading character six feet under.

The Atlanta Federal Penitentiary was set up in five tiers. Each tier had a catwalk ran in front of the cells and cell number sixteen was the shower on each tier. Sidney was assigned to cell number 5-1. One day as he was coming around the catwalk heading back to his cell. He passed another inmate who was on his way to cell number sixteen for his scheduled three-minute shower. Without warning another man came around the corner and stabbed Sidney in the chest with a homemade shank. [A "shank" is a homemade knife made from scrap metal with a piece of cloth wrapped around one end of the weapon for a handle.] Sidney stumbled back in shock—but the attacker was in for an even bigger shock when he realized he had stabbed the wrong target.

The attacker quickly disappeared. But the man in the shower witnessed the event. In a panic, he dropped his towel and ran naked down the stairs to get help.

Sidney's blue eyes drifted down to the metal object protruding from his chest. A strange feeling washed over him as he watched a red stain form on his shirt. He felt a slight twinge as he pulled the metal object from his body. Somehow the knife had stabbed through his can of Bugler Tobacco and had barely cut into his chest. It took a moment for his mind to register this information. Then he immediately began to wonder who would want him dead. He quickly came up with a list of possible enemies.

After removing the metal shard, he hurried back to his cell, bandaged the small cut in his chest, and changed his shirt before the guard could come and question him about it. When the uniformed man arrived, no one had any information. Sidney assured the guard he hadn't been stabbed and the naked man running down the hall was just crazy. If the attacker was to be punished, Big Sid and his band of thugs were going to handle it.

Later Sidney had rounded up a small posse of burly inmates and was about to hunt down his attacker when an associate came by to explain things. The attacker had stabbed the wrong target and was trembling in fear thinking Big Sid was coming after him when Sidney had just happened to be in the wrong place at the wrong time. Normally Sidney would have torn the guy apart for his mistake, but Sidney figured he wasn't really hurt so he let the man off the hook. Besides, if he made his attacker's friends mad he could fall victim to their retaliation. And everyone knew it didn't take much to get yourself killed behind the walls of the Atlanta Federal Pen. Atlanta had a reputation for brutality. The entire place was like a ticking time bomb waiting for someone to light the fuse. Sidney would choose to leave this one alone.

Every month more inmates would be attacked, murdered, and molested. It was commonplace in Atlanta. Sidney witnessed the horror firsthand, and determined he wouldn't become the next statistic no matter what it took. He began to lift weights, not to build bulk, but to build strength. His jailhouse routine consisted of dead-lifting and military-pressing two hundred pounds. way, when a fight broke out, all he had to do was to grab his assailant by the throat with one hand, and hook his forearm under the man's knee. Then the brute would lift his attacker over his head and toss him against the wall. It might not finish off his opponents, but it would knock them out for a brief moment and give Big Sid a chance to get away. Sidney knew he couldn't depend on the guards to keep him safe. All he had was his survival instincts—and he had honed them to perfection.

After bouncing from job to job at the pen, he landed a position working as a clerk in the hospital records department. This job earned first-grade pay, gave the inmate a set of coveted white clothes, and he would be on call twenty-four hours a day. This meant Sidney would get to spend a great deal of time away from his tiny cell.

His first job was to clean up the hospital's filing system. It still housed 2,800 files even though the entire prison only held 2,400 inmates. The job also gave Sidney complete access to the prison's hospital records—and a whole laundry list of hustling ideas.

Sidney would hustle everything he could to make a few extra bucks. It didn't matter if he was out in the free world or behind bars. Sidney loved the thrill of a good hustle. The hospital job gave the conman access to the prison psychiatrist and every inmate's psychiatric profiles. With the backing of the "good doctor," Sidney sent query letters to every prison in America asking what charge had caused each of their inmates to serve time in jail.

The responses soon poured in and Sidney was placed in charge of sorting them according to the inmates' convictions. Sidney soon learned arsonists were the least convicted criminals in the entire country, and not just in Atlanta, Georgia. One thing led to another and Sidney began to study the laws regarding insurance fraud and arson. He knew fully well one must first learn the law to effectively manipulate it. Years later, arson would become Sidney's forte.

At this point, one begins to wonder why this type of information was not classified, and why American prisons allow criminals to research this type of thing. This is just another example of how idle hands can lead to all sorts of chicanery or, as often quoted, "Idle hands are the devil's workshop."

While working in the medical records department, Sidney met a tall black man named Maurice Vass. He was a surgical nurse for the prison's hospital and ran into Sidney regularly. The second floor of the hospital housed a small pharmacy where the MTAs would fill prescriptions for the inmates. One day the two MTAs [Medically Trained Associates] were found bound and all the drugs had been stolen. The prison was immediately locked down while the prison officials searched 2,400 inmates. The investigation lasted three full days, but the pharmaceuticals were never located.

Sidney knew who had taken them, but of course he wasn't going to snitch on his buddy Maurice. He even knew where ill-gotten booty was stashed. Maurice and his cohort had hidden the drugs in the wall behind the large ovens. After a little time had lapsed, the missing drugs started showing up on the prison's black market. Sidney and Maurice became good friends over time and the pair stayed in touch even after they were released from federal prison.

The Atlanta prison was set up with eight men to a cell block. Sidney didn't want to live with seven other men he couldn't trust. So, he simply paid off the prison staff and they kept his cell block down to six men. Big Sid was even allowed to pick the five men he would stay with. Unless there was an emergency, or an influx of inmates, Sidney usually got his wishes. So, goes the life of a gangster behind bars.

While Big Sid's cell block was well known, there was another cell block had more connections than the small-time gangster. On the third floor in Atlanta was number thirty-two. This cell was full of big time Italian mobsters. The federal government had declared war on the mafia and they were all serving stiff sentences. They had nothing to do and quite frankly they were all bored.

Now when a mobster is bored there are only two things he can do. First and foremost, he can get into trouble, or he can find something productive to do with his time. This cell group chose option two and decided to study law. They would become unofficially known as the "Mobster Law Office" of the Atlanta Federal Penitentiary. Anyone who had a grievance about his case would pay a visit to Cell 32. The Italians there would happily take the case. They never charged for their services because most of them were very wealthy men, and besides they didn't have much else to do.

They got a thrill out of harassing the legal system, so it was a win-win situation for them.

While spending time in Atlanta, Sidney met many infamous criminals. At one point, he worked with one of the FBI's top ten most-wanted bank robbers named Fast Eddie Watkins[16]. Sidney found the man to be a fascinating case study and secretly admired the man's spunk.

April 4, 1968 the world lost a great man and it rocked the entire country. The news even rattled the prison walls of Atlanta. Martin Luther King, Jr. had been assassinated. Five days later Sidney and Fast Eddie slipped up to the third floor of the hospital and watched his funeral procession. They weren't reprimanded by the staff. Everyone mourned together.

Edward Owen Watkins was quite the character. Outwardly, he was cocky and stuck up. He was proud his name had appeared on the FBI's most wanted list. After Sidney got to know him, however, he found Eddie to be quite amiable. Eddie was serving a twenty-five-year sentence for bank robbery; the one he was caught for anyway. Eddie was so good at robbing banks he could knock over several in a single day. He only got caught because he had a heart attack during one of his robberies and was unable to escape before the cops arrived. Yet, he was so charming some of his own hostages nursed him until the paramedics arrived to help.

Another notable inmate Sidney met was Manuel Calixto Rojas De Diaz aka Carlos Diaz. Time Magazine reportedly nicknamed him the "Cuban Hawk" when he rebelled against Castro and used his own plane to help bomb the sugar mills. Diaz started out as a pilot in Fidel Castro's Secret Police, but instead of flying the plane solely for Castro's errands, Diaz also used the dictator's plane to smuggle refugees into the United States. Castro immediately placed him on his black list of pilots not allowed in Cuban airspace and issued a $100,000 reward for his capture. [17] Afterward he hoped to gain U.S.

Citizenship, but because of his past offenses under the Castro regime he was labeled a mercenary and denied. This infuriated the rebel and he began smuggling drugs into the U.S. using the plane stolen from Castro. He was arrested and sent to Atlanta Penitentiary for five years.

Diaz worked in the laundry department of the Atlanta prison and ran into Sidney on a regular basis. Rumors say he was killed some time later by Johnny "Irish" Matera. As with most mob hits there wasn't enough evidence to officially connect the murder to Matera. Despite all my research efforts over the past several years I haven't been able to find one mention of both these names together.

While in prison, being a conman by trade, Sidney quickly got into the black-market drug business. After all, he had access to all the records for the hospital. It was an open door just begging for him to pass through. The scam was simple. When the doctor examined an inmate, Sidney would make up a prescription whether the inmate needed it or not, and forge the doctor's signature. Then when the pharmacy filled the prescription, Sidney would sell the drugs to the highest bidder on the jailhouse black market. He made quite a bundle on this scheme. Inmates were only allowed to have a set amount of money with them, so Sidney would call in his lawyer and send the money out with him. Of course, the attorney received a pleasant cut from all the inmates for this service. way Sidney could amass a large bankroll and it would be waiting for him upon his release.

Most people have heard of Alcatraz prison. Many movies have been made over the years about the island fortress floating out in the San Francisco bay, and many more legends circulate the place to this day. In reality, the Alcatraz Federal Penitentiary operated from 1934 to 1963 and was quickly labeled America's toughest prison. It was often called "The Rock" and was rumored to be inescapable. Many rumors of escapes floated around stronghold, but only one man's escape has been confirmed.

The Anglin brothers and Frank Morris may have been successful in their attempt in June of 1962, but they were never seen again and no one can confirm their daring feat. The only confirmed escapee was John Paul Scott.

On December 16, 1962, Scott, along with one prison cohort, bent the bars above the latrine of their cell. They slid down a rope and dropped into the freezing 46° F. water. Although his cohort was recaptured twenty minutes later, John made it to the shore before he passed out from hypothermia and exhaustion under the Golden Gate Bridge.

After recovering in the Letterman General Hospital, the great escape artist was shipped right back to Alcatraz. Several months later Alcatraz was shut down and Scott was transferred to the same prison where Sidney was incarcerated. In his new surroundings, John Paul Scott befriended the up-and-coming escape artist, Sidney James Heard. The inmate pair worked together in the prison hospital. John was a lab tech for the prison hospital and often supplied information for Sidney's files. John was so good at his job the nearby Grady Hospital would send in specimens for John to examine. John would continue working for the civilian hospital until he was transferred to another prison.

At time, inmates were not given any notice before they would be transferred to another facility. Without warning a guard would bang on the cell's bars and tell the inmate to pack up and ship out. Within minutes he was expected to shove all his belongings into his pillowcase and be waiting at the door of his cell.

One morning as Sidney checked in for work, he received notice a fellow inmate had been suddenly transferred during the night. Sidney knew the man well and knew he was a heart patient who required daily medication. However, this information and the man's medical files were not sent with the inmate because of his quick transfer. The man later had a heart attack due to this gross negligence. Luckily the man survived, but Sidney was furious. He marched into his boss's office and demanded something should be done. They might be inmates, but they still deserved to be treated humanely.

Sidney believed every medical record should be transferred with the inmates. This would have to give the records department a twenty-four-hour notice of the inmate's transfer, and could save many lives. Sidney also knew this kind of information would yield great power to him. Of course, this information could also generate a profit. As usual the scheming criminal would observe his situation and find the best way to take advantage of it. He had learned long ago a successful conman must be an excellent chameleon. Now with the new rules in place, Sidney could give his fellow inmates a heads up before they were transferred—for a price.

One of Sidney's so-called running buddies in the Atlanta pen was an Italian named Charlie "Blue Eyes." For his privacy and *my* security, we will omit his infamous last name in this narrative. Let's just say he was well known to the Genovese and Colombo crime families in New York. "Blue Eyes" had taken the rap for a big time "underboss." Charlie went through the entire legal process knowing fully well who had committed the crime, but he kept his mouth shut and earned respect (and a great deal of money) from the "family" for his efforts. One day Sidney asked old Blue Eyes why no one would speak to another Italian inmate named Ally Romano. Sidney knew Ally was a connected man, but he couldn't understand why everyone shunned the little gray-haired fellow like the plague. The guy seemed okay to Sidney.

"We don't speak to the dead," came the gruff reply from Blue Eyes. Sidney watched the man from across the prison yard and pondered this reply for a moment.

"Hum. He doesn't look dead to me," Sidney questioned the gruff mobster sitting beside him.

"Nope, but he will be," Charlie replied. "He's messed up big time." Romano had broken "Omerta," the *La Cosa*

Nostra's sacred code of silence, and had "rolled over" on one of his mob bosses. Of course, when you snitch on a mobster you get "whacked" that is the way the business works.

Sure enough, only a few days after Al Romano was released from prison, he returned to New York and was killed execution style. Romano's gruesome murder made headlines all over the Big Apple a few days later. Whispers of mob connections circulated in all the tabloids; of course, no one dared mention any names. One might wonder why in the world the guy went back to New York, but I guess he thought the mob had enough connections to find him anywhere. I'm a firm believer in the old saying about catching a moving target, but whatever.

During his incarceration at USP Atlanta, Sidney had complete access to all the psychiatric files of his fellow inmates and he spent his free time memorizing all the juicy details. Not only did this give him inside information he could use to his benefit, it also was an educational experience for the young criminal. He would talk to all the big-time gangsters, bank robbers, and even murderers every chance he could. His young, hungry mind was like a sponge soaking up knowledge of the streets. One might wonder where Sidney's curious mind could have taken him if he had chosen another career option.

One elderly gentleman Sidney met occasionally in the hospital at Atlanta was named Mr. McVickers. This poor old man always received his social security checks at the prison and he would hoard them until his one-year sentence expired. [Now the laws have changed and Social Security benefits are suspended during incarceration.] The old man had no family and friends besides his buddies in the pen, so when he'd get out he would take his little stash and head straight for the local brothel. All the local prostitutes knew McVickers very well. They would party with him and spend his money until his bankroll was gone. After he had squandered all his money he would find a brick, chuck it through the window of the local post office, and then sit down on the sidewalk and wait for the cops to show up.

McVickers was on several medications for various health problems, so he was always sent back to the Atlanta pen where the process would begin all over again. McVickers had done this twice during Sidney's stay at Atlanta. Sidney felt sorry for the man and determined he would never let himself get in such a state.

Unfortunately, the lifestyle Sidney had chosen at a young age would eventually lose its excitement and leave him desolate, alone, and addicted to drugs. Crime, drugs, violence, and promiscuity would destroy him and when the time came he wouldn't have a choice.

Atlanta Prisoners Revolt:

During his time in Atlanta, Sidney helped lead a peaceful prisoners' revolt against the entire prison staff. At time, inmates were not given a menu for their meals. They were just given whatever so-called meal the kitchen staff could scrounge up. Not only did they not know what they were having ahead of time, they also had no way of knowing what was in their food. Sidney was not Jewish, but he ran with a few inmates who were, and they were all fed up with the prison's food. A Jew never knew ahead of time if he could eat the meal or not. According to the Jewish faith, Jews don't eat any type of pork, but pork products were often included in the meals they were served at the prison. Whenever Jewish prisoners found pork was included in the meal, they simply didn't eat. Sidney felt strongly the Jewish prisoners should not have to go without eating; besides he liked fighting the system any chance he could. So, he helped to stage an "underground" revolt.

One day at lunchtime all the inmates lined up for lunch as usual. They were ordered to not say a word as each man passed through the line and received his tray of food. Every inmate sat down at their table and stared at their food until the last inmate in line received his plate. Then, without so much as a whisper, every inmate in Atlanta Federal Penitentiary stood, scraped their plates into the trash, and headed back to their cells. No one spoke a word, and no one ate a bite.

The quiet demonstration sent the prison staff into a panic, so they locked down the entire complex, thinking someone was trying to escape. The warden began asking questions and he was quickly directed to Big Sid's cell. Sidney was often the designated speaker for such things.

"What is going on here, Heard?" the warden growled.

"It's simple, really. We want a menu for our meals," Sidney shrugged nonchalantly.

"A menu? That's all?" the warden asked with skepticism. "Why do you need a menu?"

"Well, the Jews cannot eat pork and they never know if they're going to be able to eat their meals," Sidney calmly explained. "Sometimes they might go a few days without eating because the cooks used pork." Sidney didn't know of anyone who had starved for days, but it sounded good anyway. He continued to explain even though they were criminals, they were humans and they deserved to be fed. They might even be serving a life sentence, but didn't mean they deserved to starve.

The warden took the information and went back to his office, but since the demonstration was organized and peaceful, he quickly agreed to their demands. A few days later the Federal prison implemented a menu, and a few months after the concept was implemented throughout Federal prisons nationwide. State prisons soon followed suit. When a prisoner looks at his lunch menu today, he should realize a menu is an amenity was not always provided and be thankful for it.

On one particularly bland day, Sidney was working in the hospital when a man by the name of Bobby Wilcoxson[18] walked into the hospital with a screwdriver stuck in his head. Yes, I said screwdriver in the head.

Another inmate had jumped the infamous bank robber and stabbed him with the metal object after an argument. The extra appendage didn't seem to bother Wilcoxson any. He stayed in the hospital for a couple of weeks and then was released back into the general population. Of course, Sidney quickly looked up Wilcoxson's file and found out he was one of the FBI's most wanted bank robbers. Wilcoxson was a master at disguising himself to avoid arrest. This trait had landed his story in *Reader's Digest* a feat pleased the criminal to no end. Sidney was quite impressed as well.

Sidney witnessed many horror stories while working as a clerk for the prison's hospital. If anyone needed medical attention, Sidney was immediately called to pull the inmate's files. Sidney was called upon at all hours of the day and night. One late night call sent Sidney literally running toward the records office. A man whom Sidney knew named Nemeyer had been stabbed 157 times with a shank. Sidney grabbed the man's file and raced back to the surgery room, but Nemeyer was dead before the gangster could return. Sidney steeled his expression, but his young eyes watched in horror as they readied his friend's body for an autopsy. Images of the corpse's gaping wounds would be forever burned into his memory.

Another gruesome hospital experience happened one evening when a 320-pound inmate stumbled through the door literally holding his intestines in his arms. The man had been attacked and sliced completely open with a shank. The man passed out just inside the hospital doors and fell to the floor. Sidney ran for the man's data file, and somehow the hospital surgeons could stitch the man back together. The inmate survived the ordeal and was left with quite a war wound to show off to his cronies.

Stories like these were a regular occurrence while Sidney worked at the hospital. One man came in with a tiny one-inch-long cut in the very center of his body. Surprisingly, man died before they could get him onto a gurney. Sidney wondered how the man could die so quickly since the injury seemed so insignificant. Later the doctor explained he couldn't have been saved if he'd been stabbed while lying on the operating table. The knife had sliced back and forth through the aortic heart valve and the man died almost instantly.

Chapter 10: U.S. Penitentiary: Marion, Illinois

In 1968 a guard happened to catch Sidney with drugs and a pocket full of one-hundred-dollar-bills. Of course, inmates were not allowed to have drugs; neither could they have more than $25 on their person or in their prison bank account. Because he broke rule, Sidney Heard was immediately arrested and transferred to the United States Penitentiary near Marion, Illinois. USP Marion is located 300 miles south of Chicago and about 120 miles east of St. Louis. The complex was placed in the middle of a large Federal Game Reserve. At the time, it was used for the sole purpose of isolating trouble making, high risk inmates.

This maximum-security prison was opened in 1963 to replace the infamous Alcatraz. Here Sidney's "number name" was changed yet again to inmate number 1794. USP Marion was, and still is, one of the top ten most infamous prisons in the United States. [19] He soon discovered out of its five hundred and fifty inmates, three hundred and fifty-seven of Marion's prisoners were serving life sentences or greater. (One might wonder how a person could serve more than one life sentence.) Sidney's meager fifteen-year sentence gave him the nickname "Short Timer." It was probably the only time in his life when someone referred to the six-foot-two-inch tall gangster as "short" anything. After the war zone atmosphere of Atlanta, the lifestyle in this prison blew the young conman away.

Inmates regularly had steak for dinner and hearty breakfasts every morning. Gone were the days of mashed carrots and peas; Sidney couldn't be happier—well, is unless he could get out. Life in a supermax isolation-based prison system was no picnic. Freedom would trump food any day.

Sidney started out working as a yard maintenance man. He immediately added his name to the waiting list to work in one of the prison industries; the industry jobs paid a better wage. When his name was finally drawn, he was transferred to work in the warehouse shipping industry. Next-door to the shipping department was the prison's print shop. The shop printed a little bit of everything, including FBI and DEA handbooks. Of course, these handbooks made very interesting reading material for all the convicted felons. Sidney would study the handbooks every chance he could. Years later, he would use this knowledge to fuel his underworld efforts. [Why in the world the FBI and the DEA allowed convicted felons to print their information is beyond me. Sending their literature to a free-world print shop to print copies would make more sense. That's worse than the New York Yankees giving their playbook to the Chicago Cubs.]

While in Marion, Sidney joined an activist group called the Church of the New Song. This group was run by a fellow con man named Bishop Harry Theriault. The name "Church Of the New Song" was an anagram for CONS. This so-called organization was more of a way to rally against the establishment than an actual religious gathering. It did, however, gain the newcomer access to the jailhouse gym once a week, and earned him a few more connections. Theriault had a long history of litigation against prison officials. Every chance he could he would claim his first amendment rights were being violated. Most of his frivolous lawsuits were eventually dismissed, but not before causing legal officials a major headache.[20]

Harry had a reputation as a smooth-talking con man. His silver tongue seemed to get him out of just about anything, and one time it paid off in a very big way. Two U.S. Marshals were escorting Theriault to jail and he somehow escaped from their custody. He handcuffed both officers to a tree during the escape attempt. Even with all the evidence and testimonies stacked against him, Henry Theriault still had the gall to plead not guilty of this crime in court. To top it off, when he took the witness stand, his testimony was so compelling the jury ended up finding him not guilty. Obviously, his smooth tongue didn't work every time or he wouldn't have landed in prison. When Harry heard of Big Sid he immediately recruited the big guy to be his bodyguard. If Harry ended up in a sticky situation he couldn't talk himself out of, then Big Sid's presence would come in handy.

[On a side note, in 2005, the state challenged the religion status of the Church of the New Song organization. The court was set to determine if CONS should be protected by the constitution as a religion. Challengers claim CONS is only a front for white supremacy groups, and is not a legitimate religion.[21] It should be pointed out Sidney is not racially biased in any way. He simply used the group to form new connections and to gain more amenities. In the time Sidney was there the group was never involved in anything racially biased. It seemed the only people the group was biased against were the lawyers and judges.]

USP Marion housed many of the nation's top mafia bosses, vicious gang leaders, and even violent political prisoners. One of Sidney's fellow inmates was a man named Henry Michael Gargano. As a youngster, Sidney had read about Gargano's arrest and trial in the papers. Gargano and Sidney were both from the same Chicago suburb of North Lake, Illinois. Sidney had grown up in small "mob town" until his parents moved when he was in eighth grade. Gargano was serving a 199-year sentence for killing two cops after he knocked over a bank just down the street from Sidney's childhood home. According to Gargano, the two officers shot him as he exited the building and then stood over him laughing as he bled out on the pavement at their feet.

Unfortunately, the two uniformed men didn't notice their victim was still alive and bleeding to death at their feet. Infuriated by their laughter, Gargano arose from the pavement with a machine gun and plowed through the two police officers with a barrage of bullets. He escaped day with only a bullet to the arm, but his freedom was cut short when he was arrested four days later in Indiana. Now Gargano worked in the prison's warehouse, but when he was off he loved to spend his free time painting. Sidney was surprised how good Gargano, the "North Lake Cop Killer" painted with his one good arm.

Gargano painted all sorts of things and one day he gave Sidney a painting of Clint Eastwood wearing a serape from his movie "A Fist Full of Dollars." Sidney told me it was so good it looked like one of the professional movies posters.

"I didn't plan on killin' those cops," Henry confided to Sidney one day. "They just stood there laughing and swearing at me like I was some piece of trash on the street."

Whether he was just trying to smooth talk a youngster, or he believed his version of the story I don't know, but the newspapers described a very different scene.

It is reported on October 27, 1967 Henry Gargano, Clifton Daniels, and Ronald Del Raine took over the Northlake Bank, held twenty-two hostages, and stole over $80,000.[22] On their way out of the bank two officers were pulling up out front in response to the silent alarm. The bank robbers opened fire upon the officers before they could even exit the vehicle. When two more officers arrived, they received a barrage of bullets.

When the gunfire ceased and the dust settled officers John Nagle and Anthony Perri were dead.[23] Gargano and Daniels escaped in a vehicle, but the third Ronald Del Raine was arrested at the scene. Gargano was found four days later in a fishing cabin in Indiana. He allegedly offered a local doctor $25,000 to fix his arm, but the doctor refused and called the local authorities. He was too weak to fight and instead was carried out quietly on a stretcher.

After the arrest, all three criminals were sentenced to 199 years. To make matters even worse Gargano allegedly told a reporter from the Chicago Tribune, "I don't feel any remorse about those dead cops. When you get hit in a shootout it's a fair confrontation, like Vietnam. It can't be helped." And in 1981 when he gave an interview he had the same lack of remorse.[24] What made him suddenly care about the murder he committed? This interview only a few years after Sidney's release is what leads me to believe it was all a fabricated tale to woo a young man.

Six years after he met Sidney in Marion, Henry would lead a team of five men in a daring escape from the supermax prison. They were recaptured a few days later and five more years were added to his sentence. He was then sited with two more escape attempts in 1978 and 1985, and then in 2000 he was caught with drugs. Despite all this he was almost released on parole in 2010.

The parole board was immediately hit with a tsunami of letters pleading for the Northlake Cop Killer to remain behind bars. 6,000 signatures came from Northlake alone. Finally, his parole was revoked and eventually Gargano died of a heart attack behind bars on October 13, 2011.[25] No one will ever know if he was truly remorseful, but his actions certainly didn't appear to be. I'll leave the decision up to you.

Marion was all about offering programs to their inmates to help them conform into society once released. In 1969, Sidney confessed to a fellow inmate by the name of Richard Bryant he never graduated from high school in

Chicago. Remember, he was in the Florida Prison System by the tender age of eighteen. Sidney always regretted not getting his high school diploma. His mother had been so proud of him back when he was a football star in school, but his bad behavior had gotten him expelled and then his mother had passed away. School had suddenly become the least important facet of his life at time.

Now eleven years later it had regained its importance. Bryant volunteered to help Sidney study for the G.E.D. (General Education Development) exam. Bryant was in prison for murdering two FBI agents. Whatever the circumstances for his incarceration Bryant was a good friend to the young gangster. With help from the convicted murderer, Sidney Heard passed his exams and finally received his coveted diploma at the age of 26. It was quite an achievement for Sidney—one his mother would have been proud of.

Eventually Sidney earned another job when the warden learned of his educational background and his above average IQ. The warden quickly assigned the inmate to a clerical job in the payroll office where Sidney printed all the inmates' payroll vouchers. The peculiar thing about this office job was every coworker Sidney had was a convicted bank robber. Al Barubi, Jesse James Roberts, Richard Stokes, Cary Ethridge, and even Fred Deusenberg were all employed in what was called "Bank Robber's Row," aka the prison payroll department. His civilian boss was a man named C. R. James, who claimed to be a distant relative of the infamous outlaw Jesse James. All Sidney's jobs provided the gangster with insider knowledge, and of course he used this power to manipulate his surroundings. Working in the payroll department was no different.

Sidney told me the prison's kitchen was run completely by mafia guys. If you weren't a Made Man you could forget about working in the kitchen. A mobster we will call "Sam" ran the entire kitchen staff. He was a small man, only about five-and-a-half-feet tall, but the man's psychiatric files shocked Sidney. This little man weighed around 150 pounds was labeled as one of the mob's biggest "button men." [Button man is another term used by gangsters for a hired killer or a hit man.] Sidney did some research and found the man was suspected of over seventy different homicides, but he was never convicted.

Sidney talked to Sam some time later in his cell. He asked him what "button man" meant even though he already had a good idea. Sam smiled at the tall, young man before him. Sam explained by shaping a gun with his hand and feigned pulling a trigger.

"I may be small, but it doesn't take much to do this," Sam added. "Never judge a book by its cover." Sidney pondered this advice and never forgot the mobster's menacing words, nor the evil glimmer in his dark eyes.

Life inside the maximum-security prison was like a small city. Every inmate had his responsibilities, his chosen hobbies, and his running buddies. As usual, every inmate behind bars had a specific identity. One man could be the janitor and would become his identity. Another man might be the cook. Another may be labeled as the "prison's troublemaker." Sidney wore his usual identity of a well-connected, well-educated Chicago hustler. His assumed connections would earn him respect and other prison amenities.

His education would earn him the top paying jobs behind bars. Top pay was not all much. It was more of a status symbol. Sidney was extremely young in comparison and therefore found himself constantly having to reaffirm his identity for the older guys.

One day Sidney ran into the famous New York mobster, Paul John "Franki" Carbo[26]. Carbo was serving a twenty-five-year sentence for conspiracy and extortion against the National Boxing Association. In reality, Carbo was part of the infamous Murder, Inc., but the law couldn't prove any of so they got him on extortion. is the way it worked back then. The FBI might not be able to take down the mob with the big crimes, so they would find a way to trap them with a small crime, and then slap them with a massive sentence. This was before the RICO act would change the game in the FBI's favor.

Carbo was jogging on the track when he noticed Sidney smoking on the sidelines. He stopped and challenged the young hustler to a mile-long race. Sidney thought he could out run the middle-aged Italian so he agreed. But, Carbo knew the youngster's lungs had to be weak from nicotine. A few minutes later when Sidney was hyperventilating at the three-quarter mile mark, the middle-aged mobster was laughing at him from the finish line. From point on Sidney never smoked another cigarette. With damaged pride, he went straight in and gave all his cigarettes to his cellmate.

Everyone knew Sidney was a hustler, so one time another connected man requested a bottle of Vodka from Big Sid just to test his metal. Sidney found himself in a tight spot with that request. Obviously, no one had Vodka behind bars, but his identity was of a big-time criminal with connections. If he didn't deliver the man's request Sidney's reputation would fall apart. So, the desperate young man bribed a prison guard and had him bring in a coveted bottle of the Russian brew. When Sidney delivered the Italian man's request he earned more than just a few brownie points; he reaffirmed his identity. is how the system worked behind bars. Your identity is your life.

One of Sidney's favorite quotes was taken from Ben Franklin. *"The investment in knowledge pays the best interest."* Sidney loved working in the payroll office. The job provided insight into each prisoner's personal information. Such knowledge was power in the gangster's hands. Sidney found many ways to manipulate this power and hold it over the heads of his fellow inmates.

At this point in the narrative it would be easy to class Sidney as some sort of inhumane criminal where every desire was centered around money and sex. In reality

Sidney had several so-called "normal" hobbies and interests as well. Sidney was a member of the Historical Society while incarcerated at Marion. Professors from area universities would come in and give lectures of various sorts. Like many history enthusiasts, Sidney was fascinated with ancient Egypt. He had collected several books on the subject and at one time he even had a small collection of fairly valuable artifacts. As usual his mind absorbed the lecture like a sponge. He might still be incarcerated, but for hour his mind was lost in the fantasies and mysteries of ancient Egypt.

Over time, Sidney grew close to his civilian boss C.R. James and after a while the man's wife would make lunch for Sidney along with her husband's. The two men would sit in the office and play gin rummy through the lunch hour instead of taking a trip to the mess hall. This saved them a trip and the home cooked food tasted incredible to the inmate. This friendship would prove to be beneficial when Sidney was released a few years later.

During the winter holidays the prison hosted a sporting event of various sorts. Handball tournaments were Sidney's forte and he earned several little handball trophies throughout his stay at Marion. They might not be worth much, but to him they might as well have been Olympic medals. The hard-nosed gangster proudly displayed his trophies in his cell and bragged on them every chance he had.

After four-and-a-half years, Sidney was finally paroled back to Tallahassee, Florida, to face his parole violation. Remember, he was still on parole from Florida for holding the guards hostage during his last escape attempt at Raiford Prison. Of course, getting arrested in New York for bank robbery broke his parole agreement. Really? Who would have thought such a thing?

Sidney knew with his study of law procedures, since of the winning of the *Gideon vs. Wainwright* case, he could also get this case overturned. Not one of the eight men charged with crime had an attorney present to defend them, so he decided to use fact to his advantage.

Sidney was soon transferred to Florida's new receiving department in Lake Butler. He knew the routine all too well; a uniformed guard stripped each inmate of their clothes as the Sergeant barked orders to the crowd of naked men. Humiliation worked as a great deterrent. Honestly Sidney wasn't too humiliated. After working out at Marion he was in the best shape of his life.

"Have any of you been here before?" the guard yelled over the crowd.

"Yes, Sir," Heard replied. It had been six years since Sidney had left Raiford, weighing a measly 175 pounds. Being well over six feet tall gave him the appearance of a string bean. Now, after lifting weights and playing handball at Marion, Sidney weighed in at a muscular 245 pounds. The young string bean had morphed into a hulking brute.

"What was your number?" The guard yelled looking over his paperwork.

"001818," came the reply from Sidney.

The guard dropped his paperwork on the nearby table and glanced up at the large man standing before him.

"Wow, Heard. You have really grown up. I sure would hate to get in a boxing ring with you now." Of course, these comments only bolstered the young man's ego. Never mind it had only been a few years since he was here in the first place.

After the receiving process was completed, Sidney was assigned a cell, a set of familiar blue clothing, and a clerk job in the prison's warehouse. Any prisoner had any semblance of an education got a clerk job. While working in the warehouse, Sidney ran into an old Raiford acquaintance by the name of Charlie McCarthy. Back in the days past, the two had been fairly close-running buddies. As a teenager, Sidney had even looked up to the vile criminal with a degree of respect.

Sidney soon lost his admiration for his old friend, however, when Charlie began to brag about a secret murder he had committed many months earlier. Over time, Charlie told Sidney all the gruesome details of how he had beaten a man's head in with a claw hammer and ditched the body in an old fishing cabin. Charlie was proud the case was still unsolved and gloated in his sordid success.

Sidney's stomach turned, but he dared not show any emotion in front of the murderer. From moment on, Sidney looked for a confidential way to tell the authorities about the unsolved murder case. night in his cell, Sidney prayed to God his lifestyle would never put him in a parallel position.

Sidney enjoyed the thrill of being a hustler, a gangster, and even a conman, but he never wanted to hurt anyone. In his own twisted way, he never realized stealing someone's livelihood was hurting person. Sidney's entire life revolved around hustling money and showing women a good time. To him, life was nothing more than a big game. The seriousness of Charlie's case weighed heavily upon his mind. He thought about the victim's family and wondered how he would feel if he were in their situation. He knew he would have to do something.

Sidney agreed to testify against the cold-blooded killer and on November 2, 1971 Charles McCarthy was convicted of the murder. The judge sentenced the hired killer to an additional life sentence.[27] McCarthy was already serving one life sentence for another murder he had committed in 1959. Sidney figured at least the victim's family could find some similitude of closure.

Sidney Heard prided himself on not being a snitch, but in this case, he felt good about his decision. [I'm still unclear how someone can serve more than one life sentence, or why the murderer was let out of prison in the first place. In my opinion if he had served the first life term instead of being paroled, McCarthy wouldn't have been available as a hired killer. Obviously, they didn't ask my opinion. I guess the parole board didn't have psychic abilities. Or maybe their crystal ball was broken. Any way we really can't blame them for trying to give someone a second chance I suppose.]

On December 22, 1971, Sidney's sentence was overturned and he was a free man once again. Once he was released he bought a bus ticket and headed straight to Anna, Illinois. C.R. James, Sidney's former boss at Marion, hired the ex-convict just before Christmas time. The James family welcomed him gladly and even gave him Christmas gifts during the holiday.

C.R. and his dad owned an entire city block of stores, bars, and pool halls. C.R.'s family even owned a horse ranch where they dealt in Arabian horses. Sidney was invited to work in their surplus store and to run a poker game in C. R's pool hall. For once in Sidney's life, he felt like he was part of a family—and this family was not "mob" related. Well, is unless you believe C.R. was a distant relative of the infamous Jesse James.

Sidney's happiness was not to last, however. When the parole board heard the news of his move to Anna, they demanded he move away immediately. He wouldn't be allowed to live close to the Marion maximum-security prison. Although Sidney was not allowed to live in Anna with his friends, he would still drive there every weekend to play poker and gin rummy. He would stay with the James family for a few days, but leave before he had to report to his parole officer.

After being forced out of Anna, Illinois, Sidney had no choice but to return home to his dad's house near Chicago. Sidney swallowed his pride, packed his bags, and moved back home to the suburb of Glen Ellyn, Illinois, with his father and stepmother Ana.

He caused quite a disturbance when he walked through their front door cold day in January. Ralph Heard had been so ashamed of his son's bad behavior he had told his entire family Sidney was dead. Sidney's poor grandmother was near tears when she learned of his return. His father might be ashamed of him, but Sidney's grandmother was always quick to forgive her beloved grandson.

When he was arrested in New York, Sidney had sent home a suitcase filled with $10,000 cash and a diamond ring. He had taken great pains to hide the money inside the lining to avoid detection. When Sidney returned home he soon discovered his dad had stolen the money and had pawned the diamond out of his son's ring. Anger flared behind Sidney's steel blue eyes, but he clenched his teeth and kept his mouth shut. It was not the first time his dad had ripped him off, but Sidney swore he wouldn't give him the chance to do it again.

Sidney chalked it all up to karma and continued with his life. He got a factory job making a whopping $3.50 an hour. An Italian connection rented him an empty apartment in Westmont, Illinois. Sidney couldn't afford furniture, but at least he was a free man and he was out from under "daddy's" roof. An empty apartment sure beat prison any day. He was used to having little in the way of personal possessions, but at least the bathroom was his alone and he didn't have to share it with four other men. After living like a caged animal, the apartment felt huge.

Sidney acquired a car from another set of connections. The 1965 Oldsmobile was piled under a snow bank, but the owners told Sidney if he could dig it out and start it, he could have it for $200. After a little bit of work, he could start it. So now the gangster had an apartment and a car—life seemed pretty good. Now all he wanted was a bankroll and of course a girlfriend would be nice.

One uneventful Saturday in January 1972, Sidney decided to check up on his old friend Maurice Vass. Vass was from St. Louis, Missouri, and the two had been close in the pen. Maurice said he would drive up and see his old friend the next weekend. The sharp dressed man showed up at Sidney's empty apartment and was surprised it was quite literally empty. The place might be empty, but Sidney still wore a three-piece suit, a clip-on tie, and a trench coat. [It is at this point Sidney explained to me gangsters and street thugs never wear a real tied tie. If someone comes after you, you don't want the assailant to be able to suffocate you with your own tie. Nope, clip-on ties were the best bet. Who knew?]

Maurice knew Sidney could use some money so he asked his old buddy to back him up on a deal in Chicago and offered to split the take with him. Sidney readily agreed to go along with the plan. The two men top ten Maurice's car and headed to 63rd Street on the west side of the city.

The large white boy was extremely nervous when he realized where he was going. At time a white man had never been seen on 63rd or at least not for long. Sydney new fully well if he stayed too long the police might just find his body in a dumpster somewhere. Of course, Sidney kept his anxiety under wraps. Maurice stopped the car in front of a rickety dump of a house. The moment the two hoods stepped from their car, Sidney heard a pedestrian yell, "Roller!" at the top of his lungs. Sidney watched in amusement as dozens of people literally tripped over themselves trying to get away. They weren't cops; they were about as far on the other end of the police spectrum as a person could be. He had been accused of many things, but being a cop wasn't one of them.

Sidney followed his friend up five flights of rickety stairs. The apartments had no doors or windows. People were laying everywhere; some were unconscious and others were dead. He quickly realized he was the only white boy in a "shooting gallery" on the wrong side of town. [A shooting gallery is a rundown usually condemned building used as a drug house. This one happened to be where Maurice planned to score some heroine.] Sidney steeled his nerves and pressed on.

At the top of the stairs the two men were ushered into a shadow-filled room and offered chairs around a tiny table.

The dealer and a few of his cronies sat across from them. Everyone had their eyes glued to the massive blue-eyed white man. Maurice slid a .357-magnum across the table to Sidney.

"I'm going to try this stuff out, and if I die I want you to kill this M...F... and everyone else in this place." [Maurice used several more expletives and a few non-politically correct descriptions we will not mention here.] Sidney nodded in agreement and with a steady hand picked up the weapon. Every nerve in his body was on high alert as he waited for his friend to give him some sort of signal. Of course, they hadn't discussed Maurice's business beforehand so Sidney had no idea what the signal could be. Outside his cool blue eyes were menacing the half stoned men, but inside he was panicking. *I can't shoot anyone.* His mind was racing with exit strategies. Every one of them ended with him killing someone or being shot. His stomach turned, but his face remained unemotional. When Maurice's head dropped to the table, Sidney cocked the hammer back on the magnum and pointed it between the seller's eyes.

"Oh, no, man, I'm fine. This is good stuff." Maurice smiled and laid a hand on Sidney's shoulder. "I guess they can live another day." The two men slowly stood and plowed their way through the house full of strangely contorted bodies and back to their car. In the car Maurice turned to Sidney. "You were really going to shoot the place up weren't you?"

"That's what you said to do," Sidney replied coolly. He would never admit his real thoughts on the matter. He was just glad to be off the hook.

Maurice had another "job" to do in town, so Sidney agreed to help. This time Maurice wanted to "knock over" a check-cashing place. Maurice knew the place well and told Sidney exactly what to do and where to find the money. Sure enough when Sidney made the owner of the place hit the floor he found the cigar box full of cash and the man's gun laying on top of it. Maurice and Sidney split the take and went out for a nice steak dinner at Mr. Kelly's. Now Sidney had a bankroll, but he didn't dare spend it. He waited patiently and filled his apartment gradually so no one would notice he now had money. He still had to check in with his probation officer and showing off his ill-gotten gains would be a quick ticket back to the pen.

A few weeks later Sidney called to talk to Maurice, but Mrs. Vass answered the phone instead. She informed him Maurice had done a job in Michigan and had killed a couple of people in the process. Like so many other friends of Sidney's, the man would spend the rest of his life in prison.

Unfortunately, Sidney's criminal legacy was well known throughout the small Chicago suburb of Westmont northwest of the city. And, although his mobster counterparts approved of his ways, society as a whole did not. This proved true when a young Dolly Parton look-alike named Donna caught his eye at a local bar. He had flirted with the waitress for quite a while, but she refused to date him because of his reputation. He was a little disappointed, but persistent nonetheless.

A few days later Sidney was driving through the snow-filled suburban streets and noticed a woman wading through the deep snow wearing a pair of white knee-high boots and a mini skirt. He pulled over and offered her a ride. Low and behold, it was Donna. She gladly accepted his offer of a ride—and a little more than a ride back at Sidney's apartment. Two months later the couple was married.

Rental houses were hard to find in the Westmont area, but Sidney was finally able to find a house for them. The house was missing sheet rock in a few rooms, so Sidney made a deal with the owner to fix up the house in exchange for discounted rent. Sidney enjoyed remodeling houses, and it saved him a few bucks. Donna was happy enough with the place and it had enough room for her young son. Now Sidney had a family of his own.

It was no secret Ralph Heard was ashamed of his son's criminal activities, but now Sidney was married, had a job, a stepson, and an apartment. So, Ralph swallowed his pride and decided to help them out a bit. As a member of the Moose Lodge, Ralph had a vast assortment of connections. When a genteel woman told Ralph, she needed help hauling off her antiques, he immediately thought it would make a good job for Sidney. The house was over a hundred years old and rumored to be part of the famous Underground Railroad helped slaves escape to freedom during the Civil War.

When the newlyweds arrived in Glenn Ellen, Illinois, they were expecting to haul away a few little things. They knew the house had already been partially emptied by local antiques dealers. The couple never dreamed they would anything of real value. But, they had been told they could have whatever was left if they hauled it away. The top two floors had several old lamps and other little things, but Sidney was blown away when he stepped into the untouched basement. The old crevasse was lined with brick walls and the floor was dirt, and more importantly the professionals hadn't rummaged through the vast treasure stored there.

Here Sidney found a goldmine of antiques including old barber chairs and clippers, chests were brought over from Germany, and even old Civil War memorabilia. The historical treasures ended up filling five U-Haul trailers. Sidney was officially in the antique business now. Unfortunately, the new homeowners leveled the historic landmark building once it was emptied, effectively destroying all its vast history. It is unfortunate the local historical society didn't catch wind of this before the building was destroyed. No one will know for sure how much history we lost when house was demolished.

Sidney and Donna quickly started selling their new treasures to anyone was interested. Everyone with an eye for antiques was interested in purchasing the valuables from the pair. They had little knowledge about the antique business and were selling them for little of nothing. But it didn't take them long to realize the true value of their bounty. So, they began bouncing between flea markets and antique stores to sell the precious old items, learning their true value as they went.

In 1972, Sidney packed up his wife and her son, his dog, and his grandmother and headed to Amarillo, Texas. The lone star state would never be the same.

Chapter 11: Amarillo

On October 9,1972, the Heard clan mounted their belongings on a two-wheeled trailer and covered it with a large plastic tarp. Mattresses were slung on top of the roof of both the family's station wagon and their 1965 Oldsmobile. Sidney and the family's dog were in the lead car with Grandma. Donna and her son Jerry followed close behind. The peculiar parade slowly inched its way southward toward the dusty plains of northern Texas. When the weary bunch finally arrived, Donna's parents welcomed them with open arms. Then they quickly snatched the mattresses from the tops of the cars and hid the tacky orange trailer inside their garage. They didn't want the neighbors to talk.

Sidney's grandmother was a licensed practical nurse and quickly found a job as a live-in nurse for an elderly, disabled patient. While Donna spent, the days looking for a house to buy, Sidney searched for a legitimate job, and finally wrangled up a job as a carpenter. It paid a meager salary of four dollars an hour, but it was justifiable work. Donna soon discovered houses around Amarillo at time were radically cheaper than in the Chicago area. It didn't take the newlyweds long to get into the business of flipping houses.

Being an ex-con can be difficult on one's credit rating, so Donna hunted around until she found a real estate dealer by the name of Jodi Roach, who owned Major Realtors. She thought if they could get a good realtor on their side it would make it easier for them to purchase a home in their own name and build their credit. However, Donna made the mistake of telling Roach about Sidney's past, so the real estate dealer took out a second loan on the property hoping Sidney would default. He never did. The deception bothered him, still he was grateful someone had given him a chance to prove himself.

A small three-bedroom house at 5101 S. Bouy in Amarillo became the Heard residence for the next few years. It was a nice little place with a fenced-in backyard. It seemed Sidney had finally found his proverbial "white picket fence." He had a family, a home, a job, and there was no barbed wire in sight. He kept taking over the payments on any house he could find for sale and by the end of 1974 he would amass a grand total of forty-two rental houses.

Sidney bounced between jobs for the next year or so, but he could never find just the right one. One day he happened to be waiting in line at a lumber supply store when he overheard someone say they needed help mounting a basketball hoop onto a garage. Sidney immediately stepped up and offered his assistance. He followed the customer to his home and easily completed the task. An hour later he returned to the lumber company and asked if they knew of, or ever had requests for, any other carpentry jobs. The cashier quickly wrote down Sidney's contact information and agreed to pass it on to anyone in need of a handyman or carpenter. This would soon turn into full time work for the newlywed man.

Sidney decided he didn't like earning a mere concession amount for each project, so he hired a few workers and started his own construction company. With one trip to the lumberyard, the concept of Heard & Sons Construction Company was born. After a while, Sidney hired enough workers to make up a couple of crews, so he started paying them as sub-contractors. increased his profits while cutting back on his work schedule at the same time. Meanwhile, Sidney kept his house flipping side-job with Donna. He was doing what he called "pretty well" for himself, and doing a job honestly for the first time in his life. Living according to the law was starting to feel natural for the born and bred conman, until a client came into the lumberyard to ask Sidney for an estimate on a fire-damaged home.

An estimate sounded harmless enough, but when Sidney realized how much money could be conned out of an insurance company from a fire, the sparks started flying again, in more ways than one. After careful planning, a vacant rental house, owned by Sidney Heard, mysteriously caught fire. Like clockwork a check was in the mail within 30 days. The ill-gotten insurance payoff was used to invest in other more legitimate business ventures of the now active arsonist. Any illegal money the gangster would acquire he would launder through one of his legal businesses or through gambling in Vegas. It was a simple scam seemed to have no consequences.

Eighteen more fires would burn throughout the state of Texas over the next decade. Sidney assured me he never set fire to a home with people living there. He never wanted to hurt anyone. It was all about the money. Sidney loved money, but he was not willing to kill someone for it. Instead, he focused his fire-starting talents on warehouses full of miscellaneous flammable materials, empty rental houses, and an occasional business for a financially strapped owner. Each arson job would earn the so-called family man a nice paycheck, which could be easily laundered into his legitimate ventures. Later on, one such arson would make Sidney's name appear on the cover of the *Amarillo Globe/Times*, but for the time being, life was rolling smoothly for Sidney Heard.

The chicken and the city boy:

While most of this tale is quite serious in nature I must take a moment for a bit of comedy. This is one of those stories happened to come out in an interview many years after Sidney's retirement from crime. For all his criminal knowledge Sydney had no idea when it came to raising chickens.

A big two-story farmhouse came up for sale outside of Amarillo and Sidney jumped on the opportunity. He packed up his family and moved to the country. He found a renter for his property on Bouy St and began the process of settling into his new rural home. The farmhouse was nestled on a few acres and included a few out buildings. It needed repair, but was no problem for carpenter Sidney. It was at this point the Chicago native city-slicker decided to become a chicken farmer. Don't ask me why. Who knows the reason. He immediately went out and purchased twenty white laying hens for $2.50 a piece from a local farmer. He was not sure if he had received a good price, but he loved fresh farm eggs.

"Don't I need a rooster to get eggs?" Sidney inquired rather naively. A large grin crossed the old man's face. He shrugged and handed the leather-clad gangster a rooster.

"Sure. If ya want one. Here, you kin have this 'un for five bucks, mister."

Sidney paid the man and drove home all puffed up and proud of his new chickens. A few days later one of Donna's co-workers sold her eighty more laying hens for a dollar each. Soon, the couple had fresh farm eggs coming out of their ears. So, they did the logical thing... they started selling eggs. However, one night Sidney couldn't sleep and decided to take a walk outside and check on his chickens. A few minutes later he came back into the house to find Donna wandering around the house looking for him.

"What's wrong honey?" she yawned rubbing the sleep from her lovely eyes.

"I don't understand this," Sidney grumbled, confused. "How are we getting so many eggs with only one rooster? I went out there and dang rooster was not doing anything. He was sound asleep."

Donna immediately busted up laughing and Sidney couldn't understand why. "Oh, sweetie, you don't need a rooster just to get eggs." She rolled her eyes and shook her brunette head before heading back to bed. "You only need a rooster if you want more chickens." Sidney soon followed her to bed after washing the proverbial egg off his face. He was now truly a chicken farmer.

As time passed Sidney slowly begin to lead a double life in Amarillo. With Donna and "Little Bear," Sidney was the picture-perfect husband, father, and businessman; or at least he tried to be. Parenting was something completely foreign to him. Still he thoroughly enjoyed being a family man. In business, however, Sidney was slowly slipping back into his old ways. "Kickbacks" were quickly becoming merely another necessity of his business and Jodi Roach would quickly become more than an above-board real estate partner. Any time Jodi needed a little extra cash, she would ask Sidney if he would drum up another scam and give her a kickback on it. At one point, she even asked him to knock off one of her aggravating renters. Sidney rejected notion. He was surprised how many people automatically thought if you were a criminal you are also willing to kill someone. This is one line Sydney would never cross.

While a good hustle seemed to be his favorite hobby, Sidney thoroughly enjoyed horse racing. They even acquired four horses of their own to become part of the racing scene. Of course, Sidney used his expert gambling knowledge to earn his family a good paycheck. All the couple's horses were registered under Donna's name. Sidney, being a convicted felon couldn't legally own a racehorse. One of their favorite places to race was at the racetrack in Raton, New Mexico.

One opening weekend in Raton, Donna Heard became somewhat of a celebrity when one of the Heard horses won two races in a row.

Sidney got his old friend Scott Cameron to go in with him on purchasing a thoroughbred racehorse named "Waleeta El." The horse had been fathered by a champion racehorse by the name of Skipper Bill, and it was beautiful. The only problem was it refused to be broken and it couldn't run. After sending it to a couple of different trainers Sydney finally found someone who could at least break the horse and train it enough to not throw its rider. Hoping to see results the new trainer pitched it in a race against a 14-year-old horse and Waleeta El still lost.

The two-year-old horse was eventually deemed un-trainable. Hoping to receive some sort of return on his investment, he "hopped up" his lousy horse and ran him in a rigged race in Oklahoma. Here the laws were more relaxed and he knew the winning horse wouldn't be tested for drugs. After "winning" the race, Sidney quickly unloaded the animal on the first unsuspecting victim he could find. He never paid Cameron for his share. When I reached out to Mr. Cameron for an interview I never received a response and this could probably be the reason why. Unfortunately, Mr. Cameron would pass away on February 19, 2015.

One evening during the racing season, Sidney was sitting in a bar when a huge three-hundred-pound man jumped a rather small jockey named Little Mike. When Sidney saw what was going on, he quickly donned his hero personage and took down both the big man and his accompanying son to save the little jockey. This act would forever earn Sidney the jockey's favor. Little Mike and all his jockey friends quickly befriended the gangster nicknamed, Big Sid. Of course, Sidney used this connection for his benefit when he was placing his bets on the horses.

During the spring and summer months, Sidney and Donna would race their horses at the Raton racetrack. The racing circuit would cut through Albuquerque, New Mexico, and end up at a racetrack named Sunland Park near El Paso, Texas. Sidney always had the best box seats wherever he went, whether his horse was running or not.

One day late in the summer, Sidney and Donna entered the park and were making their way through the crowd to pick up their tickets at the box office when they ran into one of the park's security guards. When the guard turned to look at them, Sidney was surprised to find it was Mr. Baker, one of the guards from Raiford Prison in Florida. Baker had retired from the Florida State Prison and had moved out to Texas after his wife had passed away. The man was surprised to see Big Sid doing so well.

Late one night, back at their home in Amarillo, Sidney's phone rang out through the quiet Heard home and proceeded to wake all its grumpy occupants. The caller was Jodi Roach and she was demanding to speak to Sidney immediately. sparked a firestorm would ultimately destroy Sidney's perfect little daydream life. Donna suspected Sidney was having an affair with Jodi, and quickly cussed out the realtor for calling at such a late hour. This didn't set well with the hotheaded real estate agent, so the vindictive woman went throughout Amarillo, telling every banker in the city Sidney was an ex-con convicted of bank robbery.

Literally overnight Sidney's credit rating was shut off completely. His businesses instantly began to crumble alongside of his marriage. He tried to reassure Donna there was no affair going on with Jodi, but the damage to his marriage had already been done. Financial woes piled high on top of his marital issues. Sidney struggled to keep his life together. Bankers canceled his business credit lines overnight. Within one day Sidney was almost bankrupt. Taking the bad advice of friends, he sold every asset he could to build up a stash of cash, and then filed for bankruptcy.

Even with the favorable intervention of his parole officer, Sidney couldn't re-obtain a line of credit for his construction company. Reluctantly, he sold the business and began to search for full-time employment. If prison had taught the young con anything, it was life could be worse. Besides, he had a family to think about; for now, anyway. That, too, would eventually fall apart.

Chapter 12: Straddling the fence

A short time after his bankruptcy was finalized, Sidney contacted one of his many "business connections" and landed a job as a construction superintendent for an apartment complex. Over the course of six months, Sidney built, bought, and sold anything he could to make ends meet. Some such business ventures were legal, and some otherwise. He dealt in everything from antiques to marijuana. is the bad thing about straddling the fence; you will eventually fall to one side or the other.

One Saturday afternoon in 1976, Sidney came home to a very distraught wife. She looked up at him through tear-stained eyes and requested a divorce. Although, shocked by her sudden decision, Sidney politely agreed to a divorce to appease his wife. The couple sat down at the kitchen table with a piece of paper and divided up their belongings. Still a little confused, Sidney walked out and went to the nearest bar to find solace in beer and cheap women. Meanwhile, Donna packed up her belongings and took her son with her to her mother's house. Sidney didn't understand, but he had decided long ago if a woman didn't want to be with him he was not going to force her to stay.

No amount of free love and alcohol could fill the hole left in the gangster's heart by Donna's absence. Instead, Sidney found himself hopping between women and failed business ventures like a rabbit on steroids. Along the fast track, Sidney picked up a girl named Linda at a local night club. The two quickly hit it off while Sidney waited for his divorce to be finalized. Linda was beautiful, wild, and liked to party. She was just the type of woman the gangster needed to get over his second failed marriage—or so he thought.

Just before the final divorce papers were to be drawn up, Sidney received a phone call from a local alcoholic rehab facility. His soon to be ex-mother-in-law was calling from there to inform Sidney Donna had been checked into the facility and desperately wanted to speak with him before the divorce was final. [Donna's mother also wanted to know if Sidney's insurance would still pay for Donna's care since they were technically still married.]

Still a little heartbroken, Sidney made the trip across town to see his soon-to-be ex-wife. It was at this meeting Sidney learned the truth behind his sudden divorce: During the chaos with Jodi and the bankruptcy, Donna had cheated on him a man by the name of Boots.

Boots was the owner of the Gulf gas station in Amarillo. Boots had flirted with the beautiful woman for months, but Donna had always shrugged it off. Unfortunately, when she suspected Jodi's infatuation with Sidney, she decided to drown her sorrows by hooking up with the flirtatious business owner. The distressed woman still didn't believe Jodi was merely her husband's business partner.

Afterward Donna was afraid Sidney might kill her illicit lover, so she quickly tried to end their marriage before he discovered the truth. Although she had given up drinking years earlier, guilt drove her back to alcohol. As an ex-alcoholic, it didn't take long before she found herself washed back into rehab. The couple's divorce would be finalized on what would have been their fourth wedding anniversary, March 29, 1976. It wasn't the way he wanted to spend his anniversary, but he decided to drown his sorrows in the arms of his new girlfriend.

Sidney's new found feelings for Linda did little to ease the pain left by his cheating wife. The strange part was Sidney had been faithful this time around. Usually he would have torn the man apart, but this time he shrugged off Donna's transgression and continued his affair with Linda. However, Donna would never get too far away from Sidney. No matter who she was coupled with, if she was in town she found time to sneak away from him and climb into bed with her ex-husband Sidney. It didn't matter to Sidney either. Now he was "free" to sleep with any woman he chose—and he still could have Donna on the side. It was a win-win situation for the promiscuous gangster.

After the divorce, Sidney was left with his house in the country and two rental houses in town. He didn't have any wheels, however, so he borrowed a truck from his boss to use for transportation. Unfortunately, the apartment complex job he had been working on was soon completed and Sidney found himself out of work again. But no matter what his situation was, Sidney was born with a strong desire and determination to work. So, he called property owner and former cohort J.C. Lane and asked him for a job. Lane owned several double duplexes and apartments. Rental houses are constantly in need of repair, so he hired Sidney to be the apartment building's maintenance man.

The Death of Ralph W. Heard:

Only a few months after Sidney's divorce was final, he received a phone call from Chicago informing him his father had passed away. Although Sidney never had a good relationship with his father, he knew he would be required to make an appearance at the funeral. At this point in his life, Sidney didn't have much of anything. He had just suffered through a difficult divorce and an even nastier bankruptcy, but he was not going to go home like that. He scrounged up a small bankroll [don't ask how] and rented a nice car. He got all dressed up in his suit and diamond studded jewelry and drove the thousand miles back to Chicago. He waltzed into his dad's house in Glen Ellyn, Illinois, looking very much the part of a wealthy, well-connected, businessman.

In 1975 the law in Chicago stated his father's estate would be divided up between the widow and the children. Ann Tiller Heard would receive half the estate and the rest would be divided evenly between her three stepsons, Sidney, Jerome (Jerry), and David. Sidney knew he could come into some serious money. His father's house alone was worth half-a-million dollars, but he thought about the eighteen years his stepmother had spent by his father's side. Sidney knew Ralph would have died with nothing if he hadn't married the well-off woman nearly two decades earlier.

At the funeral, Sidney cornered his two brothers and "persuaded" them to give their share of the inheritance to Ann. The two men reluctantly agreed to their brother's demands. Sidney stood up in front of the crowd of people at the viewing and informed them he and his brothers were relinquishing their inheritance to their stepmother. There were few times in Sidney's life when he felt money was not always the most important thing. But this time he knew his step mom would be taken care of, and made him feel good. Besides, he earned a lot of respect from his father's friends for his efforts. And, we all know who his father's friends were.

Sidney hopped in his rented Cadillac and drove the thousand miles back to Amarillo, with his big, bad gangster persona still intact. His family would never know how broke he was at the time. All through his life Sidney wore the Chicago gangster persona well. Although he was not technically a mobster, he had connections of all sorts with them. This would help him in some circumstances, and hurt him in others. Either way, Sidney was a good actor and he played his part well.

J. C. Lane, knowing Sidney's past, approached him one day about hiring someone to torch one of his rentals had been losing money. Of course, Sidney was broke and couldn't turn down such a deal. Now a desperate man, Sidney agreed and earned a nice paycheck for his trouble. This relationship change, however, would lead to more "torch" (arson) jobs, and more insurance fraud. Sidney would spend the next few years building houses for Lane, and occasionally burning down others. Either way, he was making enough money to support his lifestyle.

During time, Linda took Sidney on a trip to New Mexico. There they ran into a group of jockeys Sidney knew from the time he was betting on horse races with Donna. The group of jockeys hovered around the six-foot tall gangster; it was quite a humorous sight. The jockeys and Sidney quickly caught up on each other's lives and the group offered the broke hustler a deal. He was told to meet with his old friend, Little Mike at the fifth horse race. Sidney agreed and showed up at the fifth race at the allotted time. The deal was a simple numbers game. The top ten jockeys would make a deal and six of them would hold back their horses. This would leave four possible winners. Then Sidney would pick the first and second place winners and place his bet. He had a fifty/fifty chance of winning the big money. This numbers racket earned him a sweet $3,500 bankroll all in one weekend.

Two weeks later, Linda called Sidney and told him about a Cadillac she found at her ex-brother-in-law's car lot. As the owner, he could come up with a good deal for the couple, and Sidney drove away in a 1971 Cadillac.

It's at this point Sidney stopped to explain things to me. Texas "outlaws," he said usually loved to parade around in their Lincoln town cars. The Chicago bred conman refused to fit into the southern criminal mold. Nothing would keep him from his black leather jackets and his "Cadi's." Honestly this Midwestern girl wouldn't want either a town car or a Cadillac, but I do love a good looking black leather jacket.

Life was starting to look up again. One of Sidney's former bankers even offered to give him a $2,500 credit line to help re-establish Sidney's credit. Bankruptcy law states a person cannot file for bankruptcy again within seven years after filing the first time, so Sidney was a good candidate in the banker's eyes. Sidney was more than grateful for the financial break. As the old adage goes, "*it takes money to make money*," and now Sidney had a credit line to do just that.

An associate by the name of Bobby Jones approached Sidney a few days later and offered him a deal on a pool hall. The previous owner was looking to lease the property and retire. Jones offered to put the loan in his own name if Sidney would run the place, and pay him a percentage of the profits. This sounded like a good deal, so Sidney became the proud owner of Tiny's Pool Hall. Now Sidney was raking in paychecks from the construction company with J.C. Lane, plus his pool hall, and of course his drug deals on the side.

Over the course of a few months, three other bars became available for lease. Sidney jumped at the opportunities. He hired a few pretty bar maids to run each establishment. Across the street from Tiny's Pool Hall was a bar named El Sid's. Donna hung around the place, and ended up marrying the owner's son. Of course, also put her near her old flame. As usual, Donna kept the affair with Sidney going on the side even after her marriage to another man.

Juggling all his business ventures for Sydney to keep a tight schedule. He would close his bars at 2 a.m. After making sure everything was locked up tight, he would go home and sleep for a couple of hours. And, then he would go to work for J.C. Lane's construction company during the day. Alcohol and marijuana held his sleep deprivation at bay—at least for a while.

Generally, Big Sid never took out the trash, but one morning after closing something made him change his routine. Instead of leaving it for the girls to do, this time the big man took out the trash himself. He lifted the lid and started to toss the bags into the dumpster. To his surprise, he noticed a human foot sticking out from under a pile of trash in the dumpster. He immediately called the Amarillo police department. He told them to hurry, because the trash truck would come by at four. The officers rushed right over and determined the man had gotten drunk and passed out in the dumpster. It turns out the hard-nosed gangster had saved a man's life.

Tiny's Pool Hall had the only regulation-size pool tables in Amarillo at the time. Once a week, the Amarillo Police Department would descend on Sidney's pool hall and practically take it over. This ritual was fondly referred to as "choir practice" throughout the local precinct. They would shoot pool, party, and sometimes pass out from heavy drinking. Since they were all over the legal limit, Sidney would offer to drive them home, and earn himself some brownie points with the local officers. It was always a good idea to stay in cahoots with the local authorities, especially if you were a gangster. Sidney firmly believed in the old adage, "keep your friends close and your enemies closer." This friendship would pay off when he was arrested a few years later. To further his connection with the police Sidney was a regular contributor to the Local Policeman's fund.

When the Presley & Taylor law office moved in across the street from the pool hall, Sidney seized the opportunity and, through the appearance of his fine character, "bought" himself a couple of attorneys. He would send them clients of various sorts, and then when his business ventures crossed the legal lines, they would happily get him off the hook. Of course, they were paid handsomely for their legal services.

Many big-time pool players and local celebrities visited Tiny's Pool Hall over the years. Even the famous poker player Amarillo Slim[28] visited the pool hall on a few occasions. While most players were charged a quarter per rack to play pool, and a few dollars to use the gambling table, Amarillo Slim walked in and laid a hundred-dollar bill on the counter. Needless to say, he had dibs on all the tables, and he could play as many rounds as he so desired.

During this hectic time, Sidney decided to take a night off and check out the competition's pubs. Exhausted with the routine of long hours, the big man needed a night to relax and party. He bounced from one bar to another and noticed a woman with "Bette Davis" eyes who seemed to be bouncing along the same path as he was. She told Sidney her name was Carol, and her husband owned several tree nurseries in town. Carol and Sidney hooked up for a while evening, and then parted ways in time for Sidney to close all his bars at 2 a.m.

The next morning found Sidney's curious mind pondering his evening with Carol. Rummaging through the telephone book's yellow pages his eyes lighted on Howard Nurseries. Later day Sidney tracked her down from the address listed in the phone book and found she was at home alone. She was painting her front room in nothing but her lingerie. *"Afternoon Delight"* was blaring from her speakers from somewhere in the house. She quickly ushered him inside, and after a long sensuous lap dance Sidney's rambunctious relationship with the wild side of Carol Howard began. On one hand, she was a well-mannered RN who worked at a local nursing home. In the community, she was the respected spouse of Mr. Howard, but on the other hand she loved the excitement of gangster life.

Now in the Northern states a professional criminal is called a gangster. If he is a Made Member of the *La Cosa*

Nostra he is called a mobster. Of course, everyone knows the Italian mobster stereotype has been made famous by Hollywood films. But, in the South, a criminal is simply referred to as an outlaw. Of course, Hollywood has a stereotypical Wild West outlaw as well. When Sidney migrated south he found himself in a strange underworld. The outlaws had traded in their horses for town cars. They still wore the typical tan-colored leather duster with the cowboy boots, but they showed off their wealth and power with their massive town cars.

Being a born-and-bred Chicago rowdy rouser, Sidney refused to fit into Amarillo's criminal mold. He liked his three-quarter length black Brazilian leather jacket, his diamond bejeweled watches, his gaudy pinkie rings, and of course his fedoras. True to gangster style, he enjoyed wearing his wealth. Even his fedoras had to be cocked to the side of the head at the perfect "ace/duce" angle.

Unfortunately, Sidney couldn't find a single store sold black leather jackets in the entire state of Texas. This aggravated the gangster, so he decided he was going to have a real "gangster's coat" even if it meant he had to drive all the way back to Chicago.

One cold day in January, the frustrated gangster packed up his new girlfriend Carol and the pair made the long trip to Chicago (in a Cadillac, of course). He wanted to show his girl how a connected man buys a coat back in his hometown. They soon found themselves on State Street where the slogan was: "What you want to buy for the price you want to pay." Sidney waltzed into a store, found a leather coat priced at $499, and offered the African American cashier $200 cash. The cashier took one look at the cold hard cash in Sidney's hand and smiled.

"You got yourself a coat, brother," the cashier quickly snipped off the security tag, and handed the coat to the illustrious gangster. Now Sidney had his leather jacket, and Carol was more than impressed with her gangster boyfriend.

Of course, he purchased a few shiny baubles for his new girl before leaving town.

Chapter 13: Scams, Crime, and Drugs

During Sidney's stay in Amarillo, he "acquired ownership" of a topless biker bar named Tucker's Inn. Acquired simply means Sidney ran the business while someone else's name was on the deed. Being a convicted felon, Sidney found it a lot less complicated way. Sidney already owned another bar in town and the vending machine representative had told him of Tucker's Inn. The owner had his license, but couldn't find any dancers. Sidney had no problem finding girls and had several hired within the week. The biker joint was situated along HWY 287, and had quickly become the hangout for local Harley riders, shameless bare breasted women, and drunkards of all sorts. Here Sidney would earn the majority of the profits from more than just the beer sales.

Although the bar was for bikers of all sorts the local chapter of the Bandidos quickly took over the establishment. Sidney kept a wary eye on the crowd and tried to keep them contained. He knew fully well what this volatile group was capable of. For those of you who are unfamiliar with the Bandidos, they just so happen to be the second largest outlaw biker gang in the world right behind the Hell's Angels.

While some Bandidos are law abiding citizens, many more make their living running an international Methamphetamine operation. Drugs, sex and violence are their way of life. What started out as a local motorcycle club for ex-Vietnam veterans quickly became a thrill seeking, drug smuggling biker gang. Sidney knew all this and let them pretty much have the joint to themselves, but always tried to keep the peace.

The topless bar made headlines one evening when an idiot with a Harley Davidson jacket waltzed into the cram-packed establishment. No one had ever seen the man before, so immediately made the local rowdy crowd a little nervous. Everyone, including Sidney, wondered if the guy was an undercover cop of some sort. The cops were aware of the Bandidos criminal enterprises and had tried to infiltrate their group before.

One of the group's leaders quietly sent one of the bar customers outside to check out the man's bike to see what he was riding. Low and behold it was a Kawasaki. While the bikers got the out-of-towner drunk and plied him for information, a few burly thugs slipped outside. When the man stumbled out of the bar several hours later he couldn't find his bike. The drunken Bandidos jeered as the man wandered off into the darkness on foot.

The next morning a camera crew from the local news station found the disassembled bike resting precariously atop the HWY 287 sign. It hadn't been broken or damaged in any way. It was merely disassembled. Every bolt and screw had been taken out. The reporter commented, "The good times don't roll in Amarillo if you ride a Kawasaki into a Harley Davidson biker bar." The bike remained atop the sign for several days until the city officials finally sent someone out to clean up the mess. Sidney and the rowdy crew at the bar got a good laugh out of that one.

Sidney explained to me every good career criminal must maintain a legitimate facade. To accomplish this, one purchases a business and keeps it clean; not of dust, mind you. Sidney chose to use his fondness of antiques as his front, and opened Sid's Swap Shop down on 6th Street. Here he could buy, sell, and trade antiques and collectables of all sorts. He hired an English woman named Ann, who happened to be fond of porcelain dolls, to run the place for him. Ann would run the legal business deals in the front of the shop, while Big Sid ran his own "business deals" from a small office in the rear part of the building.

Texas law required the business owner to file a police report for anything was purchased from an individual such as guns, jewelry, and electronics. To avoid this with his underworld associates, Sidney would have Ann forward these kinds of deals to the big man himself. He would pay cash for the hot items and sell them in the swap shop, but wouldn't add them officially to his inventory. Ann new anyone who asked for Sidney personally should be sent directly to the boss. This would also mean Ann wouldn't have the knowledge to make a proper witness if Sidney was ever arrested.

When the money started rolling in Sidney decided to open Sid's Best Burgers down the street, because the cantankerous gangster couldn't find what he classed as a decent hamburger within the immediate area. The so-called renowned businessman followed up by purchasing a Phillip's 66 gas station, and then a trim molding company, which he aptly named Trim Tex. The molding company served two purposes: it provided a legitimate business he could launder his money through, but it also provided the trim molding his arson clients needed to fill their warehouses.

Sidney never torched an empty building. would be pointless, considering most of the buildings were rented, or had a mortgage on them. The way an owner or renter made money by arson was to fill the building with contents. Then, when the insurance company paid out, Sidney's arson clients would list all these over-priced items as being lost in the fire. If the owners were lacking in the contents arena, Sidney would offer his trim molding. way Sidney received the arson fee, and a nice kickback from providing the molding. Sidney would make money at both ends of the deal.

All these businesses were along 6th Street which was a part of the historic Route 66. This meant not only could Sidney service the local crowd but he would also have a steady stream of tourists to run through his businesses.

Now after a few months Sidney owned three businesses along the route. Business was booming and money started pouring in. Life was good.

On one of his many money laundering trips to Las Vegas, Sidney ran into an old running buddy from the Florida State Penitentiary. Sidney was sitting in a restaurant on Fremont Street when he looked up and there was the illustrious Frank Beck. Frank had made himself a millionaire within a couple of years after leaving prison. He could beat anyone at blackjack so he started casino hopping. He would win $200-$300 at one casino and then hop to the next one. Beck never wanted to win too much money and draw attention to himself. By the end of the day he would be several thousand dollars richer. The health nut used his winnings to open a top of the line health spa and fitness center. After Arnold Schwarzenegger hit the scene, fitness was becoming more than just a money-making fad and Frank Beck was one of thousands of people to profit from it. He had come a long way from conspiring with Sidney to escape from the Florida State Petitionary.

Although his life was a selfish one, there was a few times Sidney felt he had helped someone. One hot Texas afternoon Sidney was sitting in the back office of Sid's Swap Shop. Suddenly, he heard a bunch of ruckus next door at Ray's Coin Shop. Ray was a kind old man who owned both buildings, and had graciously leased the rooms to Sidney. Sidney knew the man well and kind of liked the guy.

Big Sid rushed next door to discover two men had stolen $8,000 worth of coins from the kind old man. Sidney, feeling rather heroic, jumped into his Cadillac and raced down the street after one of the petty criminals. When he caught up with him, he pulled up beside the man's car and grabbed the man by the shirt and yanked the thief out of his vehicle. He slammed the man's face against the hood of his Cadi and pulled a pellet gun from his pocket. The 177-caliber pellet gun looked just like a model 29 Smith &

Wesson 357-magnum. Because Sidney was a convicted felon, he couldn't carry a magnum, but the petty thief didn't know that. The man's eyes grew wide as the big-time gangster handcuffed him and threw him in the back of the Cadillac. (Don't ask where the handcuffs came from. You don't want to know.)

Sidney proudly escorted the man back to Ray's Coin Shop and handed him over to the local police who had just arrived on the scene a moment earlier. Sidney gave an official statement, but refused to give a videotaped interview and asked his name be stricken from public record. Sidney would find out later the city wanted to give him a citizenship award. This never happened, however, because a FBI task force was investigating Sidney without his knowledge.

The town quickly dropped the whole idea of an award after a firm request by the task force. Sidney couldn't care less. He didn't want publicity; he was just helping a friend. The last thing he wanted was his face plastered all over the news. But word of Sidney's good deed leaked out and night when Sidney went to play bridge, the entire building exploded with applause as he walked through the door. Sidney waved them off nonchalantly and enjoyed a night of playing cards.

Sidney's Introduction to the Cocaine business:

Up until this point, Sidney had dabbled in marijuana deals, but he had never dealt with hard drugs. However, all changed one evening when an acquaintance named Bruce Buchanan phoned Sidney and complained about a bad cocaine deal he had been a part of. Everyone in town knew Sidney had connections with the underworld and they would come to him whenever they had any sort of problem in arena. Although he hadn't been an Italian Mob Boss in Chicago, he was considered Big Man On Campus in Amarillo, Texas—and he enjoyed every minute of it.

Bruce complained he was getting ripped off on his cocaine dealings and asked Sidney if he could get him a better deal on the illegal powder. At first Sidney refused, but later he telephoned a Mexican friend nicknamed "Baltimore." Sidney confessed to his friend the cocaine business was out of his element and he had no idea how much money could be made with drug. Baltimore laughed and explained the basic business practice of every cocaine dealer in America:

The package of pure cocaine would come from Mexico with a price tag of $1,700 per ounce. The dealer would also purchase Lidocaine at $100 per ounce. Then the dealer would mix the powders half-and-half before selling the diluted product for $2,000 per ounce. That would leave the dealer with a $2,200 profit. If the dealer wanted a bigger payout, he would simply mix more Lidocaine into his product before distribution.

When Baltimore ran the numbers by Sidney, the money-obsessed gangster couldn't refuse. Sidney didn't consider how many lives would be destroyed by this action. If he could see into the future, he would have seen his own life desecrated by the evils of cocaine. Twenty years later, Sidney would confess it was the worst mistake of his life, but at this point in his illustrious career, all he could see was the money.

In fact, after spending his entire life emulating the *La Cosa Nostra* [mafia], Sidney would break one of the family's most basic principles: most big time mob bosses wouldn't get mixed up with drugs—not officially anyways. It doesn't matter how much money could be made. It was a rule, and yes, even mobsters have rules. There are too many eyes on the drug business and too many lines could lead back to the big man. Usually, if a boss found one of his associates sneaking around making drug deals the associate would be killed.

But, no matter the ramifications, Sidney informed his friend he wanted in on the cocaine business. Baltimore agreed to call in a cousin of his with ties to the Mexican Mafia. He would hook Sidney up with his first drug deal. A few days later Sidney and Baltimore traveled to McAllen, Texas, and checked into the Hilton Hotel. Underworld heavyweight and Mexican diplomat (we will call him "Big J") was heading into the states, but he informed Sidney the Hilton was full of undercover D.E.A. agents. If they wanted to make a drug deal, then they would have to move to the nearby Caballero Hotel. Big J informed Sidney the Mexican Mafia owned the Caballero and the deal could be made safely there. So, Sidney and his business partner checked out of the Hilton and moved their belongings over to the recommended Caballero. There they waited to be contacted by the big man himself.

The two men met with the Mexican diplomat at the appointed time, and Sidney was nervous. He didn't dare show it, but Sidney hadn't sampled cocaine before, and if he looked "green," Juan might think he was a cover-up cop and kill him on the spot. So, Sidney told Baltimore to spot for him. [This meant Baltimore would sample the cocaine as well, and then give Sidney the nod if it was the "good stuff."] The first meeting went well and Sidney lived to tell about it.

After sampling the merchandise, Sidney was sent home with his first run of the illegal substance. A few months later he was purchasing it by the kilo for ten grand and clearing over forty-grand a month in his drug deals alone. He was making thousands of dollars—and destroying hundreds of lives at the same time. But this fact never crossed his now drug-diseased mind.

Casa Blanca Credit Card Scam:

During his heyday Sidney Heard ran so many illegal scams even he forgets a few now and then. Basically, anything would make money outside of murder was on the table. At the time credit cards were still new and the processes weren't well protected leaving them vulnerable to predators. Bill Lankford was a man with a plan, and a perfect cover story. He was a professional florist who owned a small floral shop in town. No one would ever suspect a man who arranged flowers for a living would have any ties with a professional criminal. It was Bill, however, who proposed a credit card scam to Sidney one evening over a cold beer. Bill had learned all credit card transactions had a carbon copy usually ended up in the seller company's trashcan. carbon receipt contained all the information a criminal would need to steal a person's entire credit limit. Of course, Sidney jumped on the idea. He and Bill spent the next hour sipping beer and planning their next scam.

The setup was simple—too simple. Bill, Sidney, and a man we will call "Mac" headed out to Oklahoma City to set up shop. There they opened a front business they named Casablanca Fans. Back in Amarillo, Sidney hired every derelict, drunk, and vagabond he could find to bring him carbons of credit card receipts from local dumpsters. He paid them a dollar for each carbon copy they brought in. Of course, every panhandler in town would take advantage of kind of deal. Nowadays credit card companies have security measures would have noticed a trend with Casa Blanca Fans and would have stopped them dead in their tracks. But in the late '70s and early '80s no one noticed all the customers for this company came from one general area in Amarillo, Texas. With the lack of security Sidney's scheme worked out nicely. All he needed was to wait until he had a big enough stash of carbon receipts to start the process.

Every two weeks or so, Sidney would drive to the Alamo Bar in his shiny white Cadillac. True to his gangster roots, Big Sid would conduct a "sit-down." ["Sit-down" is mobster slang for a business meeting held by a boss in a public place. John Gotti was famous for having his "sit-downs" out on a busy New York sidewalk.] Early in the morning, the gangster would sit at his usual table in the back, order his usual breakfast, and conduct his business in plain sight. The bar opened early and with their cheap breakfast special it was the perfect place to work. At eight a.m., stragglers of all sorts would randomly file into the bar looking for their payday. They would slump into the chair across the table from the sharp dressed hustler and offer him whatever they could find to sell.

Everyone within a ten-mile radius knew when the big man's caddie was parked outside the Alamo Bar, deals could be made inside. Sidney made deals on everything from diamonds to pistols and, of course, credit card receipts. At one point a large black man brought in a garden seed spreader. It still had the store tags on it and Sidney wondered if the man had swiped it from someone's yard. Although he didn't need a seed spreader, the man obviously needed the $5 so he bought it. Sidney was more interested in the credit card receipts and soon he had enough personal information and credit card account numbers to steal a small fortune.

It was a surprisingly easy scam. The thieves would call the credit card company posing as a representative of Casa Blanca Fans, claiming the cardholder purchased a few hundred dollars' worth of designer ceiling fans. The credit card company would issue an approval code and the fake manager of the fraudulent company would skip their way over to the bank and get the cash. They repeated this procedure for three weeks, until they knew people would soon start receiving their statements in the mail. Over this short period, the nefarious trio swindled a total of $28,000 from a wide range of hardworking people.

They quickly closed shop in Oklahoma City and drove four hours away to Dallas, Texas, with the intent of repeating the easy-money scheme there. They rented a building so they would have a business address and then started opening checking accounts. After opening three new business accounts under a new name, the account representative asked me if she could have a copy of his driver's license. Every other place just glanced at the fake ID and wrote down the information. When the lady went to make a photocopy of his ID, Mac got spooked and the entire operation was canceled midstream. Mac was afraid for the bank to have a copy of his picture.

Sydney had set up a fake ID business quite a bit earlier. He had a photo studio set up in one of his many warehouses, and anyone could come in and get their picture taken. Then the boys would apply the photograph to a counterfeit Texas identification card and add any name the client chose. Sidney was always in need of a new counterfeit drivers' license. The scheme was not a huge moneymaker, but he could make a quick buck from anyone including teenagers who wanted to get into bars to professional criminals like himself. Sidney told me he was never too worried about making hundreds of thousands of dollars in one deal. He would rather make several thousand dollars over a course of time. These types of deals are easier to float under the radar of Justice, or so he said.

Hot Cadillac Scam:

Sidney had a friend, Gary Balboa, who owned a business called Balboa Paint and Body shop. While most of Gary's business was legit, he also liked to deal in stolen Cadillacs for a little extra cash. Gary would acquire a "junk" title on a Cadillac no longer existed, or was beyond repair. He would then give Sidney the year, the make, and the model stated on the title. Sidney would then turn around and send one of his lackeys to Dallas, Texas. There the gopher would rent a Cadillac of the same year, make, and model, using a phony driver's license (provided by Big Sid). Then Sid's employee would drive the now stolen car back to Amarillo. Sidney would deliver the hot car to Gary, who would quickly shave off the vehicle's identification number, or VIN, and replace it with the same number on his junk title. After a good paint job no one would know the difference. All this would be completed before the rental company even realized their car had been stolen.

Gary would sell the Cadillac as a refurbished vehicle for eight or nine thousand dollars. He would then pay Sidney a $2,500 finders' fee, and earn himself at least five grand for his trouble. Sidney would pay his hireling $500, and would still make a profit of two thousand dollars by the end of each deal. Sidney sent his man to Dallas regularly, but made sure not to do it often enough to raise any suspicion. Sidney paced every con he pulled far enough apart to avoid detection. This way it would take authorities years to tie everything together, and in the end, they never caught on to all the deals he had working.

Chapter 14: Amarillo by Fire

Sidney quickly realized defrauding insurance companies with arson could make large sums of money, and there seemed to be no limit on how far he could go with this scam. Never mind those types of "business ventures" drive up the cost of insurance and steal money from hardworking middle class people. In my research, I have found criminals tend to live what I call a "relative-morality" existence. In other words, "the crime I am committing is not as bad as the crime he committed, so I am okay." They are deceived into thinking they are above the law, and they can always buy themselves out of trouble. Sometimes they can, but it will always catch up to them in the end.

There weren't many security measures in place to protect the insurance agencies at the time, thus making them an easy target. The process of defrauding insurance companies in the '70s was a cakewalk. A client would approach Sidney about hiring him to set a fire. Of course all his advertising was done by word-of-mouth it wasn't like a professional arsonist could take out an ad in the Yellow Pages. Big Sid would charge a set fee of $5,000 per arson. He was to be paid half the fee up front and the rest was collected after the building was torched. Sometimes he would offer to fill the client's warehouse with items for them to raise their insurance claim. He would ship in a couple of loads of reject molding at a cost of $4,000, but he would charge his clients $6,000. This scheme would earn the gangster a smooth seven grand for each job. With this scam, Sidney could earn money from both ends of the deal. It was One-Stop shopping for the arson consumer.

Sidney explained many years later at the time there wasn't such a thing as a Fire Marshall. They would have one of the officers casually walk through the building and try to figure out where the fire started. Sidney's weapon of choice was turpentine. He would always soak various electrical items with it such as coffee pots in a restaurant, or even the electrical box itself. Most lumber used to build the structure contained a small amount of turpentine, and this made his accelerant indistinguishable. The untrained officer would site an electrical failure and the insurance company would be forced to fork over thousands of dollars.

Over the next decade Sidney committed twenty arsons, earning him approximately two hundred grand, yet he was never convicted of any of them. [Sidney even forgets a couple fires now and then, but he assured me there were at least twenty, but possibly more.] He would eventually make a plea bargain in exchange for his testimony in the arson trials of his accomplices, and all his arson charges would be dropped. Frankly, if you have heard one story of lighting a match, you have heard them all. So, to avoid redundancy, only a few of Sidney's more memorable arsons will be highlighted in this narrative.

One of Sidney's regular customers at Tiny's Pool Hall was a concrete finisher named Rodney Horne. The poor man was in love with Kathy the barmaid, but she wouldn't give him the time of day because he was broke. The two men started talking about Rodney's problem over a cold beer, and soon Sidney offered the dejected man a deal he couldn't refuse.

Sidney proposed and of course, Rodney was all for it. With a bankroll Rodney could ask Kathy out on a real date. He had been ogling her for weeks now, and was desperate enough to go along with just about any scheme Sidney could come up with. Sidney had recently come across an opportunity to purchase a truckload of secondhand molding and trim an extremely low price. It might be difficult to turn a profit on the junk trim, but if it were burned he could collect insurance money. The arson was planned for a warehouse storage complex in Amarillo, Texas. Sydney laid out his plans to Rodney one night at the bar.

"But place is loaded with video cameras and it has a 24-hour guard on duty," Rodney tried to reason with the gangster. The owner's security measures didn't bother Sidney at all. In fact, he relished the challenge. Sidney studied the layout of the complex carefully, and soon came up with a plan to reassure his nervous cohort.

Rodney was to rent a storage unit inside the gated parameter. Unfortunately for the warehouse owners, Sidney happened to own another warehouse abutted the entire complex. A small access road ran in front of Sidney's storage warehouse, giving the professional arsonist easy admittance to the guarded complex without being seen. The scheming criminal then filled Rodney's warehouse with 300,000 square feet of reject-molding and cheap construction material. After the building was filled with approximately $4,000 worth of molding, Rodney insured the contents for $30,000, and the stage was set.

At around six o'clock, Sidney covertly entered Rodney's storage unit, soaked the contents with lighter fluid, and drilled a small hole through the ceiling. Meanwhile, Rodney planned to leave on an out-of-town fishing trip. He didn't want to be anywhere near Amarillo when the fire was set on his storage unit.

Around 2 a.m. the next morning, Carol, Sidney's girlfriend at the time, backed a station wagon up to Sidney's warehouse. She then climbed out of the car, and began sifting through her boyfriend's belongings, pretending to be searching for something. This would have looked completely normal to any passersby. It was not like they had too many people pass by at hour anyway. Carol thoroughly enjoyed the wild side of Sidney's criminal activities and had assisted him on several other arsons and scams over the years. The fact she was married to another man never bothered the gangster.

Sidney climbed up onto the roof of his warehouse and made his way across to the roof of the rental complex. He slowly crawled across the joined warehouse rooftops to avoid any attention until he reached Rodney's unit. Then Sidney lit a few cotton balls soaked in lighter fluid, and poked them down the small hole he had drilled earlier day. Gravity pulled the tiny fire starters down onto the pile of molding lay on the warehouse floor below the hole, just as he had planned. Sidney swiftly scampered back across the rooftops as fast as he could without being seen. He could see a small puff of smoke rising from the tiny hole as he climbed off the roof of his own building a moment later.

Carol hastily whisked her arsonist far away to her aunt's house in Albuquerque, New Mexico, so he, too, would have an alibi. The fire investigators never determined the actual cause of the blaze. It was eventually blamed on another unit two doors down from Rodney's. That unit had been filled with boats and had gas cans lying around everywhere. Four different units burned night, but Sidney's warehouse was safe and sound. With their alibis in place, Rodney easily grossed a nice check for $30,000. Of course, the two criminals never thought twice about the other storage unit owners. They may or may not have had insurance, but all mattered to Sidney was the cash in his pocket.

After the thrill of the crime and the lack of consequences, the two arsonists decided they were far from being through with starting fires. With their need for an adrenaline rush, they soon conjured up a scheme to burn another warehouse in Clovis, New Mexico. On their way to scope out the area, Sidney noticed a billboard advertising Burns Insurance Company. Noting the irony of the "Burn" title, the arsonists promptly acquired fire insurance on Rodney's warehouse from the un-expecting insurance company. The routine was typical. Sidney filled the warehouse with second-rate molding costing $6,000, overbid the estimate to the insurance company for $41,000, and set the place ablaze on January 21, 1978.[25] [29] Of course, the two men made sure they were out of town when the fire department was called out.

After collecting another large chunk of the insurance company's money, Rodney bought a brand-new bass boat and the two men took a trip to Mexico, towing the boat behind them. They set up Rodney's Winnebago camper in a small compound-like village and enjoyed a couple of weeks relaxing and drinking by the waters of El Diamond Lake.

During the second week of their vacation, a group of local hunters talked the American tourists into joining them on a jaguar hunt in the nearby mountains. Of course, the drunken Americans were up for a little adventure and quickly agreed to tag along. Sidney doubted they would even see one of the large cats, but he was bored with sitting around the camp.

Rodney and Sidney decided they needed warmer clothing to travel in the mountains, so they headed into the little village nearby to purchase supplies for their trip. After purchasing food, the two men went shopping for serapes, the brightly colored shawl-like blankets Mexican men wear over their shoulders. When the small Mexican serape-vending woman looked up at the massive American gangster before her, her eyes widened with surprise. She shook her head; her dark locks bouncing around her shoulders.

"No serape para Oso Grande! (anyone so large)"

The nickname stuck and Sidney became "Oso Grande" to all his Mexican Mafia friends from then on.

The local hunting party assured the tourists they would kill a jaguar. Sidney became a little skeptical, however, when he saw the man's jaguar-call. It looked more like a round oatmeal box with a leather strap tied around it than a hunting-call for the large cats. Still, the two men trudged on trying desperately trying to keep up with the sixty-year-old native as he hacked a path through the dense foliage with his twelve-inch blade.

Soon the sun dropped below the horizon and a chill cut through the night air. The Americans listened as the little old man plunked on the leather strap of the jaguar-call. Much to Sidney's surprise, after a few moments of "calling," the hunting dogs started barking like crazy. The hunters let the dogs run, and after a brief chase a large jaguar was stuck in a tree.

The native shot the cat down from the tree with a 38-caliber pistol. With pride in his eyes he turned to his companions. Then he let the two Americans haul the 150-pound cat out of the woods. Pictures were taken when the triumphant hunting party returned home. The large cat was sent to a taxidermist and it stood mounted in a restaurant in Monterey, California for a long time. I am sure the animal rights activist groups would have had a field day with the Americans if they had known, but as usual, the thug didn't care. Now he had a story to tell and he could always say he ate jaguar meat for dinner in Mexico. To him it was just another tale to woo the ladies.

Sidney vs. "Creeper Weed":

Sidney's arson business affected the entire community, and there were many "ambitious" folks willing to take advantage of the situation. One such individual was Mr. Nicholson. He owned a small fleet of heavy equipment. His specialty was cleaning up the mess after a disaster such as a tornado, a hurricane, or perhaps an arsonist by the name of Sidney Heard. Sidney knew the man well and had done business with him on a few occasions. At one point Nicholson found he had over financed a dump truck and he knew he could never sell it for enough to cover the loss and still make a profit. Of course, Sidney wasn't the only con man who could think up an insurance scam. He was, however, the man with a reputation for shadiness. When Nicholson needed a "job" done, he called on Big Sid. Nicholson took out a policy for twice as much insurance on the dump truck as he should, and then promptly called the Amarillo Arsonist. He offered the gangster a thousand dollars if he would make the dump truck disappear.

Nicholson sent his dump truck into the shop for repairs one Friday afternoon and left a spare key with Sidney. After the shop closed for the weekend, Sidney slipped in and stole the unwanted vehicle. By sunrise Saturday morning the truck had crossed the border into Mexico with one of Sidney's so called associates behind the wheel. The truck wasn't even reported missing until the following Monday morning. By then Sidney had made an easy grand and Mr. Nicholson had already filed the theft with his insurance company.

Now Sidney had smoked, and dealt marijuana for years, both behind bars and in the free world. When his Mexican associate offered to pay him for the stolen dump truck with "weed" he readily agreed. The associate drove off in the dump truck and left Sidney to look after his Cadillac. Stashed in the car's trunk was ten pounds of what his associate called, "creeper weed." Sidney had never heard of the stuff, so when he got home he decided to try it out.

Sidney sat in his house for quite a while and waited for his "high," but it never came. Furious, he decided he would have to hunt down Mexican as soon as he got back into town. While he waited to exact his revenge, Sidney decided to drive the borrowed Cadillac to the post office around the corner. By the time he reached the building the "creeper weed" had finally caught up to the disgruntled gangster. He started to reach down to open the door and realized his mind couldn't order his body to budge. Luckily, the "paralysis" was only temporary.

When Sidney finally dropped back down into reality, he found himself sitting in the Cadillac waving and shouting at all the pedestrians like some sort of crazed lunatic. Sidney didn't have any trouble unloading the creeper weed on the street after experience. It made him a nice profit as well since he sold it for $400 per pound. This simple job earned him five grand and all he had to do was drive a truck out of a repair shop. This was the type of job Sidney liked the most; maximum payout for a minimal effort. More importantly the job left very little evidence would point back to him.

Amarillo Arsonist vs. Bandido Biker Bar:

Late one Sunday evening in 1978, Sidney and a few of the bikers at his bar were bored and decided to check out some of the bisexual girls at the gay bar down the street. Heterosexual men were welcomed in the bar; however, they were not welcome to take the girls home. Of course, Sidney's group didn't care about the rules and found themselves a few stragglers to take home. Afterwards some of the local lesbians got mad and formed a full-scale, Texas-style posse. The angry mob proceeded to storm up to Sidney's bar and pelt the front windows with every rock they could carry. The Amarillo Police Department (mostly

Sidney's police friends, mind you) quickly filed a lengthy report of the vandalism on Sidney's behalf, and bemoaned the "poor, defenseless" bar owner. While most people in town quivered in fear of the Bandido Biker gang, the Lesbian Posse took them head on without worrying a bit.

The protesting and vandalism continued for a few days until Sidney's scheming mind came up with another bright idea. He had grown tired of running all four bars, and decided it would be a good time to get out of the bar business for good. He had already gotten rid of the other three bars he managed, and this bar had become more trouble than it was worth. Besides, the best gangster is a faceless one, and this bar was starting to get too much publicity. So, the professional arsonist struck again. Late one night he set the building ablaze, raced home, and got in bed with his girlfriend Carol.

The cops showed up a short time later informing him his bar was on fire and it looked like arson. Carol put on a good show, and donned the part of a panicked girlfriend. The fire department was called out, but all was left of the biker bar was a burned-out shell. The local reporters asked Sidney if he thought the girls from the gay bar down the road could have set the fire. Sidney mumbled something about not going to blame anyone, but they got the rap for it anyway. Once again, Sidney was off the hook. It seemed the Amarillo Arsonist would never be caught.

Karma might let you run with the rope for quite a way, but be forewarned you'll always get tangled up in it in the end. And, the end would come soon for the slick witted Amarillo Arsonist.

El Toro's Arson—Amarillo, Texas:

In November of 1978, James Lane, owner of El Toro's Restaurant, hired Sidney to torch his declining business. While Mr. Lane was the actual business owner, he had taken on a partner. After a while Lane decided he wanted out of the joint business deal, but couldn't find a way to break his contract without losing a great deal of money. So, Lane decided on another course of action. He knew his partner would drop out of the contract if the business just so happened to burn and would make him a bunch of money.

Lane had already purchased a "business interruption" clause in his insurance policy. This clause meant the insurance company would pay Lane for any fire damage, and also for any missed income during the repair process. Lane asked the Amarillo Arsonist to create enough smoke damage they would have to close the restaurant, but he didn't want to burn the building completely burned down. This would effectively release Lane from his contract with his partner, and make him a large profit to boot. It seemed like the perfect scam.

On the night of February 27, 1979, Sidney simply opened the restaurant's electrical control box. He quickly soaked the wires with a combination of lighter fluid and turpentine, lit a match, carefully laid it inside the metal box, and closed the door.[30] The wires quickly melted and the heat from the flames went into the walls of El Toro's, causing major smoke damage throughout the entire building. The local newspaper reporters praised the local fire department for saving the building, but Sidney smirked at news. If he had wanted the building reduced to ash it would have been. So, Lane was out of his contract with his partner, and the insurance company paid him for all the time the restaurant was closed for repairs.

Obviously, the insurance company was not informed of the arson scheme, and they weren't told the restaurant's business had declined to such a state it had been losing money for months. This fact and many more would eventually come out in full detail on the witness stand many years later.

In 1979, Sidney also teamed up with Lane to set fire to a warehouse stood a mere three blocks away from the downtown Amarillo fire station. While most criminals would flinch at the thought of setting fire to a building so close to the fire station, Sidney relished the challenge and couldn't wait to pull it off. Lane had purchased the large glass-fronted warehouse months beforehand. The entire contents of the warehouse were worth no more than $6,000, but again an insurance policy on those contents was taken out for forty grand. Another $80,000 policy was taken out on the warehouse building itself along with the two neighboring rental houses also owned by Lane.

Lane was not content with merely stealing from the insurance company, so he decided to get his local bank involved. He paid a visit to the un-expecting financial institution and acquired a loan for $70,000 and put the warehouse up as collateral. He knew whether the arson was proven or not, the bank's insurance company would have to pay off the lien holder. Since Lane only paid $30,000 for the warehouse and the rentals originally, this deal made him a smooth forty-grand before the match was even lit. Unknown to the money grubbing criminals, stealing from the bank would be classed as a Federal offense and now the FBI could get involved. That torch job would come back to haunt Lane and Sidney many years later.

Sidney paid a visit to the building late one Friday evening. He made his way to the back of the building where the natural gas valve was located. After a few minutes of tampering with the valve, the fumes of the flammable gas started filling the space between the warehouse roof and the artificial ceiling. Five-gallon drums filled with turpentine were strategically placed around the room. After making sure everything was in place, Sidney quietly closed the door behind him, hopped in his pickup truck, and nonchalantly drove away.

Early Sunday morning just after 1 am Sidney's red pickup slowly cruised down the freeway off ramp and parked under the nearby bridge. A Springfield 30-06 military rifle was slung across the hood of the truck. Sidney had left a light on in the back of the doomed warehouse to serve as a target. Adjusting for the strong wind speed and the high Texas humidity day, he fired a phosphorous-tipped tracer bullet into the room through the warehouse's front glass window. The 150-grain bullet zipped through the darkness at 2,650 feet per second (or fps) before piercing the glass window. The gunman straightened his shoulders and waited; nothing happened.

The building was made of concrete blocks and Sidney could see the flaming bullet bounce off the wall inside the building through his scope. But the building still didn't blow. He took aim at one of the turpentine-filled barrels he could see through the glass and squeezed the trigger again. This time the turpentine ignited and the explosion ensued lifted the warehouse roof four feet above the building. Sidney could see the fire in his rear view mirror a mile away as he stashed his rifle behind the seat and headed home to get a good night's sleep. There would be plenty of time to pick up his paycheck tomorrow. For now, all he needed was some sleep

1979 was a big year for the pugnacious criminal. Sidney had been flirting with a girl named Suzanne for over a year. The tall lean Vicky Lawrence look alike worked at a local bank and Sidney made every excuse he could to stop by and talk to her. She kept telling him he was too mobish, but finally his charisma won over and she agreed to a date with Big Sid. It was a good thing, too, because the promiscuous gangster had just broken up with his crazy lover Carol. A few weeks earlier after an overdose of partying and booze, Carol had crawled out of bed and tossed on her raincoat. Sidney stared at her and wondered if she was smashed enough to go outside wearing only the waterproof jacket over her birthday suit.

To his surprise, she reached into the pocket of the overcoat and pulled out a snub-nosed .32-caliber pistol and pointed it directly between Sidney's blue blood-shot eyes. He knew the gun well. He had bought it from his ex-wife when she was low on cash and had given it to Carol a few months earlier as a gift. *Is she going to shoot me with my own gun?* Sidney's anger flared as he stared down the wrong end of the gun's barrel. Without many options, he steeled his nerves and waited.

"What are you doing?" he asked Carol, trying to sound nonchalant. "Put gun down."

"I am trying to decide if I should take a long walk, or if I should just shoot you in the head," Carol replied coldly. Needless to say, Sidney encouraged the drunken woman to take the walk. The moment she was out the door, he threw on his clothes and headed for his Cadillac. was the end of his rambunctious romp with Carol Howard.

Suzanne was different from most of the women Sidney had dated. She had three kids and a good job. She lived, however, in a tiny one-bedroom house behind her parents' place. By now Sidney was growing tired of his promiscuous lifestyle and was looking for a real family. Maybe Carol's outburst five months earlier had a hand in his decision—who knows? But after a few weeks of pleasantries, Suzanne poured out her troubles on Big Sid during a dinner date. She told him her ex-husband was trying to sue her, charging her as an unfit mother and take her children because of her financial situation. Although she worked at the bank, she was not making enough money to move out of the small house on her parent's property. And her ex was using this information to his benefit.

Sidney, again suffering from his "Hero's Complex," quickly swooped in to the rescue the beautiful woman. As fate would have it, Sidney knew the judge in Suzanne's case and had even supplied drugs to the prosecuting attorney indirectly through one of his many associates. The gangster pulled a few strings in the justice system on her behalf. And a few days later he asked Suzanne to marry him. She quickly agreed.

When her court date finally arrived, she stepped up onto the witness stand armed with enough evidence of

Sidney's wealth to floor her legal opponents and her ex-husband. She showed the judge pictures of Sidney's nice home and told of her engagement to the wealthy benefactor. The judge ruled in her favor and she could maintain custody of her children. Sidney Heard and Suzanne Davis were married on August 31, 1979. Within a matter of months, Sidney had become a husband and a father of three. His daydream of a family had finally been realized—or so he thought.

Unfortunately, money, beauty, and even political connections still couldn't buy Sidney's happiness. So, he set his sights on becoming the perfect husband and stepfather, which meant no more girlfriends on the side and a little less partying. He would have to be content with the company of one woman. This would be a change for the promiscuous bachelor, but he was willing to change. Unfortunately, in a senseless argument one day, his lovely new bride let a nasty little secret slip from her angry tongue.

"I only married you to keep my kids anyways," she yelled from the other room. The words hit the hardened criminal square in the chest. He wondered momentarily if Suzanne loved him at all or if she had merely used him for his money and power. Yeah, it hurt the man, but he refused to care. Instead, he decided to make her eat her words by sleeping with every beautiful woman he could find. Oh, he stayed married, but the marriage vows were nothing to him now. Besides, Suzanne Davis had a very wealthy father who also had many political connections. No need to throw all away, or so Sidney thought.

As with any professional criminal Sidney had his own sense of morals and standards. He had always considered himself to be the perfect husband. If his wife towed the line, then so would he. He took his marriage vows seriously as long as she didn't tick him off. However, once Suzanne confessed her true feelings, he didn't feel the slightest bit obligated to her. To her credit, Suzanne stayed with Sidney for over eight years—even through another one of his prison terms. Whether it was obligation, money, or genuine affection, no one will ever know.

Everyone has heard of the old saying, "it's a small world." In Sidney's case this rang very true. Back in 1973 a man named Mark Davis had ripped off the gangster. At time, Davis tried to cheat the gangster out of five grand. Sidney stormed into the man's office and explained in true mafioso style if he didn't get paid, everything Mark Davis owned would go up in flames. For some strange reason Davis quickly changed his tune and finally paid the angry man his due. Who knew several years later same arsonist would end up marrying Davis's daughter? Suzanne had disowned her father long ago and rarely had contact with him. Yet Sidney still found the situation quite amusing.

Breckenridge Arson:

This time, Sidney's partner in crime was his old buddy William (Bill) Lankford. You may remember Lankford was the flower shop owner who dealt with Big Sid on the side. Like most professional florists, Lankford used Scotch Broom Weed in his floral arrangements regularly. He paid individuals from around the world to harvest and store the weed for him while it dried. Somehow, however, Lankford ended up with a barn full of molded broom weed sitting right on the town square in Breckinridge, Texas. Instead of writing off such a hefty expense he decided to get paid for it with insurance fraud.

On June 17, 1980, Sidney meandered through Lankford's large barn doors in the wee hours of morning. He casually strolled to the back of the barn, lit a cigarette and threw the lit match into the mountains of dried broom weed. Unknown to Sidney, broom weed is extremely flammable. Once lit, it can't even be stamped out because of the plant's high oil content. Within moments the entire room was engulfed with flames and Sidney found himself in a race against death itself.

It took every ounce of strength he had to race towards the front door before the fire reached the only exit. Flames warmed his back and nipped at his heels as he slammed the barn doors behind him. His eyes were glued to his rear-view mirror as he sped away. He could still see the light of the raging fire miles from the Breckenridge Square. Safe at home, he could still feel the fiery fingers of death at the nape of his neck. For most people a brush with death would make them change direction, but Sidney just shrugged it off. It was not anything a good dose of booze, "weed," and cheap women couldn't fix—or so he thought.

L&L Properties Arson:

In early 1980, J.C. Lane once again hired Sidney to torch a duplex he had purchased under the name of L&L Properties. This time Sidney was too busy being a family man, so he hired an accomplice named Marvin McFarlin to do the job for him and offered him a cut of the take. After the plan was in place, Sidney scooped up his wife Suzanne and his three stepchildren, and together they headed off on a family vacation in the Bahamas. The family shipped out on April 27, 1980.[31] The plan was simple, but Sidney should never have relied on someone else to do his dirty work. The inexperienced arsonist bungled the job and the building was only partially burned on May 1, 1980.[32]

Lane was furious, and Sidney promptly cut McFarlin's fee in half to appease his boss. Of course, Lane and his son still settled with the insurance company for several thousand-dollars. McFarlin's blunder would also draw extra attention from the local authorities. All this would be outlined in the *Amarillo Daily News* several years later when it came to light on the witness stand.

Arson right under the cop's nose:

Late one rainy evening Sidney was busy "hamming it up" with a local undercover cop at the Caravan bar in Amarillo. Sidney always liked to make a good show with the local police department. He would buy them drinks, have dinner with them, donate massive amounts of cash to the local police department, and basically anything he could do to keep them on his good side. Tonight was different, however, because Sidney had accepted a contract to burn a restaurant. He knew he had to find a way to skip out of the bar and do the job without the cop knowing he had left. So, he came up with a great scheme.

A beautiful girl was working the bar night and Sidney started talking about "how good she was in bed" to all the guys around. After a while he informed his drunken companions he was going to "get a piece of that" and quickly ushered the girl back into the office, but not before buying the entire house a round of drinks. Once inside the office he locked the door and told the young woman his plan, or at least part of it. He was going to leave out the back door, and she was not to open the door to the bar under any circumstances. She was to make noise pretending she was having the time of her life. He assured the girl he would make it well worth her while when he returned. She nodded and shooed him out the back door without asking any questions.

Sidney hurried out to his car and raced across town to the doomed restaurant. The owner had given him a key, so he just opened the front door. He turned on all the coffee pots, sprayed them with lighter fluid and turpentine, lit a match, and locked the door behind him. He hurried back across town and re-entered the bar through the back door. He promptly paid the girl and invited her to party with him later night in his apartment. The infatuated woman readily agreed. [Of course partying with Big Sid meant sex and cocaine. If he wanted a woman, he just offered her a little free powder.]

When the fire department was called out, the notorious arsonist was busy drinking beer next to the cop at the bar. I would say is a pretty good alibi, wouldn't you? Sidney got paid for the arson, the owner got paid by the insurance company, and the woman got paid with free drugs and a night with the infamous gangster.

Sidney's Diamond scam:

During his marriage to Suzanne Davis, Sidney bought and sold diamonds to the owner of the Underwood Insurance Agency. He happened to meet the insurance representative while waiting at the Bank of Southwest to pick up his wife for lunch. He mentioned he was in the market for diamonds and Sidney said he could get his hands on some. chance encounter started a five-year business relationship and a brand new con idea for Big Sid.

Above the bank were several office spaces, and Sidney, now an insurance scam artist, rented one of them. Mr. Underwood was just as much a conman as Sidney Heard. He would sell people insurance policies, but then he would just so happen to forget to file the policy. If someone came in with a claim they would quickly discover they were uninsured. Sidney sold Underwood black market diamonds for a couple of years without a hitch until Mr. Underwood decided to pull this scam on one of Big Sid's associates. Of course, the associate knew who to complain to, and when his "boss" heard of the raw deal he was furious.

Once the unsuspecting insurance agent crossed onto the Big Man's territory, Sidney decided to retaliate. The gangster had recently sold a 2.2 VVS diamond, and he still had the paperwork for the $25,000 rock. So, he contacted Mr. Underwood and asked him if he would be interested in purchasing the expensive jewel for a measly five grand. Of course, the man was interested. Underwood quickly agreed to pay the conman the meager fee. Sidney delivered a cheap cubic zirconium diamond in a black case just before Mr. Underwood was supposed to head out of town. Sidney knew the man would take a running trip to Dallas to have his jeweler look over his latest investment.

Just as Sidney planned, Mr. Underwood immediately took the case with the gem to his jeweler. Come Monday morning Mr. Underwood was back in town and demanding answers from the conman. He claimed Sidney had tricked him into paying five thousand dollars for a forgery.

Sidney stormed into the scoundrel's office later afternoon and threw a cussing fit on the man. "How dare you accuse me? Do you know who I am? Do you know what I can do to you? I've always delivered the goods, haven't I?" Sidney argued with the man. "I don't appreciate someone accusing me of fraud. Now where did you take diamond?"

"I took it to a jeweler in Dallas," the man mumbled.

"Don't tell me you left it with the guy?" Sidney bellowed his eyes flashing fire. [Not only was Sidney a good gangster, he was also a pretty fair actor. Of course, he wouldn't win any Academy awards for his performances, but he did earn quite a bit of money over the years.]

"Yes, I did," Underwood admitted rather sheepishly. Finally, the man agreed the jeweler must be at fault. He never knew Sidney had scammed him from the beginning. He even continued to purchase diamonds off Sidney for the next couple of years. That's the way Sidney ran his business. No one messed with him or his associates.

Chapter 15: Hit Man/No Kill

A friend named Earl Sampson approached Sidney one evening about torching one of his warehouses. This time the doomed building was in Tyler, Texas. Of course, the serial arsonist agreed and outlined his normal plan along with his standard payment procedures. Just before the fire was to be started, however, Earl got nervous and brought in his crooked attorney, Hudson Moyer. Sidney didn't care who paid him as long as he received the money. So, Sidney finally agreed to bring in the "third wheel." When all was said and done, each man was supposed to receive five grand from Earl's insurance policy.

A few weeks after the fire, Sidney asked Earl for his payment only to discover the insurance company had sent the check directly to Hudson. Earl hadn't even received his own cut of the payment, and was pretty upset by it. Sidney encouraged Earl in the true "gangster style" to phone his alleged attorney and find out what was going on. The tall black-clad man sat quietly while Earl called his attorney and put Hudson on speakerphone. When Earl asked the attorney why he hadn't made the payment due, Hudson started cussing rather loudly. The blue-eyed gangster bore holes through the nervous man with his killer expression, but never spoke a word.

"I will pay f%&$ing Heard whenever I f%&%ing please!" Hudson yelled through the phone and slammed it down.

Earl turned a worried glance toward the eerily calm man sitting before him. Big Sid coolly stood to his feet, carefully straightened his jacket and his tie. Then quick as a wink he grabbed Earl by the front of his shirt and dragged the little man up to his face and halfway across the desk.

"So help me, Earl, if you warn Hudson I'm coming after him, you will not see the sunrise. You understand?" Sidney growled.

Earl quickly nodded, afraid to speak. Sidney dropped the man on top of his desk and left the building in a fury.

The irate arsonist quickly phoned a couple of his friends from the Mexican Mafia and headed over to the attorney's office determined to collect the debt. The three black-suited men stormed into the modestly decorated law office a few moments later. One well-armed mobster guarded the front door, while the other held a gun aimed at the secretary's head.

"Don't even think about calling the police, lady," the gunman warned the terrified woman.

Big Sid stomped through the small lobby. Fire flashed in his steel blue eyes, as his long fingers clenched his weapon. Sidney's size twelve boots crashed through Hudson's inner office door a moment later. Sidney whipped out his handgun and aimed the barrel right between the man's eyes. Hudson hit the floor at the very sight of the angry gunman. Without so much as a word, Sidney grabbed the large desk, picked it up and shoved it toward the little man cowering behind it. The massive desk landed squarely across the attorney's chest, pinning him to the floor.

The livid gangster calmly stepped around the upended desk and knelt by the man's head. Sidney pushed the barrel of his gun against the man's temple until he could almost feel the man's heartbeat reverberate through the steel shaft. He watched as beads of sweat formed across Hudson's forehead.

"Where is my money, Moyer?" Sidney snarled in his deep, baritone voice. The panic-stricken attorney lay gasping for air on the floor.

"I will get it. I swear. Will you just let me get my checkbook?" Moyer begged the fearsome man wielding the gun.

"Where is it?" Sidney questioned the man, not wanting to let him up.

Hudson nodded toward an open desk drawer. Sidney rummaged through the papers until he found the man's checkbook. Then Sidney helped the man free one arm from under the desk and held the checkbook for him while he made out the check. After the check was complete he tore out the check, tossed the checkbook on the floor next to the man's head, and calmly walked out of the room politely closing the door behind him. His black-clad thugs followed the man out of the building and back to the car. And yes, he left the poor attorney under the desk. When Sidney went to cash the check afterward the bank teller commented on Moyer's sloppy handwriting.

"Wow, he must have been really upset when he wrote this one," she noted trying to make small talk with the black-clad man before her.

"Oh, you know how he is. He hates to let go of money," Sidney replied casually. He turned and quickly exited the bank before the teller could see the evil grin cross his face.

Strangely enough, Hudson didn't hold any hard feelings against the gangster. It wouldn't have done him any good anyway. To Sidney it was just another business deal, and he had gotten his point across. No one messes with the big man—ever.

A few months later Hudson approached Sidney in a restaurant to ask him to run a scam for him. Without a word Hudson slid a white envelope across the table toward the conman and walked away. Everyone in town knew Sidney could quickly turn over $10,000 to make a profit. So, individuals who were seeking more interest than the banks could pay would simply slip the man an envelope with ten grand inside. Six months later the envelope would be returned holding twelve grand.

Of course, Sidney could roll the money over a half-dozen times within six months and make himself three times the original amount. No one knew what Sidney was doing with their money, only they would get a $2,000 increase on their investment in an extremely small amount of time. There was not a finance company in town could offer kind of interest. And Sidney, being the "kind hearted" soul, was obliged to help.

On April 4, 1975, the *Amarillo Daily News* reported Hudson Moyer's daughter, Katina, had been abducted from her high school parking lot. The lead suspect was a former Amarillo Police officer named Jimmy Paul Vanderbilt.[33]

Moyer spent several long days in a panic until they finally found her body. The teenager had been severely beaten, sexually assaulted, and her dead body dumped. The distraught father pushed for the death penalty during the trial, but the killer got off with a mere life sentence. Hudson vowed to get revenge on the "dirty cop" raped and murdered his child, as well as on the attorney got Vanderbilt off the hook.

Filled with rage and desperation, Hudson approached Sidney once more, and this time it was personal. This time he wanted to pay Sidney to knock off the cop and the prosecutor. Sidney felt sorry for the man, but still refused the briefcase filled with twenty-five grand. Unknown to the distraught father, and at time state representative, Sidney really wasn't a violent person, and had never killed anyone. The Chicago native only donned the cutthroat persona when absolutely necessary. Moyer would have to continue to mourn the loss of his daughter for the rest of his life; all the while his tax dollars were supporting his child's murderer. Although Vanderbilt was behind bars, his very existence tormented Moyer. He would go to his grave never finding closure for the death of his daughter.

Chapter 16: Krugerrand Gold Scandal

In the fall 1981, Sidney sat in his office late one evening bored with promiscuity, arson, and gambling. He picked up a copy of the *Wall Street Journal* and one article caught his scheming eye. A large quantity of African Krugerrand Gold coins had been stolen in Canada a few days earlier. What really drew his attention was the fact the coins hadn't been recovered. Although Sidney had never heard of coin before, he quickly did some research and found out the small token accounted for ninety percent of the worldwide gold market in 1980.[34] He quickly contacted his former cohort Bill Lankford and the two came up with a scheme to counterfeit the gold coins and pass them off as the hot items mentioned in the newspaper.

Sidney went out the next day and purchased one of the $700 coins from a local dealer. He took it home and studied it carefully under a magnifying glass. He noticed each gold coin didn't look exactly the same as the others because of the different grades of gold. However, the gold coins all measured twenty-two-penny weight. There is no other substance weighs the same as gold, making gold coins extremely hard to counterfeit. This fact did little to detour the determined criminal. Sidney's conniving mind thrived on the challenge.

Through trial and error, Bill Lankford found the California Emblem Company and together they created a dye of the coin made from synthetic bronze. However, the honest emblem company wouldn't make the mold without the word "copy" on it to legitimize the coin. The sample batch weighed in at a fourteen-penny-weight. Sidney went out and purchased a gold-plating machine from some associates. Then, after the word "copy" was carefully filed off the coins, Sidney simply plated them with liquid gold from an $85 bottle of the semi-precious liquid. This unbelievably simple process was repeated until the first batch of counterfeit Krugerrand coins was complete. Sidney then placed each coin in a plastic sleeve, and now the counterfeit coin's weight rivaled of the original gold coin.

At the time, federal law stated it was illegal to counterfeit any coin of legal tender. Sidney quickly twisted this legal verbiage to his advantage seeing an African gold coin was not technically legal tender in the United States. Although the coins were highly valuable to collectors, they didn't possess any purchasing power in this country. However, after Sidney's scheme and a few others were busted, the law was changed to state it was illegal to counterfeit any coin of the realm. change in legal jargon paved the way for Sidney's prosecution later when he was arrested in the fall 1981.

Sidney contacted a former accomplice named Dave Merchant, and asked him to put the word out on the street to see if anyone was interested in buying some "hot" Krugerrands. Of course, they were not hot; they were counterfeits, but the underworld dealers didn't know it. A few days later Dave sent word to the boss he could get a loan from Robert Ringo, the president of Tascosa National Bank for ninety grand if he would put up 300 of the African gold coins as collateral. Of course the money-grubbing gangster agreed to the deal. He would have been better off selling them on the street corner. The counterfeit ring might not have grossed half a million dollars, but at least it wasn't against a federally insured bank. Now the FBI would get in on the investigation.

In early October of 1980, Sidney waltzed into the Tascosa National Bank clad in a three-piece suit, looking every bit the part of a wealthy businessman. His cool blue eyes watched the bank president count the forged coins, fill out the financial paperwork, and then hand them a check for ninety grand. Although he had been duped by the fake coins, Ringo's biggest mistake was in agreeing to avoid submitting the necessary paperwork to report the currency transaction. Federal law states all transactions involving currency totaling more than $10,000 must be reported. Of course, Sidney didn't want the transaction reported so he coaxed Ringo into foregoing the process. Ringo would later resign as bank president because of this scandal.[35]

Dave Merchant was paid $40,000 for his efforts. Sidney took the larger cut since it was his racket. (Of course, when Sidney was later arrested on the Krugerrand scandal, he claimed it was not his deal at all.) Over the course of four separate transactions, the counterfeiters took the bank for over $270,000. For the first time in Sidney's life he felt like he had finally made it to the big-time racket. With kind of "dough" he could compete right alongside his mobster counterparts back in Chicago. He might be rolling in a new income bracket, but his financial step up would quickly result in his downfall.

Meanwhile, Dave introduced Big Sid to a man by the name of Rasha Siegal. Siegal was supposedly a broker for the Iranian government working out of Dallas, Texas. Siegal informed the gangster he had five million dollars from the Iranian government and was looking to purchase as much gold as he could find. Sidney was skeptical until the Middle Eastern man to him to his bank and showed him a safety deposit box stuffed with American currency. Sidney's scheming mind quickly went to work. I'm sure if he had been a cartoon, giant dollar signs would have popped out of his eyeballs.

Instead of forging another batch of coins, Sidney decided to have Ringo's bank robbed. The FDIC would repay the bank; the Iranians would have a batch of fake coins; and there would be no evidence against Sidney if he ever got caught. The plan sounded perfect at the time. As usual, the consequences this international incident could have caused never crossed the gangster's mind.

While the Iranian deal was cooking, Bill Anderson called Sidney and told him he was broke and wanted in on one of his deals. The two had done plenty of business together before, so Sidney let him in on the Krugerrand scheme. Anderson found Ventura Jewelers who offered to put the so-called "collectable coins" into gold necklaces. Unknown to Sidney, this decision to bring Bill Anderson in would lead to the downfall his vast underworld empire. Ventura Jewelers was a front business for an undercover informant with the FBI.

The counterfeit Krugerrand coins seemed to be an easy scam, so Sidney decided to broaden his horizons and counterfeit Suisse bars as well. These one-ounce gold bars would be made from the same synthetic bronze as the Krugerrands. The California Emblem Company would only make the bars with the word "copy" on them. Authentic

Suisse credit bars are labeled with a reference number. This number is matched to a list in a Swiss bank. To authenticate his fake Suisse bars, Sidney hired a woman to print ten thousand fake certificates for his counterfeits. The serial numbers on his certificates wouldn't match any numbers in the Swiss accounts, but by the time the owner discovered fact, Sidney and his crew would be long gone.

After the forged authentication papers were ready, Sidney used an engraving machine to put the serial numbers on the fronts of his gold plated bronze bars. As with the Krugerrands, it was hard to match the weight of an authentic Suisse bar. The original Krugerrand weighed 21-penny weight, so Sidney had his counterfeits made a little larger than the original to rival the real deal in weight. Afterwards, Sidney placed them in a plastic sleeve. This helped throw off the weight a little more.

Sidney's plan was to sell the fakes to an associate in Chicago for $800 apiece. With ten thousand forgeries, he figured he was going to make a killing. Unfortunately, this scam never got off the ground. Unknown to Sidney, his Krugerrand scheme was falling apart and he would be arrested before he could pass a single "gold" bar.

On February 1, 1981, Sidney made the scheduled trip to Houston to make the exchange with a representative from Ventura Jewelers. His wife Suzanne and a couple friends, Gary and Gayle Balboa, traveled with him. The group checked into a local hotel, using one of Sidney's favorite aliases: Sam Hill. Being from Chicago, Sidney always wore diamond-studded jewelry. One of his staple accessories was a 14kt gold necklace with a small diamond-studded pendant shaped in his initials S and H. Any time he needed an alias, Sidney would don the name Sam Hill. In his mind, it was a play off the old saying, "What in the Sam Hill...?" It also fit with his jewelry, so it was a win-win for the gangster. Ironically a few years later, Sidney would run into a Texan named Sam Hill.

"Sam" couldn't sleep the night before his big job at the bank, so the two rowdy men sat up drinking and snorting drugs all night long. Being his normal cautious self, Sidney left everything, including his hotel key, with his wife Suzanne, and told her to call his attorney if he didn't return or call within an hour. Gary knew what to do if his friend got into trouble, and the gangster knew he could trust him. Having a friend you could trust in this line of work was vital to Sidney's survival and he found friend in Gary Balboa. With one last look at his beautiful wife, Sidney slipped from the hotel room.

He drove his rental car through the streets of downtown Houston toward the designated bank and parked down the street from a side entrance on a one-way street. He wanted the car close by in case he needed to make a quick escape. Sidney climbed out of the car and casually waltzed down the sidewalk and entered the bank main entrance, just in case he was being watched. An arrest team was waiting just beyond Sidney's peripheral vision. He couldn't see them, but he found it was always best to be cautious in his business.

Bill Anderson and the representative from Ventura Jewelers greeted Sidney warmly as he entered the bank, but the long-time gangster was still on edge, in case something wrong. He stood aloof from the men, waiting for the slightest signal of foul play. His cool blue eyes constantly cased the bank when no one was watching him. If this exchange went well Ventura Jewelers had already made plans for a second more lucrative change to happen later day.

"Are these real?" the undercover informant asked Sidney about the coins before the deal was completed. The jeweler was a criminal as well, and was working through a plea agreement of his own. Sidney's eyes shot to the man. It was the moment of truth. Was this the signal he had been waiting for?

"Hey," answered Sidney nonchalantly, "there is gold on them. If you don't want them, give them back. Here is your money." He pulled the money back out of his pocket and handed it back to the man. With his smooth gangster mumble, no one would catch what he said until it was played back in court. This comment would save Sidney's bacon later during the trial. Right now, all Sidney could think about was getting away from the man as fast as possible. The man shook his head and handed the money back to the gangster.

With the deal complete, and the cops not having any real evidence, Sidney skipped out the side door of the bank and headed to his car. He had used the front entrance upon arrival and the cops were waiting for him there, so he was unknowingly saved by his standard precaution. He had narrowly missed the trap set by the state officers, but his pockets were greased with $35,000 of the state's buy-money—and they were determined to get it back. He returned to his hotel and waited for the call from Bill. If the jeweler approved of the merchandize they would call with a new time and place for the second exchange.

He didn't have long to wait. Bill called within the hour. Sidney was to meet him at the Republic Bank building in two hours. Sidney agreed to bring more coins for another exchange. Sidney left the $35,000 with Suzanne. Again, he warned her to flee to Amarillo if anything went wrong. She was afraid to keep the cash, so she gave it to Gary for safe keeping until the heat died down. Gary and his wife headed back to Amarillo and waited for Big Sid's next move.

Sidney met the informant two hours later, but again the sting went bad when the undercover agent took them into the vault, claiming he didn't have enough cash with him. The entire transaction was videotaped, but their voices were too muffled inside the vault to make a clear case. Again, Sidney would be spared in court by the undercover informant's bungling. It wouldn't save him from being arrested, however.

The local authorities descended upon the pair of counterfeiters the moment they left the building. Sidney and Bill were arrested on the sidewalk just outside the bank and taken to the county jail. Sidney could hear the police talking among themselves in the room next door as he waited alone in the interrogation room. A few months earlier a conman had tried to sell counterfeit Krugerrands to the Mob. The man was brutally murdered and the fake coins were scattered over his remains as a warning to anyone who would try to cheat the Mob in the future.

Sidney, of course, hadn't heard anything about case, but with his Chicago connections, the police assumed he was involved in the grueling murder.[36] The *Amarillo Daily News* reported on Thursday, March 5, 1981, the Houston Police Department was investigating the possible connection between four grueling mob murders and the counterfeit ring, which was run by Sidney J. Heard. Here Sidney also learned his good friend Bill Anderson hadn't set him up after all. Ventura Jewelers had agreed to set him up as part of their plea agreement. His buddy Bill Lankford would also turn state's evidence later during the torturing months of legal battles in an effort to reduce his own sentence.

Sidney tried to con his way into getting out of jail on bail. He assured the officers he was not the leader of the counterfeit ring. He claimed to have purchased the phony coins from an Amarillo man. He told the police about all his reputable businesses in Amarillo and assured them he could make bail if one was set for him. Sidney claimed he had a bill of sale proved he had purchased the coins from a dealer and loudly professed himself as a victim. Unfortunately, this precious piece of paper would be stolen from Sid's Swap Shop a short time later. What Sidney didn't know was the extent of the FBI's knowledge on the matter. They had been investigating the case for nearly a year and they knew exactly who the ringleader was.

Sidney was eventually released on a $2,000 cash bond and a $20,000 surety bond.[3] The officer informed him he didn't have to show up in court the next morning, and he was free to head back to Amarillo if he so desired. However, when his attorney Bill Taylor heard about comment, he hit the roof. Taylor quickly informed his client of the Houston Police Department's scam.

"Of course they don't want you to show up in court tomorrow," said Taylor. "Then they can claim you skipped town and issue a warrant for your arrest."

When Taylor realized how badly the Feds wanted his client, he decided to call in a few well-known legal reinforcements. Then not only did Sidney show up at court the next morning, he showed up with five attorneys in tow, including the famous Don Ervin. The judge, noting Sidney's legal muscle, quickly ordered the wanted man to be released on bond.

The group's next stop would be the Secret Service. Unknown to Sidney, counterfeiting Krugerrands was considered a federal offense since it compromised national security. It was a good thing he didn't sell them to Iran or it may have started WWIII. Sidney's attorneys tried to arrange a plea agreement. The federal prosecutor Shirley Lobel, unaware of Sidney's enterprises, contacted the local authorities in Lubbock, Texas. The moment she mentioned Sidney's name, a heated response exploded through the phone line.

"Heck, no," declared the contact. "We will not agree to a plea bargain for Sidney Heard. That man has been under federal investigation for three years for arson, drug trafficking, and a dozen other racketeering charges." In the end this investigation would include a joint task force of the FBI, the Secret Service, the Internal Revenue Service, the Bureau of Alcohol, Tobacco and Firearms, the Postal Service, and the Texas Department of Public Safety intelligence division as well as several state and local agencies. This massive task force had one goal in mind and was to take down Sidney's organized crime ring. Their investigation would finally end after fifteen long months.[37]

Sidney was re-arrested after the illustrious recommendation from Lubbock, and had to go through the entire bargaining process again. He eventually made bond and was finally allowed to return home a few days later. His attorneys warned him the Lubbock police would most likely try to arrest him again before his arraignment in Houston. The prosecutors desperately wanted Sidney to appear before the judge in chains.

When the plane made a stop in Dallas, Sidney skipped off the plane and headed straight to the public restroom. There he sat in the tiny stall for half an hour staring at the graffiti sprawled across the door. Meanwhile, the officers lying in wait arrested another man fitting Sidney's description. The man was held for twenty-four hours before the Houston authorities arrived. The airport security personnel were given a good tongue-lashing and the innocent man was released. All the while the real Sidney had ducked past them.

Chapter 17: The Feds wage War against Sidney

Sidney knew by now the FBI was after him big time, so it was reasonable for him to assume his phone would be tapped. He decided to throw the cops a "bone" and call his wife Suzanne anyway. He quickly explained to his confused wife he wouldn't be coming home night. Instead, he told her he was going to go skiing in New Mexico where he could lay low until the heat died down. Much to Suzanne's credit, she didn't argue with him or ask any questions. She just said okay and hung up the phone. Maybe she was intimidated by the obvious police surveillance around the house, but whatever the case she never expected to see her husband later evening.

When Sidney finally arrived at the Lubbock Airport he contacted a Mexican associate for assistance. The associate rented a car for Big Sid in his own name and picked up the boss at the airport. The man drove Sidney around through the back roads to his house and literally dumped the displaced gangster in his own back yard. The associate returned the rental, and the cops staking out Sidney's home had no idea he was even in the state much less a few feet away from them.

Sidney hopped over his backyard fence and made his way through the yard toward his back door. A moment later he nearly scared his wife half to death when he beat on the sliding glass door. Suzanne and Sidney's grandma were both afraid to answer the door when the dogs started barking, but eventually Suzanne peeked out the kitchen window and, seeing it was Sidney, let him in the house.

After the excitement died down Sidney had his wife call both of his attorneys under the pretense of explaining things to the confused woman. They arrived early the next day expecting to find only Suzanne in the house. Both were shocked to see the fugitive sitting at home, right in the middle of a massive stakeout. Together Sidney's attorneys devised a scheme to get him to his court date on Tuesday morning without being spotted by the police who had planted themselves all around the neighborhood.

An FBI car was waiting across the street; an unmarked Chrysler waited down the road; and a county cop car was parked just outside Sidney's front door. Sidney did have one advantage however; Suzanne's Cadillac was safely parked inside her garage out of view. Sidney knew there was a big rodeo going on in Houston over the holiday weekend, so he decided to drop his gangster look and opted instead for a cowboy disguise.

Much to Sidney's chagrin, he traded his leather jacket for a western-style shirt, which he tucked into his uncomfortably tight-fitting blue jeans; a bolo tie was wrapped around his neck. He shoved a cowboy hat down low on his forehead and took off his beloved diamond pinkie ring. Sidney finished off his costume with a pair of borrowed glasses. The problem was, he couldn't see through the prescription lenses. So, he quickly popped out the glass, and his outfit was complete. When his own dogs barked at him, Sidney knew his disguise was perfect. It may have looked perfect, but it was terribly uncomfortable.

Sidney climbed into the trunk of his wife's car. With a grin, she closed the trunk lid upon her folded up husband. [I have no way of backing this up, but this is probably the only time in history a gangster willingly climbed into the trunk of someone's car.] Suzanne tossed a slight wave to the officers as she slowly backed out of her driveway. She nervously watched the rear view mirror until the cops were well out of sight. After making sure she hadn't been followed she pulled the car over in a secluded spot on a nondescript back road to let her husband out of the trunk. He stretched his aching legs and climbed into the passenger seat. Suzanne delivered him to the Lubbock airport a few minutes later. Sidney took a flight into Dallas and then another on to Houston. It was a pain to have so many layovers, but it was the only way Sidney could shake the Feds were tailing him.

After Sidney boarded the plane, his eyes scanned the crowd and lit on two drunken cowboys. With his target found, he pulled his cowboy hat further down over his forehead and casually introduced himself to the two men, not by name, but by buying them a few drinks. By the time the plane landed, Sidney had two very drunk compadres. The three "cowboys" easily waltzed right by the two officers who were busy looking for the gangster Sidney Heard at the Houston Airport. With his new-found friends, Sidney crossed the lobby, casually strolled out to the parking lot, and hailed a cab.

Despite all the efforts of law enforcement, Sidney proudly showed up at court the next morning without handcuffs. The judge ordered Sidney to get all his criminal records together. Before the invention of the Internet, this was a daunting task for a professional criminal. Taking it all in stride, Sidney packed up his family and spent the next few weeks traveling back to Florida, Georgia, and Chicago to round up his rap sheet. He knew he couldn't outrun the law forever, so he figured he might as well enjoy a little family time along the way. The Feds continued to trail the wanted man and his wife every step of the way, hoping to find the missing Krugerrands, or at least trick him into giving them a reason to re-arrest him.

By now Sidney knew his friend Bill Lankford had gone rogue. The task force had caught Bill at the airport a few days earlier with a batch of the copy Krugs from the California Emblem Company. They hadn't been gold plated yet, but it was enough evidence to arrest Lankford. So, when Bill called one evening asking about the counterfeit coins, Sidney knew the Feds must be listening in on their conversation. Being of an ornery nature, Sidney decided to throw the eavesdroppers some heat. He quickly started ranting and raving to Bill about how he was going to fly to Chicago and give every black man he met one of the missing Krugerrands.

"I would like to see the Feds try to track down five thousand black men in Chicago," Sidney laughed wholeheartedly.

He didn't intend to give away the coins at all, but this would keep the Feds hopping for quite some time. Sidney went on with his telephone rampage and told Bill how some of "his Mexicans" had bugged the courthouse; how he had some "plants" in the jury box; and how Sidney had this case in the bag. [Of course, Sidney assured me none of this was true.] Bill mumbled a short reply and quickly hung up the phone. Sidney was told later the Feds had spent $10,000 going through the courthouse trying to find his listening devices, and had to replace every juror before the trial could commence. The blowhard gangster got a good laugh out of bit of info. And just to make the Feds sweat a little more, Sidney sent a few of his Mexican friends to drive around the courthouse several times a day. The intimidation worked on the media, and everyone thought Big Sid was going to "walk free."

Sid's Swap Shop Burglarized

Late one evening, Sidney stashed a load of silver in a drawer of his desk in the back of Sid's Swap Shop. Along with the silver in the desk was a small cigar box full of receipts and other important papers. Also in the box was Sidney's bill of sale supposedly proved he had purchased the coins from his buddy Bill Lankford. In reality, the paper was signed under duress. Sidney had coerced Lankford to draw up a fake bill of sale as an insurance plan in case Sidney ever got caught with the counterfeit Krugerrands. He assured his friend he would never have to use it, but wasn't the plan now.

Not long after Sidney closed shop, a lone figure slithered toward the back door of the building. A small hole was cut into the door with an ax. An arm slowly reached through the opening and carefully unlocked the door. The next morning Sidney found his desk had been ransacked; the silver and the cigar box were gone. Sidney's employee, Ann, thought the burglar was a man named "Slim." She claimed he had been lurking around the antique store and had been rude to her on several occasions. He even went so far as to badmouth Big Sid to Sid's own employee. Of course, with all the trouble Sidney was in, no one ever discovered the thief's identity. And to him it seemed like the cops refused to thoroughly investigate the incident.

Sidney's buddy Bill Lankford was getting pressured by the Feds to help set up the big man. So, he agreed to help set up his past accomplice in exchange for a lighter sentence. Bill called and asked Sidney to stash some "stuff" for him until the heat passed. Sidney agreed and Bill brought over a box of books about crime. There were books on how to forge fake ID cards, how to embezzle money, and even how to kite checks. Sidney packed the books up to the small attic-like storage space above his garage and though no more of it. Bill told his FBI contacts where Sidney put the books and assumed the missing counterfeit coins were hidden there too.

Early morning on March 12th Sidney was out and about when his wife called. A "friend of his had some stuff to sell. Sidney told her to buy it and make sure not to take it in the house around the kids. Instead she was to stash it in the fridge in the garage. Suzanne paid the man and quickly hid the 1oz of cocaine and 4 oz. of meth behind some other stuff in the fridge.

A couple of hours later Sidney gets another frantic call from his wife stating Federal agents were at the house demanding entrance. Flashing their search warrants, they raided Sidney's garage, vehicles, and safety deposit boxes in search for evidence, drugs, and the missing Krugerrands. The *Amarillo Daily News* reported David Fredricks, a Secret Service agent, thought Sidney may have three hundred more coins, and was afraid he might try to sell them.[34] Sidney did have more coins, but as hot as they were, he didn't dare sell them.

Sidney told me he was glad they didn't have a search warrant for the house. Under his bed was a WWII Thompson fully automatic machine gun, a.k.a. "Tommy gun," three rifles, and four pistols, not to mention the two loaded Smith &Wesson handguns on either side of the bed. During the process of the investigation the news media had printed the Heard's address, so Sidney was worried someone might rob his wife while he was gone to work, and of course as a convicted felon he wasn't supposed to have any type of gun.

After two days of searching the officers never found the missing coins. Bill Lanford's books were taken, drugs were found, and a few other counterfeiting tools but the coins were no were to be found. Sidney told me twenty years later they were hidden under the stepping stones in his back yard, and not even his wife knew where they were.

Sidney was immediately arrested after their ill-gotten finds, but the officer (who had frequently visited Sidney's bars as a customer) hated to handcuff him. Big Sid went with them quietly and climbed into the back of the patrol car. His sad blue eyes watched as his perfect little life quickly fell apart. He was charged with possession of methamphetamine and cocaine. The raid also turned up evidence for the prosecution which included gold plating paraphernalia, and a counterfeit gold coin. Sidney was taken to the Amarillo city jail. He asked the officers to set a bond for him, but they refused to do anything until the next morning.

That ticked off the hotheaded gangster, so he proceeded to ask every inmate about their fines. He called for Sergeant Cook to add up all the men's fines. The total came to a mere $2,800. Sidney pulled out $3,000 cash from his wallet and paid all their fines just to tick off the men who wouldn't set his bond. Now they had to go through the process of discharging all the inmates. After that, Sidney ordered pizza to be delivered for the deputies and the other inmates who had no fines. He may be in hot water, but Big Sid still demanded respect and he would get it one way or the other.

The next morning Sidney stood before a judge he knew well. But Sidney got a sickening feeling when the man wouldn't look him in the eye. A $100,000 bond was placed on the criminal's head. Sidney kept asking the officers what happened, but none would reply. Finally, Officer Garrett informed him he would be shipped off to Randall County. He informed Sidney he was too tight with the Sheriff in Potter County, and the prosecuting attorney had asked for a change of venue.

After being hauled to Randall County, Sidney and his lawyers began working feverishly on posting the $100,000 bond. It looked like he would be released, but just as he was about to head out the door, Sidney was charged with being an accessory before and after an arson case in Lubbock, Texas. Another $100,000 was immediately placed on his head. The only problem for Randall County was the arson for which they claimed Sidney was responsible was never even committed. The FBI wanted him badly, but they didn't have enough evidence against him, and they knew it. At this point it seemed as if the FBI was determined to keep Sidney Heard behind bars even if they only had circumstantial evidence against him.

The next morning Sidney was brought before the Justice of the Peace whom he also knew well. Sidney's attorneys argued he was required to stand before a judge in Houston, Lubbock, and then again in Randall County—all in three days. The Feds wanted to keep Sidney from appearing again in Houston so they could issue a warrant for his arrest. However, Sidney's attorneys guaranteed he would be back to Houston in time; however, he had three appearances to make in just three days. When Sidney and his attorneys walked out of courthouse he had posted two $100,000 bonds plus the $45,000 bond from Houston was still on his head from before.

The camera crew from Channel 7 News met Sidney and his lawyers as they exited the courthouse. A reporter asked, "Is it true you have three court appearances in three days, Mr. Heard? Stanley Marsh (the owner of the bank Sidney took for $270,000) is betting ten to one you will be in Mexico by tonight."

statement was not only defamatory; it made one of Sidney's attorneys furious. The attorney had a friend with channel 10 News, so he contacted them to make a public statement guaranteeing Sidney's return. For the next few days the two TV stations waged a small war over the criminal's location. Sure, there were more important news stories to be reported, but at the time, the two station managers were enamored with the Sidney Heard trials.

Everyone was sure he was going to slip up and miss a court appearance, or fly the coop.

Sidney immediately flew to Houston where he fought for a continuance on the counterfeit Krugerrand case. The judge granted his request and Sidney rushed to the airport and flew to Lubbock. When he stood before the judge in Lubbock, the man shook his head angrily as he read through the charges. He quickly decided to dismiss the erroneous charges completely. He grumbled something about not letting the Feds play games on his turf. The arson had never happened. So why should a judge waste his time in hearing a case about a fire never occurred? Sidney thanked the judge then raced back to Randall County. He had made all three appearances as promised.

On March 25, 1981 Sidney and Suzanne Heard were called to stand before a grand jury to hear the evidence in the case. The jury would then decide if there was enough evidence to go to trial. The couple invoke their 5th amendment right and are released from their subpoena if they agreed to give handwriting samples, fingerprints, and have their mug shots taken. Too make matters even worse Suzanne's boss had embezzled $30,000 from the bank and was trying to tie it to Suzanne. What better person to lay the blame on than a well-known gangster's wife, right? Luckily for him the handwriting samples proved Suzanne was innocent, or very furious Sidney might have ordered his first hit.

The next morning the couple arrive at the Potter County Police Department to fulfill their part of the deal. While they are being fingerprinted the FBI raids Sidney's warehouse on 55th Avenue. They collect more evidence to bolster their case, including an $800 machine Sidney used to stamp serial numbers on the counterfeit Sussie bars. Then according to the legal guidelines, they left a copy of their search warrant on the table.

Over the next few months, the federal task force pulled out all the stops. They were still under the pretense Sidney

Heard was a dangerous, deadly mobster had been responsible for four deaths over counterfeit coins. They tried to arrest Sidney for anything and everything, hoping to force him into missing a court date. But Sidney would find a way to bypass the Feds and always ended up in the courtroom at the right time. And each time he would have to post another bond. This legal circus continued for months. All the while, Sidney was snorting as much cocaine as he could. He felt if he was going to prison for the rest of his life, he might as well not have to feel the pain. Even during the jury selection, he would excuse himself to the restroom to get high.

Sidney's attorney, Don Ervin, finally got a copy of the witness list the day before Sidney's trial was to begin. The Federal Government had offered immunity to a total of seventy-eight people if they would roll over on the Chicago native. infuriated the gangster, so he arranged a private chat with the prosecutor Shirley Lobel. Up until this point, Sidney hadn't snitched on anyone except in the murder trial against Charles McCarthy. Sidney was a firm believer in keeping his mouth shut. But when he read the list of his so-called buddies who had turned against him, he decided to fight fire with fire.

"Why are the Feds after me so hard? I have never hurt anyone," Sidney quizzed his legal opponent.

Lobel coolly explained he had several different districts after him for arson charges occurred over a period of several years. Although they couldn't get everything pinned on him at the time, they wouldn't let up until the Feds had their case together against him. This enraged Sidney to the boiling point.

He finally asked Lobel if she thought they would agree to a plea agreement if he could give her more cases than she knew what to do with. Knowing his connections in the underworld, Lobel quickly agreed on one condition: The Feds believed Sidney had killed a man in a fire years earlier. Of course, they hadn't stopped to check Sidney had nothing to do with that arson. But he had a reputation for arson, so several fires were pinned on him even after he was behind bars. If Sidney could prove he hadn't killed anyone, and if he would hand over the leftover Krugerrands, Lobel said she would agree to a deal with him.

FBI agent Ron Jennings escorted the wanted man to Dallas a few days later. The two had met in Amarillo previously, so they spent the night drinking in a Texas bar before showing up for the lie detector tests the next morning. Looking back years later, Sidney wondered if Ron was trying to get him drunk so he would slip up and confess to something. Either way the gangster had one last hurrah before the test.

Sidney's somewhat famous attorney Don Ervin met him at the Dallas police station early the next morning. Sidney went through the process of being strapped to the lie-detector device and was quizzed for a half-hour to see if he was telling the truth. After assuring the detective during the test he had never harmed anyone, he was released. He passed the test with flying colors and was sent back to Shirley Lobel's office.

ATF (Alcohol, Tobacco, and Firearms) agents Charlie Baylor and Jerry Hubbell were waiting at the table in the district attorney's office when Sidney, Ervin, and Jennings arrived. Baylor slid a bullet across the table to Sidney and told him to read the inscription on it. The letters S-I-D had been scratched into the side of the casing. When he saw it, the smooth-talking gangster sat back in shock as they explained the case against him. Hubbell showed Sidney a few autopsy photos of two severely burned men, and the light started to flicker in his brain.

"What is this?" he asked. "I have never hurt anyone— ever. I only burned empty warehouses." Sidney tried to defend himself against the false allegations.

"They were just insurance fraud gigs," said Sidney. "I know I have a bad reputation, but this gangster is all about making money. And is *it*."

Baylor and Hubbell then explained how the two men were killed in a fire connected with J. C. Lane and his son—and now Lane was pointing fingers at the Chicago native with a previous arson rap sheet. After months of chaos, the pieces of the puzzle were finally coming together for Sidney. Most people would have felt betrayed, but it just made Sidney mad. Revenge boiled in the gangster's heart and mind and J.C. Lane would pay dearly for this betrayal. The Amarillo Arsonist thought about burning down everything Lane owned, but he knew there were too many eyes on him now.

Baylor told Sidney how he had rented an upstairs bedroom from the neighbors across the street from Sidney's home at 1220 S. Bonham Street in Amarillo. The ATF agent had set up a stakeout in tiny bedroom for three months, waiting for Sidney to torch the place but he never did. Sidney had unknowingly set off a red flag when he purchased the home from his girlfriend Carol for $10 plus other considerations. (Yes, they included "other considerations" on the Bill of Sale) Then he turned around and sold the place to his cohort Dave Merchant for $30,000 the very next day. And to top it all off, Dave sold it to the Weatherly brothers for $40,000 a few days after that. Baylor was positive they would catch Sidney in the act of arson, but he couldn't have been more wrong. Sidney had already made his profit and moved on.

After hearing the entire case against him, Sidney spoke up and offered the group a deal he was sure they couldn't refuse. Everyone knew Big Sid had connections from the Chicago mob all the way to the Mexican Mafia. When Sidney offered to turn state's evidence against some of the biggest names in crime, the government couldn't help but accept. One might wonder how a man could be in such a mess and still refuse to turn to God for help. But, as usual Sidney was depending on his own ability to get himself out of trouble.

Chapter 18: State's witness

To fulfill his part of the plea agreement, Sidney reluctantly turned over 4,986 counterfeit Krugerrands and his ten thousand fake Suisse bars to the local government officials. Over the course of the investigation Sidney had told several snitches they were buried out at lake Meredith, and another team thought they might be buried near a lake in Florida. Sidney showed up to meet the task force and they were all dressed in jeans and old work clothes.

"We're ready to go start digging," said one agent. Sidney laughed and told them they weren't at the lake. They were in the trunk of shiny white Cadillac in the parking lot. Sidney still laughs about one.

He was told some time later the Krugerrands were placed on a plaque and were hung on the wall the U.S. Treasury building in Washington D.C. There they remained for many years. [When I tried to contact the U.S. Treasury department, they wouldn't confirm nor deny this allegation.] Sidney and his old friend Gary Balboa buried a box filled with 200 counterfeit coins under the concrete floor of Gary's garage as a nest egg in case they ever needed some fast cash. To the best of Sidney's knowledge, they are still there. The address will not be mentioned, however. We would hate to spark a gold rush to Amarillo, Texas. With the price of gold nowadays even the gold-plated bronze coins would be worth a small fortune.

Negotiations and court proceedings dragged on until November 17, 1981, when Sidney was officially offered a plea agreement. In exchange for a guilty plea on the Krugerrand case, the feds dropped the 13 other counts concerning his arsons and his narcotics charges. (Notice they only had 13 counts of arson. In reality, there were 18-to-22 fires flared throughout the great state of Texas. There were so many even Sidney forgets a few of them now and then.)

At the young age of thirty-nine, Sidney took a good look at his wife Suzanne, his three stepchildren, and the 125 years of prison time looming over his head.[38] He made the difficult decision to take the agreement in exchange for his testimony. Besides, it was the only way he could get revenge on the 78 people who had betrayed him. Finally, on March 29, 1982, Judge Mary Lou Robinson sentenced Sidney to seven years in the federal penitentiary. [39] He received four years for conspiracy and three years for fraud. Sidney was ordered to report to federal officials within thirty days to begin his seven-year sentence. Seven years was much better than the proposed 125, but it would still mean Sidney's free reign of criminal escapades was over.

Although he was convicted and sentenced, the local authorities didn't forget all Sidney's monetary donations to the law enforcement fund in the past. In fact, Sidney was a close friend of Sheriff T.L. Baker. Their wives had worked together at the local bank, and they often attended social events together, even sharing a few drinks from time to time. This connection proved beneficial when Sidney was sent to the Federal Correctional Institution in Seagoville, Texas. Sidney was given the best treatment in the entire complex. He had the best housing, clothes, and food. Sheriff Baker even arranged for his old friend to work cleaning guns at the pistol range.

Sidney was assigned to work with Lieutenant Richardson. He would set up targets, mow the lawn, and even test fire pistols. Sidney stayed in those near-luxury conditions for almost a year until he was called to testify in the J. C. Lane trials in Amarillo, Texas.

Revenge on Slim:

In 1982, a man nicknamed "Slim" set up a string of robberies, preying on the rich and famous around the Amarillo area. Doctors, Judges, Lawyers, and even the Federal Judge Mary Lou Robinson were all targeted.

Everyone wanted the guy but no one could seem to catch him. Unfortunately, Slim had made a grave mistake a couple of years earlier when he robbed Sid's Swap Shop. Sidney hadn't forgotten, and when word came through the jailhouse Slim was involved, Sidney made a quick call to the chief of police. A meth-addict named Jerry had spilled the beans to Sidney and confirmed Sidney's suspicions about Slim.

Jerry purchased drugs from Slim and had heard he had robbed Sid's Swap Shop. Sidney's very public case made him a target and Slim thought the shop would have plenty of jewelry ripe for the taking. Jerry also told Sidney Slim kept a book with a list of all the people he had stolen from. Most importantly he knew where to find them. All the jewels were hidden in Slim's five safety deposit boxes. Next came the task of finding a way to raid the boxes without a search warrant. To overcome this obstacle, the officers brought in the drug dogs. The dogs sniffed out Slim's boxes and the officers got a court order to open them from one of the very judges had been robbed. Slim's safety deposits boxes were raided and over a million dollars' worth of jewelry was recovered. Sidney received a nice thank you letter from the Amarillo Police Department for his efforts. [Mysteriously they never found any drugs. I guess would be considered an "oops" on their part.]

The death of Carol Howard:

One morning while Sidney was working in the gun range, a couple of his lawyers from Presley & Taylor arranged a quick unscheduled meeting with the inmate. In the meeting room the well-dressed men informed the inmate his longtime girlfriend Carol Howard had died in a car accident the night before. She was on her way to visit Sidney in jail. To make matters worse, she had left behind a will stated everything she owned was to go to Sidney Heard upon her death. She had even given him custody of her two children. His name was on her life insurance policy so a check for one hundred thousand dollars would be his, as well.

Sidney sat back in shock. He hadn't seen Carol since she had pulled a gun on him years earlier. Of course, he had met her children and was concerned for their welfare. He thought about Carol's parents and how badly it would make them feel to learn their daughter had left everything to her illicit partner instead of them, not to mention the children's biological father. Sidney's scheming mind quickly went to work for an escape option of another sort. He cared about Carol's kids, but there was no way he could take care of the two children while he was behind bars, and he knew his wife Suzanne would have nothing to do with them.

Sidney shook his head and asked the attorneys who else knew about Carol's will. The attorney informed him they were the only ones who even knew she had a will. No one else had read the document. Sidney nodded and told the attorneys to tear up the legal papers, and to make sure Carol's parents got everything, including the two youngsters.

"Do you know how much money and property you will be passing up?" the attorney tried to argue.

"Money does not matter now. I can't have kind of money while I'm in here, and I can always make more money when I get out. I want those kids well taken care of, and the grandparents are their best option."

So is how the "hard-nosed gangster" looked out for his ex-girlfriend's children. To this day, if they are still alive, they have no idea about Carol's true intentions; and neither did his wife Suzanne. Crisis avoided.

Chapter 19: Undercover Informant

After working out the details of his plea agreement, Sidney agreed to become an undercover informant on cases involving some of his prior associates. Sidney testified in the J.C. Lane arson case, the Earl Sampson trial, and the Weatherly brothers case. Afterward Sidney was assigned to work with an undercover agent by the name of Jerry Bradford. In reality, Jerry's last name was Hubbell. Hubbell was famous for working the T. Cullen Davis murder case.[40] Jerry informed the rookie an agent always uses their real first name. way when someone yells at you from across the room you immediately look up. It's a simple way to keep from blowing your cover.

Sidney also had the pleasure of working with the famous FBI agent Ron Jennings out of Amarillo, Texas. These two men had chased Sidney for years and now he found himself working right alongside them. It was quite a change for the gangster-turned-informant. As usual, Sidney observed his new situation and amassed as much knowledge as possible. He never knew when the new-found information might be of some use to him.

Sidney also spent the following few months helping build cases to bring down local drug dealers. It felt good to be on the right side of justice for once in his life. Sidney traveled to Dallas along with Italian agents named Vincent (Vinny) Caesar, and Jim Ciano. Together they took down a dealer from Trinidad who ran a large international racket smuggling heroin and hot cars. Although he was playing on the opposite side now, Sidney still found the thrill of the hustle he had always craved when he was a gangster. It was strange. He was a "good guy" now, but he still pulled the same old gangster routine. This time it was in the name of the law.

Jim Ciano was a big-time undercover agent in Sidney's eyes. He always worked the biggest undercover deals and took down some of the biggest criminals. Sometimes he would even don the character of a mob boss to bust an underworld operation. The dark eyed Italian fit easily into the mobster stereotype. So, when Jim Ciano called Sidney and told him he was working on something big, Sidney readily agreed to help.

The new informant went to see the agent first thing the next morning. He passed all the security clearances and finally found himself seated in front of the illustrious Italian. Ciano explained the FBI and DEA had set up an informal taskforce together to bust up a huge drug ring, but they needed an informant to get some inside information. The job would be dangerous, but Sidney agreed to become their inside man.

The next day, Sidney mustered up every bit of his Chicago roots and once again donned the facade of the big time gangster. It felt good to slip back into his expensive suits and diamond rings. When he topped it off with a perfectly placed fedora, Sidney Heard felt like his old self again. He boldly sauntered into the drug lord's office pretending to be after one of the man's ex-employees. The thrill of the hustle was back.

While the secretary promised to get the big boss for him, Sidney casually wandered around the office. His keen eye lit upon a photograph of two massive cargo ships. He quickly took note of the names of the ships and waltzed back out the front door before the woman returned. Six months later Ciano's crew raided one of those ships and found a massive load of drugs. Sidney was already on the payroll, so he received a big pat on the back along with his standard pay.

Later, Sidney was introduced to an undercover agent nicknamed "Cowboy." Cowboy hailed from Albuquerque, New Mexico, and worked with another somewhat famous agent nicknamed "The Red-Headed Lady," Sidney never discovered her real name, but for some reason Sidney still has a strange affinity for redheads.

He used his gangster persona to set up a deal with a couple of drug dealers called the Cruz Brothers. When the deal went down, Cowboy busted the brothers and eventually another man the Albuquerque Police Department had been after for nearly twenty years. For security reasons his name will not be mentioned in this narrative.

Sidney would be paid anywhere from $1,500 to $2,500 for each FBI job. He spent a whopping total of 32 days in prison before being transferred to the small county jail. In the low security jailhouse, he was given access to a telephone and was assigned to work on various task forces. He set up deals for everything from stolen heavy equipment to hot cars, and even drugs. On some assignments, Sidney would be let out of jail to work the case. He would carry out other assignments from behind bars as merely an informant. One deal even had the incarcerated criminal purchasing hand grenades off the street on behalf of the government for $100 apiece.

One target of the law was a high-powered Mexican Diplomat. Big Juan had given Sidney his first load of cocaine years earlier. Juan had earned diplomatic immunity from the United States government. Unfortunately, this was also a great cover for Mr. Juan's cocaine business and his dealings with the Mexican Mafia. Sidney had done a great deal of business with Juan before his arrests. Juan had even shared meals with Sidney and his wife at their home in Amarillo. Juan had also seen the media news of Sidney's arrest on the Krugerrand scandal. He offered to set Sidney up in Mexico to avoid the heat, but Sidney didn't want to leave the U.S. and his family.

When the time came, Juan agreed to have dinner with Sidney and the undercover agents, knowing full well that Sidney was now an informant. Sidney didn't like the thought of tackling the Mexican Mafia or one of his only remaining allies, so during the meal he gave Juan a subtle signal to avoid the deal. Juan knew Sidney was under duress and didn't make the deal. The agents left evening without making any arrests, and Sidney still had an escape plan if he ever needed to skip the country.

During this time, Sidney was busy testifying in the Earl Sampson Trial.[41] *The Amarillo Globe /Times* reported on Friday, July 30, 1982, Sidney testified he had been offered a contract to kill a man. Hudson Moyer had asked Sidney to take the contract, and when he refused Moyer asked Sidney if any of his Chicago-based contacts would make the hit. During this testimony, Sidney also admitted he had been offered three other contracts, all which he refused.[42]

In 1977, a Mrs. Raines wanted Sidney to kill her husband; in 1975, Jody Roach asked him to knock off one of her tenants who was suing her; and Todd Chapman wanted an Amarillo businessman killed. Sidney refused them all. On one occasion, when Sidney was broke, he took the money offered to him, tripled it by gambling on the horse races, and then returned the money stating he couldn't find the target.

During this time, things started looking fishy out at the Pantex Nuclear Plant. Security had become too lax. For those of you who may not know, Pantex is plant where they assemble and disassemble nuclear weapons. The plant is located on a 16,000-acre site just north of Amarillo, Texas. It is managed by the United States Department of Energy. When several security breaches were discovered at one of America's most top-secret facilities, the FBI was called in to investigate the case. Sidney was brought in to work alongside agent Subbert. After the job was completed, four of the department's top employees were immediately fired. Nothing else can be said about this undercover assignment, but Sidney felt he had done his country a great service and it felt great.

After assisting in the delicate case at Pantex the Department of Energy sent an "eyes-only" letter of gratitude to the parole board on Sidney's behalf. This letter ended up shortening Sidney's stay inside the prison walls. Legally after a sentence is handed down it cannot be shortened. Due to the severity of Sidney's crimes, and the amount of money he stole, government policy stated he couldn't be released before three-and-a-half years. The policy didn't state, however, where Sidney had to serve his time.

At his parole hearing, Sidney arrived alongside two legal heavyweights: U.S. Chief Criminal prosecutor Shirley Lobel, and FBI agent Ron Jennings both spoke on behalf of the inmate. Sidney was granted parole after he served six months in a halfway house in Dallas, Texas. Of course, the halfway house was a definite step up from serving his time behind bars. Sidney was more than grateful to Lobel and Jennings for their assistance. Not only would Sidney enjoy more freedom in this facility, but he could also see his family more often.

In February 1984, Sidney testified against James C. Lane in his arson trial. On the witness stand, Sidney admitted he hired a man by the name of Marvin McFarlin to set Lane's duplex afire. Sidney testified he had been offered ten percent of the $30,000 insurance payoff for his efforts. However, McFarlin didn't do a good enough job and the duplex didn't completely burn. Lane was angry and McFarlin's fee was reduced to $2, 000. [43]

After deliberating for over two hours, the 251st State District court found J.C. Lane guilty of arson. [44] Sidney was smug when he heard the news. As far as Sidney was concerned, Lane deserved it for turning on him. He would have kept their secrets to his grave if Lane hadn't turned on Big Sid.

In October 1985, Lane appealed his case to the Supreme Court, in the U.S. v. Lane, 474 U.S. 438 case. On January 27, 1986, the Supreme Court also found Lane guilty of arson and refused to overturn Lane's conviction. [45] Sidney's testimony played a large part in the original conviction of James C. Lane and his testimony was again reviewed in the appeal. The revenge tasted sweet to the savage gangster turned informant.

In 1984, Sidney J. Heard performed a tremendous service to his country, but since he was a convict in the Federal Correctional Institution in Fort Worth at the time, the world wouldn't find out about it for over thirty years. Sidney helped to uncover a plot to assassinate President Reagan while he was working as an informant in the pen. At the time, Sidney was serving as a direct line of communication between the dark underworld and the then current U.S. Criminal Prosecutor Shirley Lobel. Sidney heard whispers inside the dank walls of the penitentiary. Someone was planning to send a homemade bomb to President Reagan when he visited Dallas.

A seemingly innocent letter came to a fellow inmate of Sidney's. It was from an ex-convict in Arkansas. The inmate noticed small pin-sized holes were punched through certain letters in the message. He showed the note to Sidney and asked the well-known gangster what it could mean. Everyone inside the pen knew Sidney was "connected," but no one knew how. With his gangster persona in place, no one would believe he was working for the federal prosecutor and the FBI.

Sidney immediately began to inquire into the legitimacy of the letter. Then when he began to put the letters together, they began to outline a plan to bomb the President. Sidney instantly called the office of Shirley Lobel. A car was sent for Sidney and he was quickly ushered into the federal prosecutor's office.

Sidney laid the coded message on the prosecutor's desk, and explained the code. Sidney was thanked for his service and sent back to his cell. A few hours later Secret Service Agents descended upon a specific car just inside the Arkansas state line. The driver was quickly arrested when homemade bombs were found in his car. America would never know how close they had come to losing another president.

The missing 1727 Stradivarius:

During his run with the FBI Sidney had the chance to purchase an extremely rare violin. The street dealer claimed it was the 1727 Stradivarius had been stolen from the Dallas Symphony Orchestra in 1985. If so, it was worth over a quarter of a million dollars. The underworld conman only wanted a measly $1,000 for it, but neither Sidney nor the FBI had anyone who could identify the piece as the original. Vincent "Vinny" Caesar couldn't verify the instrument's value either, so the deal was dropped. Little did Sidney know he could have been the last one to see the priceless instrument for over seventeen years.

In 2005, a retired DSO violinist saw a picture of the violin in a London magazine called *The Strad*. It was to be auctioned off by the Bonham Company. The musician anonymously phoned the orchestra officials. The London dealer quickly did some research and found it was indeed the same violin had gone missing nearly twenty years earlier. The instrument was restored and returned to the Orchestra. The famous violin reappeared on the Dallas stage in March, 2007.[48] No one ever knew the Chicago native had an opportunity to retrieve the instrument shortly after its disappearance.

Sidney's Release:

After his release, Sidney's parole officer dropped his compensation down to $1,000 per month. Sidney was not happy about the pay cut, but he was thrilled to be out from behind bars. The FBI knew the best way to catch a con is with another con, so keeping an ex-conman on their payroll was a strategic move. At this time the FBI was juggling several cases concerning local theft rings. Stolen cars and heavy equipment were flooding the black market. Sidney was placed directly in the center of the group as a buyer.

He would buy, sell, and even trade the stolen cars and equipment for the theft ring all the while the FBI was running surveillance. After they amassed enough evidence to go to trial a sting operation would be organized. The thieves would be arrested and Sidney would sometimes be called to the stand to testify on behalf of the authorities.

Sidney always seemed to fall back on his construction abilities when he had the opportunity, and this time around was no different. When the FBI operations would slow down, Sidney would run a small construction business on the side. In 1986, Sidney was working on a new Olive Garden restaurant building in Mesquite, Texas. He knew several other contractors were also working on the project. When it came time for the restaurant to open, the owner ran back to California without paying thirty of the local contractors. Sidney was only due $3,000, but the cut still made him furious.

The gangster paid a visit to the local officials and acquired a license to arrange a picket line. The plan was set, and a large group of Sidney's rough looking associates grabbed signs and formed a picket line in front of the local Italian restaurant. [Sidney was smart enough to make sure the owner wasn't a connected man before he went on this escapade.]

Within the first few weeks of opening the restaurant started losing money. No one wanted to eat at the new Italian restaurant with a bunch of mobster-looking thugs walking a picket line outside. It didn't take long for word to get back to California and miraculously everyone got paid. Sidney was glad to have his three thousand bucks, but he was even happier to help some friends. To top it all off, he had done it legally.

Early in 1988, Sidney began to dabble in cocaine again. Sidney had moved to Italy, Texas with his wife Suzanne in hopes of starting a new life. The couple made a pact to stop doing drugs together. She was running a small antique store, he was managing his construction businesses, and life seemed to be looking up.

At this point a big corporate construction job at the DeGolyer Estate in Dallas was up for grabs and Sidney placed his $99,999 bid in alongside all the big-time construction companies. To qualify the bids each company had to provide net worth statements. Sidney's Trim Tex statements, various assets of his and his business partners (aka mother-in-law) added up to 1.6 million dollars. The announcement was made over the radio and Sidney was ecstatic to hear he had won the bid. Unfortunately, the job fell through because of some technical legalities and no one ended up with the contract.

Sidney wasn't worried about the bid because he had secretly started selling drugs again behind Suzanne's back, and Sidney's pockets were always lined with cash. All the while Suzanne was trying to be a responsible parent; he was partying with two bisexual girls from Dallas and smoking cocaine. To make matters worse Suzanne had slowly changed from her high heels and short skirts to a more sensible tennis shoes and jeans type woman. Three kids and responsibility will do that, but her sex-addict husband wouldn't have any of it. If he'd been in his right mind maybe things would be different, but from his point of view their sex life was almost nonexistent and she wasn't into partying with cocaine anymore.

Finally, after eight years of marriage, Suzanne had had enough of Sidney's drug habits and filed for divorce. A short time later, Sidney was put through a routine drug screening. When the results came back positive for drug use, Sidney was deemed unusable by his current task force and promptly dismissed. Over the course of seven years, however, Sidney had prevented a loss of two and a half million dollars. Once again, drugs had stolen Sidney's dreams, so he tried his best to quit the terrible habit. He would be clean for a while, but the lifestyle always seemed to catch up with him.

Chapter 20: Trouble and Redemption

During the 1988 hurricane season, a beautiful woman named Diane Wigert blew into Sidney's troubled life. As fate would have it, the whirlwind relationship began while Hurricane Gilbert brewed just off the gulf coast. While most of Galveston's residents fled from the island off the coast of Texas, Sidney and a few other rogues gathered into a ship-like bar aptly named the Poop Deck. Whether it was grit, gall, or alcohol the rowdy crowd wasn't retreating from nature's fury.

Diane had run into Sidney and his crowd at another bar and followed them to the new location to ride out the storm. There while the wind howled outside, they spent their evening cozied up together in a booth, drinking beer and regaling each other with stories of their life-long adventures. Diane had dated many high profile, very wealthy men. She had even met the president of the United States on the arm of one of her wealthy financiers. Sidney listened to her stories and found it flattering she would be interested in a small time ex-gangster like him. He watched her tell her stories and thought about how much she looked like Cher. At time Sidney ran a local bar called The Castaways and after the storms passed Diane would drop by the place to hook up with him from time to time.

After months of romantic cat-and-mouse games, the couple ended up moving in together in a house on Tiki Island. Although he had lost one job with the task force, Sidney was still working undercover on other jobs and he was still being called to court to testify in a few cases at the time. When Sidney received a phone call from the Feds, he would simply tell Diane he had to leave on a business trip. She never seemed to mind too much, and more importantly she never asked too many questions.

The couple loved taking road trips together all over the U.S. and ended up taking a vacation in the Branson area of rural Missouri. They stayed at the Cedar Creek Lodge and spent their time seeing all the shows along the Branson strip and shopping along HWY 76. Diane was completely charmed by the rugged countryside. Sidney enjoyed wining and dining the beautiful woman wherever they happened to be.

When Sidney's parole finally ended in April 1989, he moved to Dallas and started working with the Federal Task force doing surveillance. It was a perfect job for him. He could use his "gangster persona" to get himself into all sorts of deals, and make good money from the government if he could keep away from the drugs.

The agency began cleaning up the small fish around Dallas and its surrounding areas. Sidney found he truly enjoyed being on the right side of the law. Looking back at those days, Sidney always regretted not getting into law enforcement at a younger age. It would be one of Sidney's many life-long regrets. In 1990, the task force was officially dissolved and Sidney moved to the rural Ozarks region of Missouri with his now steady girlfriend, Diane.

The couple purchased a large three-bedroom home on Talking Rocks Road just south of what is now called Branson West. It was a lovely home with a covered deck overlooking the beautiful waters of Table Rock Lake.

Before leaving Texas, Sidney had purchased a concession stand/trailer and converted it into a mobile BBQ stand. He settled his little business on a busy street corner in Branson, Missouri, during the peak of tourist season. For a several months, Sidney served all sorts of travelers who were on their way to and from the Branson shows. Sidney even met a few of the country music legends during the process. Everyone stopped by loved Sidney's BBQ and he was making good money.

After the summer tourist season ended, Diane decided to travel to Burlington, Iowa, to visit her parents over the

Christmas holidays. Sidney had gone with her once before, but decided to stay in Branson and run the BBQ stand this time around. The tourist town usually saw a big boom around the holidays and Sidney hoped to cash in on the shopping crowd. He called her a few days later to check in. Her mother answered the phone. When Sidney asked to speak with Diane her mother yelled Big John was on the line again and wanted to talk to her. Sidney's heart sank. Big John was one of the big-money sugar daddies Diane had dated once before.

Broken hearted, Sidney immediately packed up and headed back to Texas in hopes of finding another undercover job. To this day, Sidney claims Diane was the "one who got away." It took him an entire two weeks to get over her. To most people this would sound pathetic, but in his game women were a dime a dozen and he never got too close to any of them. Two weeks was a new record for the promiscuous ladies' man.

The Texas Department of Public Safety offered Sidney a job breaking up an illegal cigarette ring. All cigarettes in Texas, at the time, were required to have a tax ID stamped on the package. Of course, there is always someone eager to make an illegal buck, so the Iranian business owners throughout Texas found a way to smuggle illegal contraband through their stores. Sidney was supposed to step in and become an undercover distributor, in hopes of catching the smugglers in the act. This job fell through, however, when the officials couldn't get enough of the cigarettes rounded up for the job. This left Sidney high and dry.

When Jim Ciano had recently retired from the F.B.I. and had started his own business. When he found out Sidney was out of work, he offered to set him up in his investigation company. Jim and Sidney had worked together years earlier. With all his experience with the FBI, Jim chose to put his skills to good use as a private investigator of sorts. Any time someone had reason to suspect embezzlement within a large company, Jim would send in one of his employees to apply for a job. After they were hired, they could be the eyes and ears for Jim's private investigation firm.

While Sidney was waiting to get hooked up on a job with Ciano, he was offered a job with the D.E.A. for $800 a week. Accepting the D.E.A.'s offer would prove out to be another terrible mistake. At this point, Sidney had cleaned up again, and was trying to start over. If he would have waited, he could have saved himself a lot of heartache, but no one can see into the future. Unfortunately, Sidney found it nearly impossible to work as an undercover agent among the drug lords without getting messed up in drugs himself. The DEA was targeting the Garcia and the Rodriquez Families who were drug dealers. Sidney already had connections with both of them, so it was supposedly an easy job to fill. Finally, an overabundance of drugs, cheap prostitutes, and money broke the ex-criminal. He began to play both sides of the fence, and sometimes the middle. The lethal combination would soon lead to his demise.

Sidney soon found it harder and harder to work as an undercover agent with the D.E.A. without taking the drugs. When a dealer wanted to find out if someone was a cop, he would simply send a couple prostitutes to the room with a load of cocaine. If the man didn't smoke the powder and hook up with the girls, he would know you were a cop. Sidney found the temptation too much to handle, and finally the man broke under the pressure.

At first he just would just do enough drugs to get in, but being an ex-drug addict, he found himself doing drugs more and more often. Of course, Sidney had no problem taking the prostitutes. He would gather intel for the DEA all the while he would be taking cocaine and distributing it himself. He'd give information about rival dealers, but wouldn't turn in his own suppliers. Eventually he would be caught.

Finding God in the Michael Unit:

This time when Sidney was arrested he was sent to serve his time at the Mark W. Michael Unit just south of Tennessee Colony, Texas. A local author once quoted the Michael Unit as the "meanest lockup in the entire state of Texas." Here the fantasy world Sidney had spent nearly fifty years creating suddenly crumbled down on top of him. At the age of fifty, Sidney no longer thought he could con his way out of his predicament. His scheming drug-fogged mind had reached the end of the road and he lay on his cot behind bars once again. All the money he had amassed had been smoked up in cocaine. All the trophy women had flown the coop, and he was left alone to face the ugly truth.

Sidney James Heard, the quick witted professional criminal, was nothing more than an out of control drug user without a hope of change. With all hope lost, the still small voice had nagged at the back of his mind since childhood now became the only voice worth listening to. All alone in his cell, Sidney finally turned to God for forgiveness and help. No angels sang in his cold jail cell. No lightening flashed. No thunder boomed, but the angels in Heaven rejoiced as the hardened criminal knelt beside his cot and finally asked for forgiveness and for Christ to come into his heart and life. Some might scoff at this thinking it was just another con, but a change came into Sidney's entire outlook on life.

As Mahatma Gandhi once said, "Prayer is not asking. It is a longing of the soul. It is daily admission of one's weakness. It is better in prayer to have a heart without words than words without a heart."

The Michael Unit was a maximum-security prison and visitors were strictly monitored, but for the first time in the prison's history they decided to host a "Family Day." The prison gathered a group of inmate volunteers and preparations began. A huge tent was set up on the prison yard and BBQ grills were brought in. The event was big enough the Kairos Prison Ministry sent several volunteers to help organize the event. Sidney was quite the grill master, so he was assigned as cook. Tom Perdue and his wife worked with Kairos and helped with the condiments for the hotdogs. This seemingly inconsequential event would produce one of Sidney's lifelong friends. Tom Perdue would become the best friend the ex-gangster could ever ask for.

Sidney would spend seven more years behind bars at the Michael Unit, but he would spend them working with the Kairos Prison ministry. [51] Kairos is a Greek word meaning "God's special time." The Christian-based, non-denominational prison ministry focuses on teaching inmates about Jesus' forgiveness and His power to change lives. The program begins with a three-day weekend workshop to teach the inmates about God and to give them hope change is possible. Hope is the key word here. Inmates without hope are less functional within the system. They tend to be more violent and less manageable. A lack of hope also hinders the inmate's capability of rehabilitation. Both prison officials and the Kairos organization work together to change the lives of thousands of inmates a year.

The Kairos chaplain, along with scores of free-world volunteers, visits the prison to select forty-two inmates for the retreat. During the retreat, the inmates would be seated at tables in specific racially integrated groups. Every table had to have men of every race to teach the inmates about God's love for everyone. After teaching and proclaiming God's word to the incarcerated men, the chaplain would give them all a chance to accept Christ into their hearts and lives. There are counseling services and literature offered to the inmates to further their spiritual growth.

Through the Kairos Prison Ministry, Sidney learned about the God he had been avoiding all his life. At his table was a free world volunteer by the name of Jim Warren. The two men shared a name, (James) but soon shared much more. Jim, and his wife Priscilla would become some of

Sidney's closest friends. Jim continued to write to Sidney on a regular basis after the weekend retreat ended. This small gesture meant the world to the softening criminal.

Kairos not only educated the inmates, it gave them a break from the mundane prison life. But it meant more for Sidney Heard. He finally felt like he had a purpose in his life and the chaos of jumping from crime to crime was a thing of the past. He truly wanted a better life and felt now he had the chance to find peace. Peace was new to him.

While Sidney was working with Kairos in the Michael Unit he met the famous Huston Oilers player Mike Barber. Barber had retired from professional sports and had started his own prison ministry. Sidney would help set up the massive tents for the revival services, help prepare meals, and anything else he could do to help with the events. Gone were the days of greed, hate, and malice. Now Sidney enjoyed helping to spread the gospel to his fellow inmates in any way possible. Barber came several times during Sidney's stay and he would always bring along someone to sing. One time the sister of the famous Gatlin Brothers sang at one of Mike's events.

One must point out at this point in the narrative, although Sidney was now a born-again Christian, he was nowhere near perfect. People tend to believe once you get saved, all the evils of your past will immediately disappear. In reality, every believer has a transitioning period. Some have a longer one than others, but everyone must go through it. And, whether anyone wants to admit it or not, everyone falls off the wagon from time to time. The important thing is to repent and to climb back on. This is a hard lesson Sidney would have to learn, but for now life seemed peaceful and good.

Chapter 21: Calvary Commission

On July 7, 1999, Sidney was finally paroled to Calvary Commission in Lindale, Texas.[51] Calvary Commission is a Christian mission organization located on 186-acre ranch. It offers inmates a chance to learn about God's Word and to find His purpose for their lives. Joe and Charlotte Fauss ran the Christian missionary school, as well as the nearby Hope Christian Fellowship church. In Lindale, the fifty-seven-year-old reformed gangster would attend missionary school at night. He would graduate a year later with an Associate Degree in biblical studies. During the day, as part of the missionary school's rules, Sidney was required to work on the mission ranch and to study the Bible. Bible classes were every morning from nine to noon. The residents were also required to read a religious book and write a book report every week. Sidney enjoyed learning about all the famous missionaries and preachers of days long ago. Seminars were held periodically and speakers would come in from all over the U.S. to give presentations.

Some of the men at the ranch grew tired of the rules and eventually leave the mission grounds, but Sidney thrived in the regimented environment. In a way, the ranch was Sidney's safe haven from the world of sex, drugs and greed. At Calvary Commission, he was separated from worldly influences and could completely focus on his desire to become a missionary.

Three weeks after his release from the Michael Unit, a group of Kairos members approached Joe Fauss and asked his permission to take Sidney off the mission property so he could give his testimony at a local church to help raise money for their Kairos organization. Of course, Joe readily agreed. Sidney gave his testimony and started out the speech with a joke his Sunday School teacher had told him back when he was only a child attending an Evangelical Lutheran church in Chicago.

"What Biblical person killed one fourth of the world's population?" Sidney asked the crowd of so-called "bible scholars," Sunday School teachers, and Christians of all sorts. When no one replied, Sidney coolly responded to his own question with, "Cain killed Abel, and was one fourth of the entire population back then."

That little joke broke the ice and Sidney went on to relate how he got into a life of crime and how God saved him on his fiftieth birthday in the Michael Unit. Sidney would continue to give his testimony at local churches and would even return to the Michael Unit to preach the gospel of God's love to the inmates. He loved to share his story with the young people he met, encouraging them to avoid the criminal lifestyle. He felt like if he could keep one teenager from trying drugs, or keep one person from turning to a life of crime his journey would be worth it.

Christmas, 1999 Mission trip to Mexico:

As summer ended and winter was quickly approaching, Calvary Commission became abuzz with activity. Everyone was preparing for the big Christmas Outreach mission to Mexico. Sidney didn't dream he could leave the country since he was on parole, but Calvary Commission had a lot of pull, and Sidney was approved to leave the country with the group. Sidney crossed the border into Mexico from Hidalgo, Texas. Calvary Commission carried 50-lb sacks of rice and beans across the border for the hungry Mexicans.

The group traveled to Reynosa, Mexico, and stayed in a local hotel. As the ex-con sat in his hotel room, he began to reflect over the past couple decades. He smiled as he realized the irony of his current situation. Twenty years earlier he was sitting in the Caballero Hotel on the other side of this same border waiting for his first shipment of smuggled cocaine to arrive. Now he was a born-again Christian smuggling food across the border into Mexico to feed the hungry. He chuckled and took a moment to thank God for his blessings before falling into a peaceful sleep.

"Father, you sure have a sense of humor," Sidney thought.

Calvary Commission supported the Josiah and Bethany Children's Home. They would bring gifts for the children; feed the hungry kids rice and beans, and even had a door-to-door ministry. Sidney was amazed by the entire experience and the support the missionary team received from all over the U.S.

Sidney and his interpreter went on a door-to-door ministry one afternoon. The former Chicago gangster was astonished by the local living conditions. Small adobe houses lined the dirt lanes. Each one had a fenced yard, but the fences were made from various wood scraps. Most fences were made from disassembled shipping pallets.

Sidney was invited into one such dwelling and was in for a big surprise. The small one room house had dirt floors with chickens running around inside the home. A couple tiny beds lined one wall. A small wooden dresser stood nearby, but to Sidney's amazement in the corner of the room sat a color-television with a remote control. Sidney shared the good news of Jesus Christ with the family through his interpreter, and soon returned to the mission.

Before the team headed back to the U.S., they visited a local prison to preach the gospel to the captives held there. The ex-convict was invited to tag along. Sidney found the prison to be quite peculiar. The guards stayed outside the prison walls. The only time they entered the compound was to stop a riot. Guards were dressed in black, so visitors weren't allowed to wear the color. Visitors were not allowed to bring any money or weapons, and they were discouraged from wearing any type of expensive jewelry. If an inmate seen what looked like an expensive watch, you might be killed before the guards could come to your rescue.

The inside of the prison was like a small village; cells were more like small houses. Inmates moved about as they pleased. If you were an American inmate however, you had to beg for food and essentials unless you had money. The prison even had a small church in the yard. The mission team had to be escorted through the prison camp by a group of Hispanics so the inmates wouldn't try to rob the Americans. The images Sidney had seen while in Mexico would be burned into his memory for the rest of his life.

Working with Kairos from the Outside:

By law, former inmates cannot re-enter a prison as a guest for at least two years after their release. After this time, had expired, Sidney, along with the Kairos leaders, worked through the legal red tape to obtain entrance for Sidney with permission to testify in the Michael Unit. The speech was to be held in the prison gymnasium. Guests were not allowed to bring anything into the prison except a photo ID to verify the person's identity. Then the group would line up in alphabetical order to go through the receiving line.

When Sidney entered, the guard ushered him to the front of the line and told him to go through first. The gym was filled with nearly three hundred inmates, many of which Sidney knew personally. As Sidney's feet strode across the hardwood floor, the crowd rose to their feet and applauded the ex-convict. It was a high moment in the roller coaster ride of Sidney's crazy life. Unfortunately, the highs wouldn't last forever. At the moment though Sidney Heard couldn't imagine a greater feeling than he was enjoying right now.

Sidney told the crowded room how the Lord had saved him from a life of crime, drugs, and debauchery. He went on to explain how an inmate might have an identity inside the prison walls, but persona is lost on the outside. Being thrown to the masses as a "nobody" is one of the driving factors cause repeat offenders to re-enter the prison society. Sidney explained to his former fellow inmates although their prison identity is lost, one could find a new identity in Christ Jesus. When his sermon was finished, he walked off the floor to another round of thunderous applause.

Sidney worked his way through the Kairos organization starting as a table leader. Eventually he worked his way all the way up the ladder and became a volunteer chaplain. As such, he could go in and out of the Henderson Unit and the Michael Unit regularly. As a volunteer chaplain, Sidney was given the opportunity to help organize a Kairos retreat for the inmates. It was such an honor for the ex-con, because he knew how much these retreats helped him when he was in the Michael Unit. Every detail of the event was special to the reformed gangster, and he made sure those details were perfect.

One Thursday morning, Sidney and the Kairos team descended upon the Michael Unit with vigor. They spent the next few hours setting up tables, sound systems, and organizing a small army of volunteers. The large tent was erected, and things started falling into place. Sidney enjoyed seeing the guards and inmates he knew so well. It was almost like a homecoming for the ex-con. He was even allowed to visit the Maintenance department where he had worked as a clerk. His bosses were glad to see him again, and were proud of what he had become through his relationship with Kairos. The group left the prison for lunch with plans to return in a couple of hours. However, late afternoon when they returned, Sidney was asked to step out of the line by a guard.

Sidney watched as each of his Kairos teammates showed their IDs and were admitted into the facility. He sat there wondering what he had done to be banned from reentering the prison he had just visited morning. The captain of the guard came over to the former inmate and shook his hand politely. Sidney remembered him well. It felt strange to be shaking his hand as a free man. The guard explained to Sidney the warden, ironically named Castro, decided not to let the ex-con in any more. When Sidney asked why, the guard shrugged and said the warden openly despised Kairos.

Castro had wanted to ban them for years, but the non-denominational organization was so powerful he couldn't stop them from coming in and preaching the gospel. The warden had previously tried to lock out the Kairos organization, so the Kairos officials went over his head and visited the director of prisons. The director so happened to be a Christian and ordered the warden to allow Kairos to carry on. Frustrated Castro did the next best thing; he used his power to ban Sidney from the premises in hopes of stopping the gospel from being spread. Whether the warden was a believer or not, the moral message Sidney was sharing wasn't causing any harm. It gave the prisoners hope of a better life and provided a moral compass to live by.

Dejected and somewhat confused Sidney called the Kairos official, who had approved his promotion in the first place, and explained what had happened. The official was clearly upset, but she informed Sidney she didn't have the authority to do anything about it. Kairos Prison Ministry was required to sign a contract with the Michael Unit before they could enter the facility. This contract stated the warden has the right to keep anyone out the prison he or she chooses. Unfortunately, the warden had complete control over the prison and whatever he said was to be taken as the law. Kairos could contest the rule, but it would only result in the entire organization being banned from the premises. Castro had them over a barrel and he knew it. Sidney would have to bow out for the good of the inmates. He would never be able to re-enter the facility.

Disappointment grew into bitterness, and eventually Sidney chose to walk away from the Kairos organization completely. He would regret the decision years later, but at the moment he couldn't deal with the rejection. Rejection was an entirely new concept for the reformed gangster. On the street no one dared to reject Big Sid, but now he felt betrayed by the people he had trusted the most. Eventually Sidney would learn Christians are just humans too; they make mistakes. But now Sidney began to wonder if he could trust his old crowd of gangsters more than his Christian companions.

Shamgar Missionary Ranch, Tyler, Texas:[52]

In the summer of 2000, Sidney was invited to join the Lobel family for their annual Fourth of July celebration. Sidney was happy to go. He and his now ex-wife Suzanne had been friends with the U.S. District Attorney and her family before and even after Sidney's arrests.

Sidney was a great grill-master and his forte was barbecue. So, when they asked him if he wanted to grill he readily agreed. He enjoyed seeing all the Lobel children now they were grown. He had barbecued for them when they were little, when he was still married to Suzanne. Sidney enjoyed renewing old acquaintances for the weekend, barbecuing for them, and watching the fireworks on the lake. It was a quiet and serene point in his life when he thoroughly enjoyed his freedom, and was thankful for the peace in his soul.

After Sidney graduated from Calvary Commission in August of 2000, he moved to the Shamgar ranch in Tyler, Texas. Sidney had done some construction work for Sister Betty while he was still working on his Biblical studies at Calvary Commission. When she found he needed a place to stay she offered him the large cabin at the back of the property for $100 a month if he also kept up the lawn. The one-room cabin had a TV with only one channel, but Sidney didn't mind. He had gotten used to not having contact with the outside world at Calvary Commission. The commission didn't allow any television or newspapers at all. The entire experience was limited to working on the ranch, studying the Bible, or going to church.

Sidney enjoyed the solitude of the cabin and spent his time praying and reading his Bible. He started a small construction company and built many buildings on the ranch and elsewhere. He stayed there for about a year.

In 2003, Sidney was asked to join the speaker's lineup for the United Methodist Church's Annual conference. The ex-gangster would go on to give his testimony in churches all across the great state of Texas. It seemed as if nothing could hold him back from his ministry. It would be wonderful if the story could end here, but unfortunately life doesn't always end on a good note. Although Sidney had become an avid student of theology, he would still have to learn one very difficult lesson. Religion is not the same as a relationship. Growing up on the streets of Chicago Sidney learned your word is your life and if you don't keep it you die. Unfortunately, this is not always the case everywhere else and sometimes the most religious person on the planet can also turn out to be cruel and hardhearted. There's a vast difference between religion and a relationship with one's Creator.

Chapter 22: Religion vs. Relationship

During his time with Kairos, Sidney worked alongside another Kairos member named Armando Reis. Armando invited Sidney to join his family while they put on a Kairos event at a church in Arlington, Texas. On Easter Sunday, Sidney joined Armando and his family at their local church and ended up sitting next to a woman we'll call Pam. He had seen her before at a few other Kairos events, and the two began to hit it off. She was a registered nurse, and worked at a local Tom Thumb grocery store as an assistant pharmacist.

Pam had been recently separated from her supposedly maniac husband, but she didn't have the money for a divorce. Again Sidney had found a so-called damsel in distress. Sidney had plenty of experience in this area, so he took her to the local library and showed her how to file the paperwork for a cheap divorce. She would later use this knowledge against him.

For the moment, however, the two hit it off and soon Pam invited him to go on a trip to Galveston with her. The only requirement was he had to check into his own hotel room. Not only was it her requirement, but it was also required by the Kairos organization. Usually the ex-gangster just took what he wanted, but now with a changed heart he politely followed the rules. This too was a sweeping change for the once promiscuous gangster. Sidney rented an SUV, paid for separate hotel rooms, and got permission from the Kairos organization to tag along. This would be the first of many road trips the couple would take together over the course of the next few months.

All the while, Pam was trying to decide where she wanted to work. She had an opportunity to work at a mission in Santa Fe, and the couple traveled out there to see the place. While they were traveling, she heard of a monastery in Chicago needed a nurse. So, she put all her belongings in a storage unit in Tyler, Texas, and asked Sidney to keep all her bills paid while she was gone. She was gone for two weeks and decided to return to Texas and to Sidney. Of course he was delighted.

At the time, Sidney was living in the cabin on the Shamgar Missionary Ranch. Shacking-up was not allowed at the ranch, so Pam stayed with a friend for the time being. Sister Betty and Pam got along well, but the highly religious woman wouldn't allow Sidney to have a female house guest overnight.

"She must be out by 9 pm," Sister Betty informed the somewhat surprised ex-convict. He didn't mind though. Betty had a motherly way about her. Sidney agreed to have Miss Pam out before his curfew.

Right down the street from the ranch Sidney noticed a house for sale. He took Pam out to look at the place and she fell in love with it. The house was a three-bedroom home nestled amongst ten acres. They impulsively decided to get married and buy the place. Everything seemed to be going in the right direction for the newly reformed gangster. He had a job, a degree, and soon would have a Christian wife.

The couple's wedding was held at Calvary Commission. The event was a huge affair. Former inmates from the Michael Unit came to see Sidney take the plunge, and fellow Kairos people flooded the place. Pam's family came from all four corners of the United States. Happiness abounded at the little church day—but it would be short-lived. If Sidney could have had the slightest inkling of his future with Pam, he would have hit the road, running for his life.

Sidney had started up a little construction company, and since his new wife was a nurse, he figured life would be easy. Unfortunately, Pam's mental and emotional state was not so simple. She hopped and skipped between jobs like a jackrabbit on steroids. She started out as a RN for a nursing home, but promptly quit when they asked her to work a double shift. Pam decided to volunteer to help handicapped children for a scant salary in hopes of eventually landing the head nurse's job. This would never happen because Pam couldn't seem to stick with anything long enough to find success.

Sidney, meanwhile, took care of the couple's finances. He never understood why Pam couldn't make it on a job somewhere. She had a musical degree from a prestigious school, so she decided to teach music to a group of Seventh Day Adventists. Three times a week she volunteered at an Episcopalian hospital. Sunday mornings she would sing in a local Lutheran choir. Sometimes she would join her husband at Hope Christian Fellowship Church at the Calvary Commission Missionary ranch.

To the outside world their life seemed to be going well, but at home things were quickly falling apart. The only time the couple seemed to enjoy being together was when they were traveling, so when Calvary Commission's Christmas outreach to Mexico came around they signed up to go. This time Sidney didn't travel with the group. He rented a car and the couple drove down alone. They took the scenic route and enjoyed the view along the way. It seemed to be the only way Sidney could make his wife happy, and for the first time in his life he genuinely wanted to make his wife happy.

The couple stayed in a hotel separate from the mission team, but traveled along with them on their daily outreach missions. This time the mission team visited what Sidney labeled as a "trash dump colony."

Sidney was shocked at the living conditions of the people living amid the garbage. The dump was larger than a major U.S. city and people had erected makeshift homes throughout the entire site. Their houses lacked electricity and running water, and the smell was atrocious. The people dug through the mountains of trash in hopes of finding scrap metal to sell for a meager profit. The locals raised pigs and fed them scrap food from out of the dump. (It was at this point Sidney decided to never eat pork from Mexico again.) The couple enjoyed the mission trip and their time there, but Sidney knew all the old problems would still be waiting for them when they returned home.

Over the course of a year, Pam had completely succeeded in avoiding intimacy with her husband, with only two exceptions. When Sidney let this slip to one of his friends at a Kairos meeting, his best friend Tom Perdue paid to send the couple to marriage counseling. When the counselor took Sidney's side, Pam refused to return for further sessions. She saw no problem with running all over God's creation doing her own thing with Sidney's money, and leaving him high and dry. She liked to gamble on the weekends without him, and frankly seemed to enjoy the company of her several cats more than her husband. Whatever her reasons for marrying the reformed gangster they seemed to have completely diminished by this point.

After months of his wife sleeping on the couch, with her cats mind you, Sidney finally had enough. He packed a bag of clothes along with his Bible and called a friend for a ride to start his trip. His own car happened to be in the shop awaiting repairs. He hitchhiked the rest of the way to Galveston, Texas. Once he reached Galveston, he called a few old friends who wired him enough money for bus fare.

After walking, hitchhiking, and bus riding for days, Sidney finally made his way back to Tyler, Texas. His friend Tom Perdue picked him up at the bus depot, and took him to Jim and Priscilla Warren's house. Sidney had built them a boathouse right after being released from prison, and had spent many months doing odd jobs for the couple as he stayed with them. Jim gladly took his old friend under their roof and gave him a place to stay. They had a small mobile home on the back of their property. This would provide Sidney with a little bit of privacy.

Pam quickly filed for divorce and tried to pull the ex-con-card on Sidney. She wouldn't let him have anything from the house, and tried to take him for everything else he had. Of course, it was not much at the time, but she wanted everything.

Sidney finally had to make a trip down to the police station. The officer informed him he had the right to get his personal belongings, and she couldn't keep them from him just because he happened to still be on parole. Sidney returned to his own home with a police escort, just to grab a few more clothes and some personal affects. It was probably the only time a gangster was given a police escort to any place besides prison.

The divorce was the straw finally broke Sidney. In a fit of despair, he went out and found a cocaine dealer and some girls. Over the course of a weekend he ended up sleeping with seven what he called "crack whores" and had blown $700 on the white powder. It was the beginning of a very low point in Sidney's life would span three years.

Through the course of a nasty divorce, Sidney discovered the truth. He had married an unstable woman with a massive amount of debt. She hadn't paid payments on her huge student loans in years and now the government had placed a $55,000 lien on their home. To make matters worse, Sidney wouldn't discover this fact until he went to file for his income taxes. No one knows for sure, but it seems like this may have been the motive for marriage. Who knows?

This news sent the struggling drug addict in a downward spiral. For a while with his sharp wit Sidney managed to keep his drug habit somewhat under wraps. He would plan his highs and lows so he could take his scheduled tests and come out clean. One man knew what was going on, but he never judged Sidney. It didn't matter how much money he asked for, or where he had to pick him up, Tom would always be there for Sidney. One day Sidney was high and trying to choose between three women when the dealer came running in.

"Look man there's a guy with a gun out here says he won't leave until he talks to you," the man reported to the dazed drug addict.

Sidney lumbered out front to find Tom there with a gun in his belt waiting for him. He tried to talk the half-smashed man into coming with him, but Sidney would have none of it. Of course, Tom never gave up and the next Sunday he made sure Sidney was in church with him. When he was clean, Sidney honestly tried to stay way and he was truly grateful for his friend. Drugs were Sidney's downfall, but Tom Perdue was his saving grace. Sidney and Pam's divorce was finalized in December of 2004, but the damage was already done.

Several months later Sidney received a phone call from a friend. He said Pam had converted to the Islamic faith. Sidney wondered how long change would last. She had been involved in every religion known to man while he knew her. It was because of her and a few others Sidney learned another important life lesson: not everyone who claims to be a Christian is a true Christian. There is a major difference between "religion" and an honest relationship with a higher power. Unfortunately, Sidney had to learn this lesson the hard way. Some people would like to judge Sidney for his next course of action, but remember what Jesus said to the harlot's accusers: *"He is without sin can cast the first stone."*

There were moments of clarity when Sidney would wake up from his drug induced nightmare and try to clean up. He would make a large amount of money and then turn around and smoke it up in a weekend. He was tired of the life and decided to take Tom's advice and start Narcotic's Anonymous.

It was a cold rainy night, but Sidney was determined to start over and arrived thirty minutes early for the meeting. A beautiful girl in a raincoat approached the car and tapped on the window asking if she could get in out of the rain. Sidney agreed and tried not to stare at the girl. She looked like she had just walked off the cover of a Playboy magazine. When she asked if she could smoke in his car, Sidney said sure thinking she was referring to cigarettes.

To his surprise she lit up a crack pipe. He asked her why she even went to N.A. Meetings. Her reply surprised him even more. She met her cocaine dealer every week in the meetings. Sidney finally told her goodbye after a long weekend of partying, sex and cocaine. If they ran out of money he would drive her to a strip club, she would dance for a couple hours, then they'd be back at the dealer's house. Sidney never went to another N.A. meeting.

A gangster's broken heart:

In 2005, Sidney spent his time working odd jobs for Jim and Priscilla. They worked for a local oil company and

Sidney made a great "gopher" for them. Finally, Sidney got an official job researching genealogies for the company. He enjoyed researching old wills and finding the graves of lost loved ones. He was making good money and would travel all over the state doing research.

Cocaine and prostitutes quickly overtook his life however. He would work a few days and party until his money was gone. It didn't seem to matter what town he was "working" in drugs seemed to gravitate to him. Days would blur into one giant crack binge.

Honestly, this chapter is extremely hard for me to write. I asked Sidney why many times during our interviews. He never had a good reply. It seems like such a waste to watch such a sharp mind be burned up with cocaine, but as a biographer I am bound to tell the story like it is and that's what I've endeavored to do. As painful as it is, I must show the highs and the lows of the life of Sidney James Heard.

During this time of partying, he suddenly started having terrible pain in his chest and arm. After the second day of pain he decided to go to the local hospital and get checked out.

After the usual battery of tests, Sidney was informed he had suffered through three heart attacks, and he would need stints put into his heart. When the doctors started to put in the stints they realized it wouldn't be possible. His heart was far worse than they had anticipated. Sidney had one heart valve totally blocked, one had a 95-percent blockage, another had a 90-percent blockage, and a fourth valve was blocked at 85-percent. Sidney would have to undergo open-heart surgery immediately.

At this point Sidney had a known prostitute living with him. His probation officer had demanded Sidney kick her out. She had a record and just the act of living with him could violate his parole, but he never made her move. Christie was supposed to pick him up from the hospital several days after his surgery, but instead she took his truck and crashed at a crack house for a few days. Without any other option, the recovering heart patient called the one man in Texas he could trust to always pick him up when he was down; Tom Perdue. Sure enough good old Tom showed up and drove him home.

Sidney was required to undergo periodic drug testing as part of his parole agreement. Right after his heart surgery, Sidney's test came back positive for drugs. He tried to con his way out if it claiming the drugs the hospital gave him was what showed up on the tests, but the parole officials knew better and it wasn't his first dirty U.A. On November 10, 2005 Sidney was called in to check with his parole officer. He was expecting some sort of reprimand, but instead he was arrested and checked into a ninety-day drug rehab facility behind bars. He was still bandaged up from his heart surgeries when he entered the facility. Once again the not-so-illustrious gangster from Chicago found himself behind bars. This time he was a sixty-three-year-old drug addict recovering from heart surgery. It was a far cry from the Bible toting fifty-six-year-old had preached the gospel to the lost in Mexico.

Sidney would be behind bars through the Thanksgiving, Christmas, and New Year's holidays. In January of 2006, the weary inmate was once again awarded his freedom. I wish I could report his life changed afterward, but after his ninety-day stint in the local jail Sidney's life of debauchery continued. He bounced between odd jobs, drugs, and women constantly.

At one point Sidney was flying down the back roads to avoid the cops and stopped to pick up a beautiful blond German woman. He said she was dressed in the perfect little "Heidi" type outfit complete with pigtails. When she got in his car he began to freak out as he noticed her shrinking and then finally disappearing completely. After his Heidi hallucination Sidney decided he might be a little too high to drive. He pulled into a friend's driveway and spent the next few hours sitting on the porch with him.

Finally, Sidney commented about the large amount of traffic in this out of the way location.

"What? There hasn't been a single car for over an hour," came the reply. Sidney was definitely wasted.

October, 2007 was a turning point for the sixty-five-year-old. After a non-stop party for the two weeks surrounding his birthday his gray eyes finally fluttered open and his mind was uncommonly clear. With the first lucid thought he'd had in three years Sidney looked around at trailer house and his two women and thought, *"What in the heck am I doing?"*

Before his divorce he was a millionaire, now he was just an old man with no hope of breaking his drug addiction. He was living with two prostitutes and one wasn't even his. He was just looking out for her because her boyfriend (one of Sidney's cocaine dealers) had been sent to prison. Sickened by his life he decided it was time for a drastic change.

In his moment of clarity, he realized he couldn't stay in Texas and hope to pull out of this. Without any thought of consequences Sidney left his house and all his earthly belongings to the girls. Desperate for a change in scenery and a fresh start, Sidney packed a bag and headed to the bus depot. He bought a one-way ticket to Springfield, Missouri and left his drugs, his women, and his lifestyle behind him. He hoped and prayed a new life would be waiting for him in the Midwest.

It was a cold rainy day when he stepped off the Greyhound bus in Springfield. The bus station wasn't where he remembered it from his visit nearly twenty years earlier. This left him stranded a few miles from the Victory Mission. He walked downtown and finally arrived at the mission. After showing his Texas ID he checked into their facility using his middle name; James Heard. He was given free room and board for thirty days. The only requirements were to help with the chores, and to attend the mission's meetings. This sounded great to the weary traveler.

The mission offered free all you can eat buffet-style meals. The standard cafeteria food looked like heaven to the emaciated drug addict. Sidney hadn't eaten in days, and hadn't eaten regularly in three years. Life was all about working long hours to buy more cocaine and sex. There was no time or money for things like food.

A local homeless man from the mission helped Sidney get his affairs in order. He helped him get his Social Security check transferred to Missouri, helped him sign up for a post office box, and even showed him how to save on a bus pass using his Medicare card. Sidney was more than grateful for the assistance. He was offered drugs a few times and each time he would reply, "If I wanted drugs I'd go back to Texas where the good drugs are." It was just a stupid line, but it kept the dealers at bay.

James, as he was now known, knew he would need to find a job. He waited for a week before he went looking to make sure the drugs were completely out of his system in case the business required a drug screening.

Sidney's first job was on the cooking side of Willow Brook Farms. His job was to cook the rotisserie chicken. His coworkers bet he wouldn't last a day in the cold damp factory. They were wrong. After a few days, they began betting he wouldn't last a month. He worked in the harsh factory conditions for nearly five months before moving on to a better job.

Although his great speaking career was over, Sidney used his motivational skills to help the homeless men around him. With an encouraging word from Sidney every man he shared a bunkhouse with at the Victory Mission found a job. It was not the mighty missionary work he had hoped for, but Sidney was thankful to have the chance to help those around him. Once again the hardened criminal began to feel the precious peace he had so foolishly forfeited years earlier.

After a few short-term jobs, Sidney landed a job working as a telemarketer. It was a befitting job for an ex-con man. As always, Sidney keeps busy and to his credit he still works a full-time job. At the time of this writing he is seventy-three and he still works five days a week. One could argue at this point America would be a better place if everyone in this country had Sidney James Heard's work ethic. Our economy should would benefit for sure.

The Gangster & the Preacher's Daughter:

In 2010, Sidney sought out a local author to write his biography. I happened to be the president of a local writer's guild and his project was referred to me through one of the members. After speaking to the illustrious mumbling gangster on the phone for over an hour I finally agreed to a meeting. Little did I know this small-town preacher's kid was in for the ride of a lifetime.

At last the time had come. Calming my nerves, I arrived twenty minutes before the scheduled time and waited with mild trepidation for the gangster to appear. An uneasy feeling nagged at my mind despite the crowded restaurant foyer where I stood. *Are you seriously going to meet a bona fide gangster alone?* I asked myself.

The tormenting thoughts raced through my mind as my eyes cased the already seated crowd. *What would this guy look like? Would he resemble a typical Hollywood gangster?* We all know the movie stereotype. I was expecting what I had always thought was a typical Italian with charisma, charm, and poise. Looking at the crowd I tried to find a man in an expensive suit wearing more jewelry than any local country boy would dare wear.

mental stereotype was blown out of the water when the tall, blue-eyed man ambled through the door and waltzed toward me. Soon after the conversational pleasantries were completed, his stories whisked me back to another time—one filled with excitement, adventure, and condemnation. For a time, my mind couldn't comprehend the magnitude of his story, or its legitimacy. *How could someone so normal looking get into so much trouble?*

After a time, I gained a better understanding of "Big Sid," as he was nicknamed back in his heyday. The now retired gangster spent the next four hours regaling me with his life story. His criminal resume included bank robbery, arson, counterfeit gold scandals, and so much more. I honestly thought he was putting me on.

Trying to act nonchalant, I asked him if he was linked to organized crime. His steel blue eyes cut into me for a long moment. Then he informed me if he had been organized he wouldn't have been caught. We laughed and I immediately knew what our book's title should be: *Unorganized Crime.*

After our first encounter, I was elated with the prospect of such a big book deal. Unfortunately, the longer I thought on the subject I was sure he couldn't be telling the truth. The tale was just too much to comprehend. Without any evidence to corroborate his story I finally wrote him a heartfelt letter explaining I just couldn't take on such a large project without any documentation.

Sidney was never one to take no for an answer even after straightening his life up. With the help of a friend he spent the next eighteen months gathering newspaper articles from all over the country. When he approached this timid author again he was armed with two large manila envelopes overstuffed with proof of his wild life. After a few more negotiations, I finally decided to take on the daunting task of detailing a man's seventy-year ride into a single narrative. I would spend the next four years of my life shocked, appalled, and confused by Sidney's actions.

"Why did you do something so stupid?" I'd ask him in interviews. He'd just grin and shrug his shoulders.

"I know it was stupid. That's just the way my brain worked back then." A deep sadness would pass through his otherwise confident expression. Most would miss the subtle change, but I have seen it on many occasions. "I'm not proud of any of this Sis," would always follow. I honestly have a hard time relating Sidney's insanity to James. To me Sidney seems like a character in a book and James is the guy I have lunch with on occasion.

Although he has recanted his old ways and tries to lead a clean moral life, Sidney still carries the scars of his former self with him every day. He may resemble a tall blue-eyed teddy bear, but I have noticed he cannot sit with his back to a door in a restaurant. He must have his back to the wall so he can constantly case the place. During our many interviews, his eyes would dart from the crowd to me to answer a question and then immediately return to the surroundings. It amazes me he can recount all the details of the restaurant days and even weeks later. He can tell me how many people went in and out, what type of people they looked like, and sometimes what they ate. I, on the other hand cannot even remember what I ate, what I wore, or sometimes even what day we had our interview. If I didn't write everything down, I'd be lost.

I had no idea what the criminal world was about, so I've spent a good deal of time researching true crime. I've watched every mob documentary, all the FBI Files, and read every gangster biography I could lay my hands on. I have noticed during my research movie mobsters always have perfectly tailored suits, but Sidney still refuses to tuck in his shirttails. I asked him about this and was informed it was from his hustling days when he tucked a gun into the small his back. Besides he informed me, it is harder for a thief to pick your pockets if your shirt tale is out. Of course, this was news to his naive biographer.

Even a simple task like a shower is a daunting task he explained to me over the phone one time. Showers for the ex-convict are still an anxiety filled two minutes. Sidney related more men were killed in prison behind the shower curtain than anywhere else. fact, the tiny space, and the lack of visibility still tends to make the man claustrophobic.

You'll never catch Sidney Heard taking an hour-long shower, and it has nothing to do with wasting water.

I have noticed although his body has aged, Sidney's survival instincts are still fully functional. You still don't want to sneak up behind him, or you just might get a fist in the jaw. While in prison he learned to sit in the mess hall with his toes barely touching the floor. One never knew when a riot would break out, or someone might slam you over the head with a lunch tray. A survivor had to be ready to jump in an instant. To this day, Sidney finds himself sitting at his dinner table with just his toes barely touching the floor. When he notices the quirk, he quickly places his feet flat on the floor trying to break the habit. People tend to believe once you are saved all the old scars are immediately removed. As harsh as it sounds, sometimes scars are left behind to remind us where we have been, and how far we have come.

Chapter 23: Love & Warrants

May, 2012 was another turning point in Sidney's new life. He was sitting on a bench near the entrance of Walmart waiting on his ride when a woman came and sat next to him. She was decked out with jewelry and a beautiful hat. They chit chatted for a minute and he mentioned her unusual hat. Come to find out Dena was a very creative person loved to spend her time making crafts and designing hats. She gave him her card before he left.

Brad, Sidney's roommate encouraged him to call Dena over the next week. Sidney's life was just beginning to straighten out and he wasn't wanting to get into anything serious. She hadn't wanted anything serious either, so Sidney broke down and gave her a call. Soon they were going out on dinner dates and over the Christmas holidays Dena invited him to tag along on a road trip to California to visit her daughter. What had started out as companionship soon blossomed into romance.

February, 2013 Sidney began working for Hometown Benefits Group Insurance company. His job is to generate leads for his employers and they have sold over four hundred policies since he started. Sidney enjoys the work and helping people find the best health insurance for their situation. Ironically after stealing from insurance companies in his wild days, now he works for them. In one loose estimate Sidney stated he had conned over a million dollars from insurance companies with his arson scams two decades earlier. Life is ironic and now the ex-conman had come full circle.

Finally, in June of 2013 Sidney and Dena became roommates. He moved his things into her lovely home in Springfield, Missouri. He helped her with the bills, keeps the yard nice, and makes a good companion for the lonely widow. They took another trip for his birthday in 2014. This time they rode the Mississippi steam boat and spent four days in New Orleans. Life was finally peaceful and it seemed all his trouble was behind him for good, but all was not as well as it seemed.

After two weeks of covert surveillance three U.S. Marshalls pull into the shaded driveway. Sidney and Dena were outside in their back yard watching their dogs play when the uniformed officers walked around the fence. They informed the surprised man he was under arrest for an outstanding warrant in Texas was nearly eight years old. March 12, 2015 Sidney was handcuffed and ushered into the back of a police car leaving his common-law wife confused and alone. Sidney was hauled to Greene County Jail to await extradition back to Texas. This was expected to happen within a few days, but in fact the seventy-three-year-old heart patient would be held for thirty-seven days before a bus from Texas would arrive. The whole process seemed insane since the statute of limitations expired, but Texas had issued a warrant for Sidney shortly after he left the state. Although the standard statute of limitations was over there is no limitation on a parole violation.

Before he was scheduled to leave, Sidney told them he wasn't feeling well and needed to see a doctor, but his request was never granted. As part of standard procedure, a doctor must see the inmates and give them a release to travel before they can be shipped off. The physician reviewed the file and released Sidney to travel without physically seeing him. What the chart didn't reveal was the extra stress of prison had weakened Sidney's already weak heart.

The bus came for him wasn't an official prison bus. It was a third-party currier service and it was scheduled to travel through several states picking up inmates before heading back to the Lone Star State. While in Memphis, Tennessee a few days later Sidney suffered a major heart attack and was immediately placed in a local hospital for four days. Doctors find a blocked artery and kidney stones. They cannot fix the blockage without open heart surgery, so they patch him up as best as they can, give him a prescription, and send him on his way.

The weak and emaciated ex-gangster was then bound to a wheelchair and was finally taken to the Diagnostic center at the James H. Byrd Unit in Huntsville, Texas. Here he would stay for five days while waiting on his transfer to a medical unit. While being hustled out to the medical van Sidney ran into an old acquaintance he had met at the Michael Unit back in the late 1990's. Lieutenant Shepherds had retired for a while and came back part time to help transfer medical patients from one unit to the next.

After an hour long drive Sidney was admitted to the medical facility at the Louis C. Powledge Unit just outside Palestine, Texas. This medical center was set up differently than a standard prison. Instead of individual cells in rows upon rows, it was one massive room with barred gates surrounding the entire room. Inside this facility the inmates were all handicapped and in wheelchairs. The "cells" were four-foot-tall cubicles about six feet wide and nine feet long.

The tiny space held a metal bed with a 3-inch thick mattress, a small metal table in the corner and a locker. Inmates were allowed one electrical outlet for a fan or a radio could be purchased at the commissary. Sidney had to do without because his card wouldn't work and it would be a couple weeks before Dena could get him some money. In the meantime, the other inmates rallied around the newcomer and gathered up things to share with him. He was offered coffee for the first time in weeks and it tasted like heaven.

He hadn't eaten much since he left the hospital in Memphis. When his new comrades found out they gladly shared their "spread" with him. A spread is another word for what some people call a potluck. It usually consisted of a mix of noodles, canned chili, in a tortilla mixed with some canned cheese. As nasty as it sounds, Sidney told me it tasted like the best steak he had ever eaten.

Unlike the standard prison community this unit doesn't have industry. The inmates aren't held in cells, but they can't go and work outside their dorm room because of their medical problems. Sidney couldn't read because he didn't have a magnifying glass and found the only thing to stave off boredom was conversation with his fellow inmates.

As usual Sidney could tell me about every inmate in detail. In Cell 1 was Mr. P. He was a one-legged preacher man had made some mistakes in life and wound up behind bars at the Powledge Unit. He prayed all the time and enjoyed discussing God's forgiveness and other Christian theologies with Sidney who resided just over the wall in cubicle two.

Cell three was a man by the name of Garcia. He had heard of "Oso Grande" and knew a lot of Sidney's former running buddies. The two became instant friends. On the other side of Garcia was the handicap accessible bathroom. On one side was a shower wall with three showers, and the other wall was three toilets. Of course it was all open so there was absolutely no privacy. Sidney didn't expect such a luxury.

On the other end of the walkway were the sinks where the inmates washed up and shaved. Up until recently every inmate had to be clean shaven. While Sidney was there the rule was changed and if you were Jewish, a Muslim, or an Amish person you could grow a beard. Sidney said he had never seen such a mass religious conversion in his entire existence. It seemed like everyone became either Jewish, Muslim, or Amish literally overnight.

Rudy was in cell eleven at the back of the building, but he always came by to check on Sidney. He helped the nearly blind ex-gangster fill out his commissary lists and took his laundry to the laundry room. It was a long way across the complex and hard for Sidney to get there with his wheelchair. In return Sidney always bought his friend coffee and cookies. Rudy loved cookies. Rudy was good at making pillows out of scraps. When he found out Sidney had been sleeping on hard lumpy mattress without a pillow he went back and made one specifically for him.

It took a week before Sidney could plow through the red tape and call home. Dena was so glad to hear from him. She told him to call every day. So, at exactly 4:50pm Sidney called her. He kept insisting it cost too much, but she wanted to hear from him. Dena spent $150/month on phone calls alone. The couple talked every night and then Dena would relay messages to his friends back home and to me. Throughout the chaos Dena never gave up hope. I guess absence really does make the heart grow fonder.

What was the reasoning for all this chaos you ask? Sidney had a few outstanding checks hadn't been paid before he had left the state nearly eight years earlier. These were paid and all Sidney's new friends and family sent letters of recommendation to the Parole board on his behalf. Dena submitted a letter in hopes of getting a medical reprieve for her beloved ex-gangster. What seemed like a small matter turned out to be a long seven-month ordeal.

Finally, on October 1st Sidney was released to a shabby halfway house made from a rundown Marriott. Six days later Sidney was released from his halfway house, and was granted a thirty-day travel permit to Missouri. Now he had to prove to the parole department he had a good reason to stay in Missouri. He went and told his parole officer he had a home, a wife, a makeshift group of family and friends, and most importantly his bosses had saved his job for him. That's right. Home Town Benefits group said Sidney had a job until the day he dies.

Sidney spent the next thirty days at home in Missouri with family and friends. He got a letter from his boss and took Dena with him to meet the Missouri Parole officer to get a pre-approval for his permanent transfer to Missouri. This was granted and now all was left was a quick trip back to Texas...or so he thought. Two weeks was all it was supposed to take to get through all the legal paperwork, and he hoped he would be home by Thanksgiving. Unfortunately, bureaucracy is never quite so easy.

This time Dena found a different "halfway" house for Sidney called Open Door Ministries out of Troup, Texas. This large plot of land had several houses on it and was owned by the Madlock family. Nearly every ex-convict on the property was a registered sex-offender except for Sidney. He didn't mind. He was just happy to be out of jail. There wasn't much to do at Open Door Ministries, but Sidney's mind was focused on getting home. He went to church on Sundays and spent the rest of the time pestering the Parole office.

During this time of struggling with the bureaucracy of paperwork Sidney called his old friend Tom Perdue. Tom was glad to hear from his old friend and had thought all these years Sidney had died.

"Now this is the old Sidney I remember," Tom told him over lunch. He was so proud of Sidney for straightening up his life and leaving the drug scene behind. The two instantly reconnected as if no time had elapsed since their last meeting.

After frantically plowing through red tape Sidney was finally granted his transfer back to Missouri late on December 23rd. He arrived at the bus station in Tyler, Texas at 2 am on Christmas Eve. After an agonizing nine-hour bus ride he arrived in Tulsa, Oklahoma only to be informed his bus broke down and would be delayed. Another bus wouldn't arrive until 7 pm. Realizing he would never make it home in time for Christmas he thought about Dena and how disappointed she would be. He said a little prayer and tried to call a friend from Springfield. No one could come and pick him up on Christmas Eve, although everyone wanted to. Desperate to get home to his girl in time for the holiday he walked outside and hailed a cab.

"How much will it cost to drive me all the way to Springfield, Missouri?" he asked the cab driver.

"$398" came the reply.

"How about $300 cash," Sidney offered. The cab driver agreed, but refused to take his old cab all the way, so he stops by his home in Broken Arrow, Oklahoma and the pair load up in his own vehicle. Together they make the 170-mile trip back to the Show Me state.

After breaking every speed limit between Oklahoma and Springfield Sidney called Dena when he was a few blocks away from the house and told her to open the garage door. A few moments later he walked up to his door at 4:30 pm. Dena raced out of the house to greet him dressed in her Christmas sweater. He wrapped his arms around her and thanked God for one more Christmas with his loved ones.

The reformed gangster from Chicago, who now goes by his middle name James, enjoys the simple pleasures of life and freedom. He has recovered somewhat and can walk well with a cane, but still needs open heart surgery. Every warm morning, he sits in his chair on the porch and listens to the birds, the breeze, and the silence. His tired eyes glance about the well-shaded yard. No barbed wire fences trap him in. No armed guards berate him now. Drugs, lust, and greed no longer cloud his mind. Life is peaceful. A quiet prayer of gratitude slips from his lips as he watches the sun rise over the horizon. He still cannot sleep in, but at least he can get up of his own free will. There are no bells ordering him around anymore. Freedom–at last.

BIBLIOGRAPHY:

1 http://www.dupagesheriff.org/jail.htm
2 *The Daily Journal* – Thursday, April 21, 1968
3 *Chicago Daily Journal* – Friday, June 24, 1960
4 *Daily Journal* - Friday, June 24, 1960
5 *Chicago Daily Journal* Friday June 24, 1960
6 *Chicago Daily Journal* Thursday, June 23, 1960
7 East Unit: http://en.wikipedia.org/wiki/Florida_State_Prison
8 Gideon vs. Wainwright:
http://en.wikipedia.org/wiki/Gideon_v._Wainwright
9http://www.bulk.resource.org/courts.gov/c/US/375/375.US.2.16.36.54.
55.60.html
10 Judge Hoffman: http://en.wikipedia.org/wiki/Julius_Hoffman
11 The Del Prado Apartments: http://www.thedelpradoapartments.com.
12 U.S.v. Samuel Desist, Frank Dioguardi, Jean Claude Lefranc, Jean
Nebbia & Anthony Sutera:
http://law.justia.com/cases/federal/appellate-courts/F2/384/889/392678/
13 http://articles.sun-sentinel.com/1991-04-
08/news/9101170948_1_fernandez-informant-slayings
14 http://en.wikipedia.org/wiki/Jimmy_Hoffa
15 De Angelis: http://en.wikipedia.org/wiki/Tino_De_Angelis
16 Fast Eddie by Neil F. Bayne and Wes Sarginson, 1983 – published
by *Leisure Books* in NYC
17 Castro's Blacklist: http://cuban-exile.com/doc_101-125/doc0110.html
18 Bobby Wilcoxson:
http://en.wikipedia.org/wiki/Bobby_Randell_Wilcoxson
19 http://newsone.com/1565605/most-notorious-prisons-in-the-us/
20 CONS: http://federal-circuits.vlex.com/vid/song-establishment-
religion-theriault-36957617
21 http://www.religionnewsblog.com/10378/state-challenges-status-of-
religion-calls-it-gang
22 Henry Gargano article written by: Earl Filskov
http://www.examiner.com/article/cop-killer-to-be-paroled-a-travesty-
the-making
23 Henry Gargano Article written by: Ted Gregory, Tribune reporter
http://articles.chicagotribune.com/2010-12-04/news/ct-met-bd-gargano-
cop-killer-parole-20101204_1_henry-michael-gargano-older-inmates-
anthony-perri/2
24 Article written by Ted Gregory
http://articles.chicagotribune.com/2010-12-04/news/ct-met-bd-gargano-
cop-killer-parole-20101204_1_henry-michael-gargano-older-inmates-
anthony-perri/2

25 Death notice: http://articles.chicagotribune.com/2011-11-03/news/chi-northlake-cop-killer-dies-in-prison-20111103_1_northlake-police-officers-northlake-cop-killer-ronald-del-raine

26 http://en.wikipedia.org/wiki/Frankie_Carbo

27 *Florida Times – Union* November 4, 1971

28 Amarillo Slim: http://en.wikipedia.org/wiki/Amarillo_Slim

29 *Amarillo Daily-News* September 5, 1981

30 J.C. Lane vs. U.S. appeal: https://law.resource.org/pub/us/case/reporter/F2/735/735.F2d.799.83-1742.html

31 *Amarillo Daily News* – February 7 & 8, 1984

32 U. S. Vs Lane, 474 U.S. 438 (1986) http://www.supreme.justia.com/us/474/438/case.html

33 *Amarillo Daily News*, April 4, 1975. http://amarillo.com/stories/110809/spe_specialsec24.shtml

34 report posted on http://en.wikipedia.org.wiki/krugerrand

35 *Amarillo Daily-News* Thursday, March 5, 1981.

36 *Amarillo Daily News* 03.05.1981

37 *Amarillo Daily News* March 19, 1981, page 2

38 *Amarillo Daily News* March 5, 1981

39 *Amarillo Daily-News* September 5, 1981

40 *Amarillo Daily News* 2/7/1984

41 *Amarillo Daily News* 3/30/1982

42 *Blood Will Tell:The Murder Trials of T. Cullen Davis* by Gary Cartwright. Published 1979

43 *Amarillo Globe/Times* – Wednesday, July 28, 1982

44 *Amarillo Globe/Times* Friday, July 30, 1982

45 *Amarillo Globe/Times* February 7,1984

46 *Amarillo Daily News* – Thursday, February 9,1984

47 Court case: http://supreme.justia.com/us/474/438.case.html

48 http://www.nationalspeedsportnews.com/racing-history/torn-from-the-headlines/black-thursday-saw-racers-arrested-in-drug-ring/

49 http://articles.orlandosentinel.com/keyword/castoro

50 http://www.playbillarts.com/news/article/6096.html

51 http://www.kairostexas.org/

52 http://www.calvarycommission.org/

53 http://www.shamgardiscipleship.org